THE DIAMONDS AND
THE NECKLACE

The Diamonds and the Necklace

A South African Journey

RICHARD WEST

A John Curtis Book
Hodder & Stoughton
LONDON SYDNEY AUCKLAND TORONTO

British Library Cataloguing in Publication Data

West, Richard, *1930*–
   The diamonds and the necklace: a
   South African journey.
   1. South Africa. Description and
   travel
   I. Title
   916.8'0463

   ISBN 0-340-43035-4

Published by Hodder and Stoughton,
a division of Hodder and Stoughton Ltd,
Mill Road, Dunton Green, Sevenoaks, Kent TN13 2YE
Editorial Office: 47 Bedford Square, London WC1B 3DP

Photoset by Rowland Phototypesetting Ltd,
Bury St Edmunds, Suffolk

Printed in Great Britain by St Edmundsbury Press Ltd,
Bury St Edmunds, Suffolk

CONTENTS

The whole world projects a darkness, its own darkness of which it is unaware, onto the South African darkness. The darkness is there, of course; apartheid is a thing of darkness. But it is there as on a stage where this ancient drama which takes place in the heart of every man . . . is produced in its most dramatic and theatrical form.

Laurens van der Post
A WALK WITH A WHITE BUSHMAN

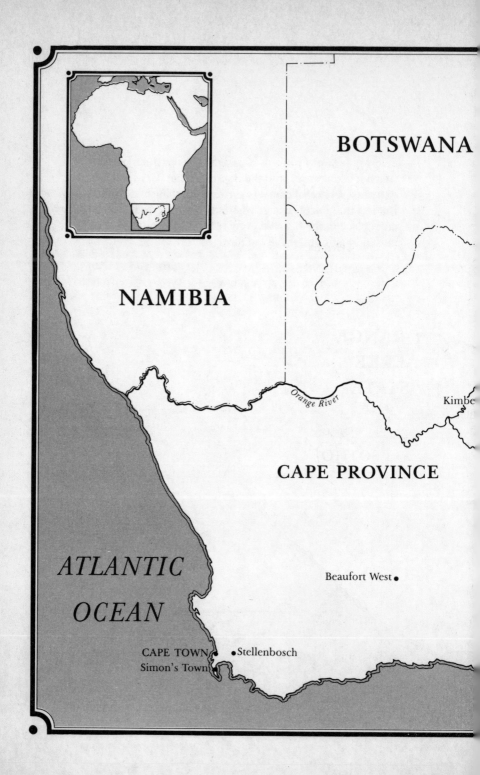

BOTSWANA

NAMIBIA

Orange River

Kimbe

CAPE PROVINCE

ATLANTIC

OCEAN

Beaufort West •

CAPE TOWN •Stellenbosch
Simon's Town

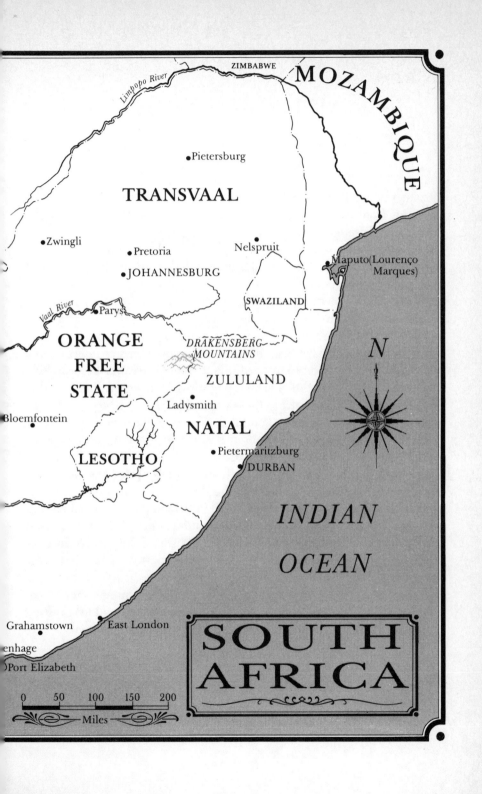

ZIMBABWE

MOZAMBIQUE

Limpopo River

•Pietersburg

TRANSVAAL

•Zwingli

•Pretoria   Nelspruit

•JOHANNESBURG   •Maputo(Lourenço
                                Marques)

Vaal River •Parys   **SWAZILAND**

ORANGE   *DRAKENSBERG*
              MOUNTAINS
FREE
              ZULULAND
STATE
              Ladysmith
Bloemfontein
•   NATAL

LESOTHO   •Pietermaritzburg
              •DURBAN

N

INDIAN

OCEAN

Grahamstown   East London
enhage   SOUTH
Port Elizabeth
                                  AFRICA

0   50   100   150   200
Miles

AUTHOR'S NOTE

Various publications have given me air tickets and or expenses to write for them from South Africa. My thanks are due to the editors of the *Daily Mail*, *Evening Standard*, *Daily Telegraph* and *Business Traveller*.

In particular I should like to thank Charles Moore, the editor of the *Spectator*, and his predecessor Alexander Chancellor, for their constant help and encouragement.

In the course of the book I have mentioned by name some of the friends and acquaintances in South Africa who helped with ideas and advice. Others, I thought, would prefer not to be named.

In this country, I have been helped by the comments of many people who know and have thought hard about South Africa. These include David Wright, Lord 'Bill' Deedes, Geoffrey Wheatcroft and the Rev Gordon Taylor, Rector of St Giles-in-the-Fields.

As is customary, I hasten to add that none of these people necessarily share my views. When writing about South Africa, you find that almost nobody does. It is a country more divisive even than Israel or Ireland.

During the Boer War, friends and families were split, sometimes for ever, between those who supported the Boers and those who supported the Empire. Passions run almost as high in Britain today. My thanks and sympathy are due to those who may unwittingly have become involved in this furious argument, not least my publisher John Curtis and my literary agent, Maggie Noach, for those tireless efforts I am especially grateful.

Above all, I thank my wife Mary Kenny (no stranger herself to controversy on matters such as abortion) for her loyalty and love during my absences in South Africa and during the writing of this book.

RW

INTRODUCTION

M Y FIRST TRIP to South Africa in 1964 was part of a long swing
through sixteen countries, beginning in Kenya and ending in
Senegal. Five of these countries still belonged to European states:
Angola, Mozambique, the Gambia and Northern and Southern Rhodesia, now Zambia and Zimbabwe. There was war in progress in only two
of the countries, Angola and the Congo, now Zaire. Most of these
countries were peaceful and happy, while Kenya, Uganda, Ethiopia, the
Gambia and Senegal were, in their different ways, delightful.

South Africa stood out from the rest. This was shortly after the
famous trial when Nelson Mandela and others were sentenced to life
imprisonment. The Prime Minister was the eccentric ideologue of
apartheid, Hendrik Verwoerd. The parliament was discussing plans to
segregate the clothes of the whites from those of the blacks in public
laundries. Johannesburg had a surreal atmosphere, not simply because
of a freak fall of snow. The police were making a series of raids and
arrests on journalists of the kind that I met every day. It was the only
place I had been in the English-speaking world where people lowered
their voices before talking politics. It was only by subterfuge that I got
to talk to some blacks, and even the hotel servants were suspicious.
When I went to visit some farms in the western Transvaal, I had to take
an interpreter, since most of the Afrikaners spoke no English.

In common with most foreign visitors, I found the apartheid system
offensive. It demeaned the Africans in their own eyes, in a way they were
not demeaned by colonial rule in British and Portuguese territories. The
black and Coloured South Africans might aspire to the vote, still more
they wanted dignity. I sympathised with such anti-apartheid measures
as stopping the tour by the Marylebone Cricket Club.

But while opposing apartheid, I always felt one should look at it in
its context. Unlike, for example, socialism or liberalism or feminism,
apartheid is not a universal credo. It is a formal response to special local
conditions; like, for example, Ulster Unionism. The apartheid features
that we found repulsive, the ban on mixed marriages or the separate

11

buses, were only part of a broader plan for holding together a country of different races, nations, languages and degrees of civilisation. Whoever rules in Pretoria, whether English, Afrikaner or black, is bound to face up to these difficulties.

Over the twenty-four years since I first came to South Africa, devastation has fallen on most of the countries north of the Limpopo. Some that I loved most, like Ethiopia and Uganda, have suffered most from famine, despotism and civil war. The Soviet Union has replaced Portugal as the foreign power in Angola. Meanwhile, in South Africa, the blacks have advanced in a way that is no less remarkable because it is generally unreported. They have attained a standard of living higher by far than anywhere else in Africa or, for that matter, some parts of eastern Europe. The government has abolished or quietly dropped most of the petty apartheid regulations that gave offence. People of different races can now work, shop, drink, and sleep together.

Yet the economic improvement of the blacks has been accompanied by a wave of violent protest, followed by violent police repression. Riots, the necklace and deaths in detention have roused the concern of the West and brought the demand for sanctions against South Africa. Individuals such as Archbishop Desmond Tutu and Winnie Mandela, wife of the imprisoned Nelson Mandela, are world figures. South Africa has become a television spectacle; and yet it is not as it seems on the small screen.

More than most countries, South Africa has to be understood in the light of its history and geography. This book is therefore a journey in time as well as through the different provinces of a huge and variegated country. Since the recorded history of South Africa does not start till the seventeenth century, the journey begins where the Dutch first settled, at Cape Town in 1652. The journey then follows the white man's progress, north and east through the Cape and Natal; it follows the path of the Voortrekkers, into the Orange Free State in the 1830s; it moves to Kimberley where the diamonds were found in 1869; north-east again to Pretoria and the Transvaal Republic; and ends at Johannesburg, where the finding of gold in 1886 transformed South Africa.

South Africa is hard to understand because it is not like any other country. Nowhere else is there such a mixture of quite different races and cultures. Even the whites are divided between the English and Afrikaans speakers. It faces the problems of Europe and the United States as well as black Africa. As I hope to show in this book, outside peoples such as Americans, Australians, Irish, Jews and Indians try to think of South Africa as an analogy with themselves. But all analogies are misleading. South Africa is a state but it is not a nation; it is at least six nations. In South Africa, unlike the United States, the different nations do not even attempt to blend in the 'melting pot'; they remain Afrikaners, English, Zulus, Xhosas, Coloureds and so on.

Anything that one writes about South Africa is likely to displease some, if not all the different racial, national and political groups. Even the names employed by these groups are fraught with contention. In the choice of names I have been influenced not by ideology but the hope of employing terms that readers will find both clear and familiar. Here are some notes on the terminology of the various peoples, roughly in order of their appearance.

The first Europeans to settle here, from what is now the Netherlands, I call by the popular name of the Dutch, although many of them were French or German by ancestry. From around the start of the nineteenth century, these people were frequently called the Boers, from the Dutch word 'Boer' for 'farmer'. Later they came to be known as Afrikaner, meaning simply African. Their patois, including English, Asian and African words was first called derisively 'kitchen Dutch' but later acquired the status of a language, Afrikaans. It became a literary language during the early years of this century.

The immigrants from the British Isles who came to South Africa from the start of the nineteenth century, were commonly called the English, because of course they spoke English, though many were Scots and Irish. The later arrivals to work in the diamond fields and Johannesburg included some Americans, Australians and people from Central Europe, some of them Jews escaping persecution. The Afrikaners lumped these people together as 'uitlanders', meaning foreigners, but all of them came to speak English, and most identified with the British Empire.

The original inhabitants of the Cape are here called by the incorrect but traditional names of Bushmen and Hottentots. I have also followed convention in using the term Cape Coloureds, for reasons that I hope will become apparent. They were not the same as the Coloureds in other parts of South Africa.

Still more confusion and argument come as one starts to write of the largest ethnic element in South Africa, which I have called both African and black. The first risks confusion with Afrikaner; the second is not quite accurate since they are patently much less black in hue than the people of West or Central Africa. Anthropologists used to call them the 'Bantu' meaning 'people'. However this term was taken up by the ideologues of apartheid and fell into disrepute.

The black South Africans also divide into tribal or national groups, which I describe in the plural, as for example, the Xhosas and the Zulus. The use of these terms is highly contentious. Conservative Africans speak with pride of their nation. The radicals claim that old tribal differences have been subsumed in a common nationhood. Many militant blacks will even deny that they have a tribal ancestry or language. They may think it insulting to call them a Xhosa or Zulu.

While some radical movements, such as the African National Congress, accept members of every race, others will take in only 'blacks'. The 'Black Consciousness' movement founded by the late Steve Biko would not accept whites, but some of its leading members today are Indians. The term Indian is used in South Africa to describe people whose ancestors came from all three states of the Indian sub-continent.

In writing of Afro-Americans in the United States, who have in the past been called 'coloured' and 'Negro', I use the present preferred term of 'black'. However it should be borne in mind that both racially and historically they correspond more to the Cape Coloureds than to the South African blacks.

When writing on such a complicated and delicate subject, one cannot avoid offending some susceptibility. If so, I can only say it was not intended.

I

CAPE TOWN

Vanished glory . . . the Cape Coloureds . . . the
Cape Town British . . . and Australia

Vasco da Gama, Drake, Nelson, and hundreds of thousands of
passengers on the Union Castle line, proclaimed the beauty of Cape
Town, seen from a ship. 'There, rising above the white line of the
houses, banked by its attendant sentinels, Lion's Head and Devil's Peak,
lifts solemnly in the air, this stupendous pile of stone known as Table
Mountain,' says the *Official Handbook* of Cape Town for 1909. 'It rivals
Gibraltar and Constantinople, Bombay and San Francisco,' wrote James
Bryce, one of the worthies cited by the Handbook. Lord Randolph
Churchill said that 'forests, groves, plantations of oak, pine and eucalyp-
tus, owing their origin to the provident foresight of the early Dutch
settlers, thickly cover the ground from the slopes of the mountain almost
to the sea. Miles of shady lanes, extending in all directions, make
riding and driving an unfailing pleasure.' The *Handbook* itself advises
the tourist: 'Bring your trout rod and your books on nature, your gun,
your volumes of Ruskin, when starting Southward Ho!' Apparently
Ruskin's *The Stones of Venice* was thought indispensable to an enjoyment
of the seashore.

There are housing estates where there were forests, groves and
plantations; the slopes of the mountain are rather bald; the shady lanes
are motorways, and you would have to go far from Cape Town before
making use of a trout rod, a gun or a nature book. A road follows the
western edge of the Cape peninsula, and the railway spoils most of
the eastern, or False Bay side, so there is nowhere to gaze at the sea in
the calm and reverent fashion suggested by Ruskin. However, I much
enjoy walking an hour or so each day on the promenade at Sea Point,
where I am staying. The shore is rocky, and anyway the Atlantic is too
cold for bathing. There are few anglers compared with the Indian Ocean,
or False Bay side. But the breeze and the smell of the seaweed bring

15

out the locals, even in winter. On warm days, numbers of black girls lie on the grass between the road and the promenade, and amuse themselves by making saucy remarks at the men, or calling out 'Left, right, left, right' to the more deliberate walkers. There is a view over the harbour to Robben Island, the island of seals, which started off as a fever station, later became a leper colony, then a lunatic asylum, and now is a prison for enemies of the state. Nelson Mandela was there before he was sent to the mainland. Like Alcatraz or Devil's Island, Robben Island is too far from the mainland to make it feasible to escape by swimming. Conditions are said to be better than they were on Alcatraz or Devil's Island. The prisoners on Robben Island are allowed to read library books, which consist almost exclusively, so it is said, of the works of Ethel M. Dell and similar lady novelists; which shows that the governor has an acute sense of humour, or none at all.

The physical aspect of Cape Town has not changed much over the eighty years since the *Handbook* was published; but you can no longer see it from a ship. Your view of Table Mountain comes from squinting sideways and upwards. What was for centuries the best known port on the route between Europe and Asia is now seldom visited by a foreign ship. The Union Castle mail and passenger line from England stayed in business after the transatlantic and Indian lines had ceased; then it too closed. Even the cruise ships seldom stop here, perhaps because of the tales of riot, perhaps in protest against the regime, most likely because it is just too far from Europe and the United States. The tankers have no need to stop at the Cape for fuel or food. Most cargo ships for South Africa go to Port Elizabeth, Durban, or even Maputo in Mozambique, because they are nearer the centres of population and industry in the southern Transvaal. The export from Cape Town of local fruit, wine and tobacco has suffered from boycotts in Europe, and most of the produce stays in Africa. During the 1930s a Cape Town journalist, Lawrence Green, wrote an enjoyable column, entitled 'The Tavern of the Seas', concerning the ships and the sailors coming to Cape Town. No such column could run today.

Coming to Cape Town by plane, or train or car, one misses the noble view but gets instead a true impression of Cape Town's isolation between the sea and the desert. Hundreds of miles of the bleak Karoo divide the Cape from the central plateau of Africa. Until the railway was built, it took more than twice as long to get from the Cape to Kimberley as it took to come from England. The west Cape coast, like the North African littoral, is separated by desert not only from tropical Africa, but from its characteristic people, the 'Bantu' or blacks. When the Dutch settled the Cape in the second half of the seventeenth century, they found Bushmen and Hottentots, but there were no Bantu for five hundred miles to the east or nearly a thousand miles to the North. Cape Town is as remote as Cairo from what we think of as black Africa. It is now a provincial outpost. It is the seat of parliament and the summer capital but only because the politicians like to get away from the heat of Pretoria. Whereas there are half a dozen flights a day from Europe to Johannesburg, there are only two a week to Cape Town. The elegant 'Blue Train' no longer runs each day from the Transvaal, and South African Railways have cut their humbler service as well. Most Transvaal people go to Natal for a seaside holiday. Only the rich or foreigners can afford to keep villas at west Cape resorts such as Gordon's Bay and Hermanus.

It is hard to recall that this dull, provincial city was once a fashionable rendezvous of the British Empire. When Cecil Rhodes, the millionaire, was Prime Minister of Cape Colony, and had given his name to what are now Zambia and Zimbabwe, he exercised power greater than most of the kings of Europe. Groote Schuur, his Cape Town mansion, enjoyed the prestige of Schönbrunn, Belvedere or the Winter Palace. Scarcely less grand was the Mount Nelson Hotel, nicknamed the 'Helot's Rest', whose pink brick façade looks out over the gardens and public buildings of Cape Town. Prime Ministers and princes stayed there. It was in effect the British headquarters during the Boer War. It was the scene of dancing, courtship, wedding reception and honeymoon for sons and daughters of Britain's aristocracy as well as the new plutocracy from the diamond mines of Kimberley and the gold mines of Johannesburg.

The Union Castle line from Britain to Cape Town was still more chic than Cunard, serving America, or the P & O ships to the East. When the owner, Donald Currie, launched the *Pembroke Castle* in 1893, he took it out on a private cruise with a party including the then Prime Minister, W. E. Gladstone, and Alfred Lord Tennyson, the elderly Poet Laureate. At Copenhagen, the *Pembroke Castle*'s captain played host at a banquet at which the guests included the King and Queen of Denmark, the Tsar and Empress of Russia, the King and Queen of Greece, the Princess of Wales (later Queen Alexandra) and the royal family of Hanover.

Lord Randolph Churchill, in praise of Cape Town, asked rhetorically why the British went to the south of Europe 'among unsympathetic foreigners', rather than coming to 'this lovely spot among people of their own race, speaking their own language and thinking their own thoughts'.

The Cape was as royalist as it was British. All of our last four monarchs visited Cape Town. The Duke of Cornwall, the future King George V, arrived here in August 1901, six months after the death of his grand-mother, Victoria. The Boer War still dragged on; indeed the guerilla horsemen of General Smuts had moved south and west in a foray that threatened Cape Town itself. The cheers for the Duke and Duchess voiced a resolve to finish the war, as well as loyalty.

A different welcome was given to their son, the Prince of Wales and future Edward VIII, who visited Cape Town in 1928 during a long swing through Africa; he had already enjoyed himself with the 'Happy Valley' crowd in Kenya. Edward's brother and his successor, George VI, arrived with his wife and family at the Cape after an African tour in 1947, one year before the election which brought the National Party to power and which foreshadowed the break with Britain. No inkling of the approaching quarrel showed in the broadcast by Princess Elizabeth, now the Queen, on her twenty-first birthday:

> As I speak to you today from Cape Town, I am six thousand miles from the country where I was born. But I am certainly not six thousand miles from home. Everywhere I have travelled in these lovely lands of South Africa and Rhodesia, my parents, my sister and I have been taken to the hearts of their people and made to feel that we are just as much at home here as if we had lived among them all our lives. That is the great privilege belonging to our place in the world-wide Commonwealth.

The British visitor still feels at home in Cape Town because it has grown as horrid as have our own cities over the last thirty years. Evelyn Waugh, in 1931, called Cape Town, ' . . . a hideous city that reminded me of Glasgow; trams running between great stone offices built in Victorian Gothic; one or two gracious relics of the eighteenth century; down at heel Negroes and half-castes working in the streets; dapper Jews in the shops.' Since Waugh wrote that, and partly thanks to his friend John Betjeman, the British have come to admire Victorian Gothic in Glasgow, Liverpool, Manchester and Bombay. The modern visitor to Cape Town mourns the destruction of nineteenth-century buildings almost as much as of those that were left by the Dutch. The planners, road contractors and property speculators have ravaged Cape Town. A motorway on stilts now runs between the sea and the city, through an expanse of waste land. Skyscrapers, housing banks and insurance companies, tower over Adderley Street. Seeing a panoramic painting of Cape Town from more than a century ago, one recognises nothing. Against this setting of Table

Mountain, there now stands a city as drab as Bradford or Birmingham. Of all the cities in what was the British Empire, Sydney alone retains its beauty.

In Cape Town, as in Liverpool, Glasgow or Belfast, the politicians and planners have razed what they called the 'slums', transferring the occupants to new housing estates. In Britain they normally went to high-rise flats, such as the 'Piggeries' in Liverpool, famous for crime, drugs and vandalism, or to the Divis Flats in Belfast, a fortress of terrorist gunmen. In Cape Town, the planners demolished the northern suburbs, including District Six, a kind of Montmartre, with its bars and brothels, its artists, writers and bohemians. But whereas in Glasgow, Bradford or Belfast, the people who had to move were distinguished only by social and economic class, in Cape Town they were a separate race, the Cape Coloureds. The demolition of District Six was not just social engineering. It fitted the new apartheid system.

The effect of apartheid on Cape Coloureds was devastating. It was very much worse than the effect on Africans. A failure to see the difference between the Coloureds and Africans explains much of the foreign misunderstanding of South African problems. Although the Cape Coloureds number only some two or three million, most of them in one province, the western Cape, their grievances against the apartheid system outweigh those of the blacks. Almost all the stories about apartheid which shocked the world in the fifties and sixties concerned Cape Coloureds. The Afrikaners themselves look differently at the blacks and Coloureds. They look on the blacks as a people of different race, language and culture with whom they must co-exist in the same part of Africa. They look on the Coloureds as distant relations by blood, religion and language. The Afrikaners have feelings of guilt about the Coloureds. Even State President P. W. Botha, who comes from George in the western Cape, is said to feel bad about what his National Party did to the Coloureds; and so he should.

It is here at the Cape that one sees the ugliest features of South Africa. Coming here certainly changed my own perceptions. Looking back at what I had written about South Africa in the sixties, I have been surprised by the lack of indignation; I wrote with irony rather than outrage. The explanation is that I spent my time in the Transvaal, where the apartheid system struck me as weird and offensive rather than cruel. By the time I came to the Cape in the late 1970s, the government was beginning to

THE DIAMONDS AND THE NECKLACE

ease the apartheid system; experience of the rest of Africa had made me more sympathetic to whites in government; yet I was angered and saddened by what had been done to the Cape Coloureds.

Here, perhaps, we should stop to ask who are the Cape Coloureds. They themselves reject the name but it is hard to think of a better one. Part of their ancestry comes from the Dutch who settled the Cape in 1652 to furnish supplies for ships going to and from their East Indian colonies. More settlers followed, including hundreds of Huguenots, French Protestants who had fled their country when Louis XIV revoked the Edict of Nantes, removing their freedom to worship. The Huguenots planted the vineyards round Paarl and Stellenbosch. Cattle farmers moved steadily north and east, to get more land, and to distance themselves from the Dutch authorities at Cape Town. These settlers wanted domestic servants, herdsmen and labourers in the fields and vineyards. The Bushmen, who constantly slaughtered the cattle, and even shot at the settlers with poisoned arrows, were loth to work either as slaves or as paid hands. The Hottentots were scarcely more amenable. The Dutch government therefore imported slaves and some free men from settlements in West Africa, from India, and above all from Java, in what is now Indonesia.

During the nineteenth century, the settlers bred with and sometimes married the women of Asian ancestry, producing a strain to which was added Hottentot and Bushman blood. Some Malays, as the people from Java were called, continued to marry among themselves and maintained their Muslim faith. You can see in the Cape Coloureds every kind of ethnic characteristic, such as the blue eyes of the Dutch, the flat broad face of the Javanese and the crinkly hair of Africa. A great many Afrikaners who pass for white have traces of Cape Coloured. The term Cape Coloured serves to distinguish this partly Asian race from what are called Coloureds in other parts of South Africa, most of whom are a straight mixture of European and Bantu.

When the British annexed the Cape in 1795, Evangelicals such as Wilberforce were trying to end the slave trade and hoped to abolish the institution of slavery. Cape Town, like Freetown in Sierra Leone, became a depot for Africans who had been released, by the Royal Navy, from slave ships bound for America. These men and women from what is now Zaire and Angola were not related by language or custom to southern blacks such as the Xhosas, Zulus and Sothos. The freed slaves became Christians, they spoke English or Dutch, and came to be treated much as the Cape Coloureds. All former slaves in the British Empire obtained their freedom in 1834. They had the chance at least of an education, acquiring skills and the ownership of a house. They worshipped alongside whites, and by the end of the nineteenth century the blacks of Cape Town, as well as the Coloured, possessed the vote, though subject to high qualification by income. And here one must emphasise, once again, that the rights and privileges of the Coloureds and some of the blacks of the Cape were not enjoyed by the native, tribalised blacks of the eastern Cape or Natal, let alone by the blacks in the Boer republics of the Transvaal and the Orange Free State.

The apartheid laws of the National Party government made less change in the lives of the blacks outside Cape Town. There had been an effective segregation of races long before the Group Areas Act. The Immorality Act of 1928 forbade sexual relations between whites and blacks. The Pass Law, in some form or another, had been in force since the blacks came to work in white settlements such as Kimberley and Johannesburg. Blacks who had never possessed the vote, or perhaps even aspired to it, were not surprised to be disenfranchised by law.

The effect of the apartheid laws on the Coloured people of Cape Town was devastating and radical. Although the blacks in Cape Town lost their vote by the Act of Union of 1910 – this was a sop to Boer opinion – the Coloureds still had a vote in 1948. Although most of the Coloureds were Afrikaans-speaking, with Dutch or Huguenot surnames, they looked to the British for protection. Many had served with the British forces during the Boer War and the two world wars against Germany. Many old Coloured men tell you with pride and affection of when they wore the King's uniform.

One of the early acts of the National Party government was to disenfranchise the Coloureds. It was not till the 1960s that Hendrik Verwoerd, the then Prime Minister, put into action his plan for the physical separation of whites and Coloureds. This involved the demolition of Coloured suburbs that had been designated as white and the transfer of the inhabitants to such distant areas as the Cape Flats. The social engineers of apartheid tried to justify to the people of District Six the destruction of what was a much loved part of Cape Town. 'It was quite true, one such person declared before the Synod of the N. G. Mission Church in 1966, that Coloureds have had to make the most sacrifices. But the Coloureds should not be sentimental and should remember that they would be resettled in new, healthy communities with all their socio-cultural amenities'. This comes from W. A. De Klerk's *The Puritans in Africa*, a magnificent study of Afrikanerdom, by one of its wisest sons. Note his mockery of the sociological euphemisms like 'socio-cultural amenities'.

The Cape Coloureds asked why District Six could not be repaired and renewed rather than flattened, to which the authorities gave a disingenuous reply. They said that the purchase cost of the land and its subsequent development would make the district too expensive for Coloureds. In fact, the resettlement of some sixty thousand people, miles away in a sandy veld, proved to be more, rather than less, expensive than the 'renewal' of District Six. The extra travelling expenses still further increased the cost of this social engineering. Moreover those who had been removed were paid in compensation less than half of the price at which it was hoped to sell plots in District Six to the new white buyers.

The apartheid system also called for the segregation of public facilities such as transport, toilets and beaches. Here again, this new indignity affected the Coloureds more than the blacks, because it deprived them of something which they once had enjoyed. In Johannesburg, where a colour bar had always existed in practice, conditions did not change much when it was put on the statute book. But the Cape Coloureds had till then been on an equal footing with whites. The segregation of beaches, of which the whites were given a disproportionate share, was also of course an issue affecting the Cape coast and Natal, where most of the Coloureds and Asians live.

The pedants of the apartheid system brought in a law for the classification of all South Africans by race. Since most of the population was obviously European or black, the classification mostly affected the Coloured who, by a later proclamation, were subdivided into Cape Coloured, Cape Malay, Griqua, Indian, Chinese, 'other Asiatic' and 'other Coloured'. The Act was absurd and sometimes resulted in heart-break. The most notorious case in the early sixties was that of Sandra Laing, who was born, indisputably white, to well-known parents, was registered as a white, and had been baptised in the white Dutch Reformed Church. Because she grew up to be dark and crinkly-haired Sandra was re-classified as a Coloured, and later married an African.

The Immorality Amendment Act of 1950 extended the prohibition of sexual relations between whites and blacks to those between whites and all non-whites. The enforcement of this law produced a string of suicides, nervous breakdowns and flights abroad. Sometimes the white men brought to the dock protested their wish to marry the Coloured girls with whom they were living. Married couples were forced to split.

The foreign press and the English-speaking newspapers gave huge prominence to these poignant 'human-interest' stories, and even *Die Burger*, the Cape Town voice of the National Party, wrote in 1962 of 'the nameless anguish caused to innocent women and children by the trials and sentences as a result of the Act'. Indeed, the Immorality Amendment Act disturbed the Afrikaners more than the English-speaking whites because the Cape Coloureds descend from the Cape Dutch settlers. They are living evidence of the sins of the fathers.

The property developers and the apartheid bigots combined to demolish District Six. Together they erected Cape Town's equivalent of the London South Bank, the Nico Malan theatre 'complex', a word that smacks of property speculation as well as sociology. The taxes of Coloureds as well as whites had contributed to this expensive folly, named after the local National Party boss; but only the whites could attend the performances. The anti-apartheid boycott of Nico Malan went on for almost a decade; playwrights from all over the world refused to have their work performed in South Africa.

The ban on a Cape Coloured cricketer, Basil D'Oliveira, led eventually to a world-wide sports boycott against South Africa. D'Oliveira had left South Africa because the apartheid laws prevented him from playing in the Currie Cup tournament between the provinces. He went to England and played for Worcestershire with such success that he was chosen for the England side in a test match against South Africa. The South African government said he was unacceptable. The Marylebone Cricket Club, which runs the England side, therefore cancelled the tour and in 1970 it announced that no further test matches would take place between the two countries till cricket in the Republic was played on 'a non-racial basis'. Once again the dispute concerned a Cape Coloured, not a black. The black South Africans take little interest in the favourite white games, cricket and rugby.

Another cause célèbre was the application of the Immorality Amendment Act and the imprisonment of the Afrikaner poet Breyten Breytenbach. In 1972, Breytenbach and his Vietnamese wife were invited back from exile in Paris by *Rapport*, the Afrikaans Sunday newspaper. The poet was given world-wide publicity for his leftish views and writing. It is an oddity of the Breytenbachs' case that whereas his country is moving away from apartheid, Mrs Breytenbach's Vietnam, under its new Communist rulers, has set about the persecution and the expulsion of the Chinese and also the children born of American fathers. Returning to Saigon in 1980, I heard how the authorities made life miserable for half-caste children, especially those of black fathers. Most of these children have since been expelled.

It was a Coloured man of Greek and mulatto descent who in 1966 stabbed to death Hendrik Verwoerd, the Prime Minister and the moving spirit behind apartheid. The Cape Coloureds are prone to acts of violence; the Coloured consumption of alcohol, especially wine, is three or four times that of the white South Africans, who are themselves hard drinkers. This habit may go back to the 'dop' system, payment in tumblers of wine, which resulted in the practice of letting the vineyard labourers drink at work.

Sex has always played a part in the unhappy relationship between whites and the Cape Coloureds. In the nineteenth century, when the Cape was under the sway of the Evangelical Churches, a stigma attached to the Coloureds because of their bastard ancestry. This was of course unfair, since almost always the white man took advantage of his position to impregnate a slave, or later a girl who had no family to protect her. The tradition persisted that Coloured girls were of easy virtue. 'It's the rich what gets the pleasure and the poor what takes the blame' was still more true when the poor were also of darker skin. The Cape Coloureds continued to live with the awareness of their bastard ancestry and the whites continued to look on them with a mixture of guilt and concupiscence. And many whites still look on Coloured girls for naughty amusement. A German I met in the Cape complained that because inter-racial sex was now legal, 'the fun has gone out of going to bed with Coloured girls, though of course we still do.' But now the Coloureds suffer a different kind of hypocrisy. Young white men pride themselves on their freedom from racial as well as sexual inhibition. They flaunt their Coloured girls in the discos or on the Sea Point promenade. But they still do not marry these Coloured mistresses.

The apartheid system proved a disaster both to its principal victims, the Cape Coloureds, and to its perpetrators, the South African government. The mass of black Africans, who care more about land, wages, rent and above all the chance of moving out of the countryside into the cities, were affected differently. The laws relating to Influx Control, which were also a feature of apartheid, were very important to blacks: however, all African countries have influx control, and most enforce it more brutally than South Africa does. In its treatment of black Africans, the National Party government continued with much the same policies as the previous government of General Smuts. In forty years of National Party rule, the Africans have made an enormous advance in standard of living, housing, and education. In the last few years they have gained a social equality with the whites which would have been unthinkable forty years ago. If the National Party was judged by its treatment of Africans, I think South Africa would not now be a pariah nation. It earned and deserved the hostility of the world for its callous and shameful treatment of the Cape Coloureds.

And it has all been to no avail. The South African government has by now repealed a large number of its apartheid laws. The Immorality Amendment Act, which was strongly enforced in the 1960s and largely ignored in the 1970s, has now disappeared altogether. The government has removed not only its ban on sexual relations between whites and non-whites but even the earlier ban on sex between whites and blacks, a law dating to 1928. The government which had banned D'Oliveira during the 1960s let in non-white sportsmen during the 1970s, and now actually welcomes them. The original cause of the boycott, Basil D'Oliveira, now has a flourishing business in South Africa as a coach for white as well as Coloured players. In October 1986, the President of the anti-apartheid South African Committee on Sport, Mr Frank van der Horst, accused Mr D'Oliveira of 'having betrayed the aspirations of millions of oppressed sportsmen by disagreeing with SACOS's code on sport'. He called Mr D'Oliveira a 'turncoat renegade on the isolation of apartheid South African sport'.

Although the Group Areas Act remains on the statute book, the Coloureds are moving back into what are in theory 'white' but in practice 'grey' suburbs of Cape Town, especially where there are students, nurses and other young people living in flats or bed-sitting rooms. But few people of any race now live in District Six, which remains to some extent a waste-land, and those that do are in houses preserved for their architectural merit. The plans for a new white suburb were not fulfilled. Some whites think it is wrong to take advantage of what they see as an unjust action against the former residents. Others regard the District now as 'creepy'. The destruction of District Six is one of the main causes of anger among people like Allan Boesak, the head of the Dutch Mission Church, the Coloured branch of the Dutch Reformed Church. He is a bitter and angry man, perhaps the most dangerous adversary of the National Party government. And who can blame him? The Coloureds have suffered great hurt and indignity from the apartheid system.

Nor can the Coloureds make common cause with the blacks. Most tribal Africans have a taboo against sexual relations with people of another race. They do not accept the children of such a union. The

Zulus enforce this taboo with the utmost severity. Once, in Lesotho, an independent enclave of South Africa, I went to a local hop, where the white girl I was with danced with the men, but I was not allowed to dance with the women. The Immorality Act, for all its harshness and dogmatism, did at least curb the sexual exploitation of African women. South African beaches may be segregated but you do not see, as you do in the Gambia or in Kenya, the wholesale prostitution of African women, and men, by West Europeans.

The Cape Coloureds, still bitter against the whites, now find their position threatened by the growing numbers of blacks. The ending of Influx Control, which was designed to limit the number of Africans coming into the cities, has meant that tens of thousands of Xhosas are moving westward towards the Cape. This immigration has grown since the civil strife in the Xhosa country of eastern Cape province. A colleague who lives in Somerset West, about thirty miles east from Cape Town, talked in dramatic language about this Xhosa invasion: 'They are pouring through the passes in their lorry-loads. There are no more police checks. They can come as they wish.' As in every country, the newest immigrants take the poorest jobs. Although they lack the education and skill of the Coloureds or of the blacks who grew up in the city, they are already proving a threat to jobs and wage levels. Some of the fighting two years ago in suburbs around Cape Town expressed the hostility between the Coloureds and immigrant blacks.

All Dr Verwoerd's plans have ended in ruin. He wanted to see the western Cape province neatly divided among the whites, the Coloureds and Asians, and barred to tribal Africans from the 'homelands', as they are called in apartheid language. But economic necessity and the rise in population find a way of destroying man-made fences. The west Cape, where there were no blacks three hundred years ago, is little by little turning into a black province.

In their cruelty to the Cape Coloureds, the Afrikaners may have been trying to get revenge on their ancient enemy, the British. The Boers started their Great Trek northwards in 1837 largely because the British government would not allow them to keep domestic slaves. Cape Town was the imperial capital and home of such hated figures as Cecil Rhodes and Alfred, Lord Milner, the two men blamed by the Afrikaners for starting the Boer War.

The Cape Town British, who voted against the National Party and did not approve of apartheid, now share with the Afrikaners the obloquy of the outside world. Every day they read in the papers how disliked they are 'at home', as some of them still call Britain. Here are three typical news items:

> The British publishers Kevin Mayhew Ltd and Palm Tree Press of Bury St Edmunds have stopped selling to South Africa liturgical and worship material, including prayer books, study literature for the ministry, Bible stories for children and Christian music books. An unnamed woman at the publishers said: 'We are writing to various outlets in South Africa . . . saying we will be unable to supply them until apartheid is dismantled.'

> Workers at the Pregnancy Advisory Service's Charlotte Street Clinic have decided to close their doors to white South African women. Annually about 75 women from South Africa come to the clinic for abortions . . . A spokesman said: 'Not to take this action would mean that we withdraw our support for those fighting for basic human rights.'

> A report from London in *Inside South Africa* says that the civil service trade unions in Britain are carrying on their private campaign against South Africa, apparently independent of the government: 'One immediate impact was felt at the passport office where key staff are quietly side-tracking applications from South Africans with dual nationality. Employees of the British Library are refusing to dispatch books to South Africa. Employees of the British Council, who have won the right to refuse South African work, have voted for its Pretoria office to be shut down.'

Like most of the boycotts, these affect the English-speaking South Africans, including the blacks, more than they do the Afrikaners. Most Afrikaners dislike the British for their imperial past, and feel only contempt for most of their new politicians, Margaret Thatcher excepted. The Cape Town British still have not learned to get on with the Afrikaners. Collecting travellers cheques one day at a Cape Town branch of the Ned Bank, I noticed some bits of cake and paper cups and other remains of a party. I asked the girl teller if she had had a good time. 'Yes,' she replied, 'but I'm English and most of the others are Afrikaans. We don't get on with each other. We have a different way.' An elderly Englishman told me of how he had gone to live in a country cottage in an Afrikaner district: 'They were friendly and gave me cups of coffee but they simply didn't accept me. I wasn't a Dutch Reformed church-goer. I spent two years trying to learn the language but almost all I picked up was a few smutty expressions I heard in the pub.'

In the early days of apartheid, the Cape Town English press, the university and the Church of England made a stand against the National Party ideologues. But now, so it seems to me, the critical spirit has atrophied into what Americans used to call 'knee-jerk liberalism'. The intelligentsia mouth the arguments of thirty years ago, or still more clamorous slogans from Trotskyism on black power, but few seek to apply these theories to the reality of Africa.

The University of Cape Town demonstrated its yobbo spirit by shouting down a distinguished visiting speaker, Conor Cruise O'Brien, whose thoughts on Africa, whether you like them or not, are always interesting and provocative. The students, both black and white, just did not bother to listen. They prefer to cling to their own half-baked certainties. Intellectual fads like Structuralism catch on in South Africa when they have long since been ridiculed and dismissed in Europe. The Cape Town English-speakers ignore the black-run countries north of the Limpopo. They do not want to hear of the famine, dictatorship and civil war that now prevail in these countries.

The Anglican Archbishop of Southern Africa, Desmond Tutu, is famous to television viewers all over the world. To many South African Anglicans he is a cause of embarrassment. They are not amused when he goes through Australia wearing a T-shirt saying 'Call Me Bish'. They resent his demand for the imposition of sanctions against South Africa. That policy is unpopular with all the white and most of the black politicians. He is rightly praised for his courage in restraining violent mobs, but none of the other black South African bishops have his flair for publicity, or so much support from the left. The one service that I attended in the cathedral was more like a TV chat show than a religious ceremony. Tutu himself cracked a few jokes. Another black bishop told a joke which had made me laugh when I heard it in *Bonnie and Clyde*, the movie; a white clergyman told an unfunny anti-semitic joke.

At a pub I met a girl who writes on religion for a newspaper. She greatly admires Tutu's political statements. I asked where he stood on religious matters. Was he high or low church? Did he favour the old or new liturgy? She looked blank and then said tartly that she did not actually go to church. The English newspapers are dull. It is hard to think that the *Cape Times* once held up the last edition to print a leader on D. H. Lawrence's death by Laurens van der Post. Even to find the news these days, one has to pore through the Afrikaans newspapers as well.

The conversation of British Cape Town constantly harps on the past. A few look at the changing scene with humour. A farmer of Scots descent, who lives on the coast to the east, asked me to take a look at the footwear of everyone in the bar where we were talking. He pointed out that the blacks wore shoes of much better quality than the whites did. 'Look at those whites and blacks together there. They get on fine. The distinction of race is going out. But there's still a distinction of class. Always has been and always will be. I remember thirty years ago there were white shepherds who used to come to our house, and they had to use the back door to drink a cup of coffee in the kitchen.' This perception on race and class reminded me of Evelyn Waugh's remarks on apartheid in one of his last books, *A Tourist in Africa*, published in 1960:

> Apartheid is the creation of the Boers. It is the spirit of equalitarianism literally cracked. Stable and fruitful societies have always been elaborately graded. The idea of a classless society is so unnatural to man that his reason, in practice, cannot bear the strain. Those Afrikaner youths claim equality with you, gentle reader. They regard themselves as being a cut above the bushmen. So they accept one huge cleavage in the social order and fantastically choose pigmentation as the determining factor. Cardinal Garcias and the Hottentot are equal on one side; you, gentle reader, and the white oaf equal on the other; and there is no passage across that preposterous frontier.

The Cape Town British pine and fret. At Sea Point, on the verandah of my hotel, the conversation is stuck in the period after the Second World War. 'The London public accepted Max Miller's humour but it didn't go down in South Africa ... Tommy Trinder, now he was the bee's knees, he was booked up solid, and yet he didn't go down well in South Africa.' Love of sport goes with fear of death: 'I'd like to go out on the bowling green ... Yes, Bing Crosby was the lucky one, to go out on the golf course.' Cape Town was once world famous for golf, so I learn from the *Handbook* of 1909, which goes into bolder type to describe the '*ancient and royal game*', played at the course at Wynberg:

> The first hole presents no special difficulties ... but if at the first drive a foozle results, the reeds in front of the tree will be found very clinging ... *The drive to the seventh* is one that calls for the exercise of much judgment for here a cart track crosses the course ... while a sliced ball seems to be ashamed of itself and seeks to hide its shame in the long grass outside the Cape Flats Railway ... The eighth was at one time an oasis in *a veritable Sahara of long reeds* ... a monumental erection with a wide trench in front of it which has witnessed more niblick work than any other bunker on the course ... this hazard which in its present form has been compared with the

Phallic monuments of Zimbabwe ... The tenth, which might appropriately be called the Red Sea ... and the eleventh ... have proved the *Majuba of many* a promising score ... [The Battle of Majuba was Britain's defeat in the first Boer War.]

World-class golfers still compete in South Africa, though normally at the Sun City resort in Bophuthatswana, which is recognised by South Africa, but by nobody else, as an independent country up in the north. But international golf cannot compensate for the loss of the international matches in rugby, football and cricket. Again and again I have heard people recall the last games played by such cricketing heroes as Barry Richards and Graeme Pollock. Sports lovers cannot work up the same excitement over the visiting scratch teams like the Australians who were here in 1986. 'Those matches against the rebel sides aren't the same thing ... I doubt if there were two thousand people at Stellenbosch last week. But I remember as a child how you'd listen all day to a test match on the radio, even if there was only one or two runs an over.'

For just one day, in November 1986, I was given a glimpse of Cape Town harbour once more crowded with splendid ships and sea-goers of many nations. The nineteen yachts of a round-the-world race moved slowly from Table Bay to start the second and much the most perilous leg of their trip, past icebergs, to Sydney, that other magnificent port of Britain's old maritime Empire. The first settlers, bound for Van Diemen's Land, had stopped at the Cape for water, meat, vegetables and some healthy exercise. Later, the Table Mountain was part of the doleful memory of the thousands of convicts who lay in shackles off the Cape on their way to penal servitude. It was on the route of the grain and wool clippers. Gold-diggers stopped here on their way to the first Australian rush and many of them, or their children, came back to the Cape to join in the diamond rush at Kimberley, or the later gold rush on the Witwatersrand.

In the last few years, many thousands of white South Africans have left for Australia, fleeing uncertainty and the threat of violence. Those who intend to remain, or who have not yet raised the money to leave, speak scornfully of the 'chicken run' or 'taking the gap', an image that comes from rugby, I think. Whatever their motives, many South Africans have decided to start a new life in Britain, the United States and above all Australia, especially its west coast. The Australian government has cut air flights to South Africa as part of its sanctions policy, but Qantas flights from Zimbabwe are booked months ahead, mostly by South African emigrants. A few South Africans have sailed all the way to Australia, for yachts are a useful way of carrying household goods. People are building yachts as far inland as Johannesburg, but most of the yachtsmen head west to the Florida town of Fort Lauderdale, where there are lawyers who specialise in helping South Africans to obtain a 'green card', the US work permit.

Not all the South African émigrés are white. Black businessmen and professional people, who do very well at present, are anxious about their future in a hypothetical 'Azania'. They know what has befallen educated blacks in most of the countries north of the Limpopo. They may have noted the 'brain drain' to the United States from black Caribbean states such as Jamaica, Trinidad and Guyana. However, the great majority of the emigrants are white, and of those almost all are English-speakers. Among recent graduates of the Business School of the English-language University of the Witwatersrand, forty-five per cent said they intended to emigrate, compared with a figure of less than one per cent of business graduates at the Afrikaans-language Stellenbosch University.

South Africans of British stock have natural affinities with Australians. Both are outdoor people, besotted with cricket, rugby, tennis, surfing and golf. Australians who come to South Africa, apart that is from the politicians and ideologues, are quick to perceive that they, in the same position, would take the same attitude to the non-whites. They also see that apartheid is dying out, that the blacks are now suffering at the hands of their own savage young 'comrades' as much as from the white police. An Australian yacht skipper, Ian Kiernan, who toured western Cape during his week's break from the race, told a local newspaper: 'I have been into the townships, and visited about fifteen shebeens. I found the black people to be very friendly and happy, though the situation among the youngsters seems to be somewhat different and I think that's where problems should be addressed. I cannot believe the stance by the international media against this country.' Probably Mr Kiernan got a truer impression of South Africa than the TV journalists who see only Archbishop Tutu, Winnie Mandela and the spokesmen for the African National Congress.

The Australian cricket team which was in South Africa when the yachts arrived met little hostility. The protesters shied bricks at the Sea Point hotel where the team was staying, poured oil on two of the pitches, and also into the swimming pool of the national cricket chairman. This fouling of swimming pools tells you much of the South African left. They are almost all from the rich, pool-owning class.

Australian yachtsmen and cricketers may be popular in South Africa, but not Australian politicians. In fact Australia may have taken over from Britain and Sweden as the symbol of the outside world's pharisaical humbug. The arch bogeyman is the former Australian Prime Minister, Malcolm Fraser, who came here as co-chairman of the grotesquely-named Eminent Persons Group. There was much delight when the news reached South Africa that Fraser had come to grief during a boozy night out in Memphis, Tennessee. 'Ex-PM loses pants in motel' was the headline in my newspaper. Some South Africans think that Australia led the campaign for a boycott against this country in order to seize the market for goods which they both produce, such as minerals, coal, wool, sugar, wine and fruit.

Because South Africa and Australia are so alike in natural resources and in the character of their people, one needs to reflect on why they turned out differently. The answer lies in geography. Australia is an island, and the whites found only a few aborigines, most of whom they exterminated. The settlers at the Cape found Bushmen and Hottentots, who were not quite so primitive as the aborigines. But the Cape is not an island. It lies at the tip of a vast and teeming continent, whose black people were moving inexorably south. Australia chose to remain an island for whites. During the nineteenth century the Queensland sugar planters tried to obtain cheap labour by 'blackbirding' or kidnapping men from the Solomon and New Hebrides islands. The British government put a stop to this practice. During the first half of the twentieth century, Canberra governments enforced a 'white Australia' policy. As late as the 1960s, Australia would not accept Coloured immigrants, even if they held British passports.

It is sometimes said that South Africa could not survive without black labour to work in the mines, to cut the cane of Natal and do the domestic chores for 'missie'. It is true that South African gold mines are deeper and therefore more 'labour intensive' than those in Australia. It is true that the companies of the Witwatersrand brought in Chinese miners during the first decade of the century. The production of gold was increasing at such a pace that there were not sufficient whites to do the work, or to enforce their monopoly. But even in England at that time, coal miners were working at almost as great a depth, and in far worse conditions, than gold miners in Africa. They fought, successfully, to exclude imported labour from British pits. If there had been no black labour on hand, the white South Africans would have mined even the deepest shafts. And the companies would have had to pay them what they wanted. Indians were brought to Natal to cut the cane because this was thought too heavy a task for white men, under the African sun. But in Queensland, where Indians were excluded under the 'white Australia' policy, whites cut cane until the recent invention of machinery for the job.

Many South Africans do not depend on blacks for domestic service. In the age of the Hoover and washing machine, a servant is now just a luxury in South Africa. If there were no blacks, South Africans would get by with occasional cleaning ladies, baby-sitters and odd-job men. It is absurd to say that all South African women are rich, spoilt darlings who would be lost without black servants.

Australia's attitude to South Africa smacks of humbug. The 'white Australia' policy was revived under a different name in 1975, when hundreds of thousands of Vietnamese fled from Communism as 'boat people', some getting as far as Darwin. The Australian government tried to exclude these refugees under the pretext that those fleeing the Communists were former bourgeois predators, drug pedlars and brothel owners – the same reason once offered for not sheltering Jews from Nazi Germany.

2

SIMON'S TOWN

By train to Simon's Town . . . Death of a Cabinet
Minister . . . 'Just Nuisance' . . . Jock

IN THE TWILIGHT of the apartheid system, it is sometimes hard for a
foreigner to discern the local customs on segregation. These vary
from province to province. In Durban, for instance, signs say what parts
of the beach are reserved for which race, though the signs are largely
ignored. In Johannesburg, until very recently there were different buses
for whites and non-whites, which meant that everybody waited twice as
long at the stops. In Cape Town, the buses are mixed, and I even noticed
two white youths stand up to offer their seats to black women. This
startled me as much for its sexual as for its racial implications. You
seldom see a man offer his seat to a woman in London these days. Cape
Town is old-fashioned that way.

Boarding the train from Cape Town to Simon's Town, I found there
to be a kind of optional colour bar. There are carriages for whites only
at one end of the train, for non-whites only the other end, with some in
the middle for people of any race. Almost all the whites sit in the whites
only carriages. They do not talk much, and read hardback books rather
than newspapers. It struck me that few people on trains in England
read hardback books. After a few stops on the journey to Simon's
Town, twenty-five miles to the south, I moved into one of the mixed
race carriages, where there were fewer people but much more noise.
As the train was running beside the shore, there suddenly came a
great yell of boisterous laughter and whistles and clapping. Startled
out of my daydreams, I looked around to find the cause of the
mirth and saw on the beach a young white man, baring his arse to the
train.

The anti-apartheid movement denounces the last remains of a colour
bar on the trains of the western Cape. Of course they are right in
principle. However, there have been ugly riots, in and around Cape

34

Town, as well as muggings. A white man, still more a white woman, could be at risk in a carriage alone with the wrong sort of Coloureds or blacks. How many white New Yorkers feel wholly comfortable in a subway, faced with aggressive blacks? How many whites on the tube in London have looked at a gang of Jamaican youths without a flutter of trepidation? The anti-apartheid theorists say that if whites feel insecure they should pay more to travel in first-class compartments. But this merely dodges the issue. Why should whites have to pay more for public transport? There are no separate classes on the suburban trains in South Africa. In Cape Town, as in New York and London, it is the poorer whites who travel by train. The professional and business classes, the ones who preach against 'racism', are those who are more likely to travel by private motor car.

The British created Simon's Town as a naval base in the early nineteenth century, during the wars against Napoleon. The long, narrow street between the sea and the mountains is lined with handsome Regency public buildings, officers' quarters, chandlers' shops and taverns. It has been spared the ravages of Cape Town, and still looks rather as Plymouth or Portsmouth must have looked when Jane Austen was writing of naval life in *Mansfield Park* and *Sense and Sensibility*. One of the great Victorians, Mary Kingsley, the scientist and explorer, died at Simon's Town. Like Jane Austen, she was a spinster and therefore, wrongly, an object of pity to her contemporaries and most biographers. Like Jane Austen, she is revered by those who have read her books. Mary Kingsley was an imperialist, a friend of Rudyard Kipling, and like him she came to South Africa to play her part in the Boer War. She found a job as a nurse to Boer prisoners in the hospital at Simon's Town. She caught from them the deadly enteric fever, and, being a proud and lonely woman, refused all medical treatment or comfort during the last torment. Like a cat, she wanted to die alone. When she was buried at sea, off Simon's Town, the coffin refused to sink. The mishap would have appealed to Mary Kingsley's humour, which was macabre and irreverent, permeating her books on the anthropology of West Africa. Mary Kingsley has survived attempts to make her a posthumous heroine of the feminists, whom she opposed in life. Nor was she, as some pretend, a victim of late Victorian piety and hypocrisy. On the contrary, her spiritual and poetic nature was crushed by a cold agnostic upbringing.

For a few years after the break with South Africa, Simon's Town remained as a British naval base. Now that agreement has ended too. The South African Navy has its headquarters in Pretoria, hundreds of miles inland. The only sailors I noticed were one squad marching by at the double, chanting a song in Afrikaans. The Cape Coloureds, who are the merchant seamen and fishermen of South Africa, do not have a respected role in the Navy; or in Simon's Town. There is a monument in stone, inscribed in English and Afrikaans, 'to the memory of our forefathers, who for many generations lived here in peace and harmony, till 1967, following legislation . . .' It is a monument to the victims of apartheid.

Simon's Town used to have as its Member of Parliament one of the very few Englishmen to become a Cabinet Minister in the National Party government. This was John Wiley, the Conservation Minister, who was found shot dead at his home on the Sunday morning of March 28th, 1987. The apparent suicide came as a rude surprise to the National Party, only six weeks before a general election. The State President, P. W. Botha, went straight to the house to offer condolences to the widow. The cameras of the South African Broadcasting Corporation (SABC), filmed the journalists waiting outside Wiley's home, some of them laughing and joking, to give the idea that the liberal press was gloating over a personal tragedy.

The life and death of Wiley show the predicament of the Cape Town English, half wanting and half not wanting to come to terms with an Afrikaner regime. After studying law at Cape Town and Oxford, Wiley went into politics with the old United Party of General Smuts, winning the safe seat of Simon's Town. With the break-up of the UP, Wiley did not join one of the new English-speaking groups, but founded his own South African Party. By the time he decided to join the National Party, he had enough friends in Simon's Town to hold on to the seat. However, many Cape Town English regarded him as a renegade. In particular he fell out with the English-language press, which he accused of left-wing bias. As well as holding authoritarian views, Wiley was crude and bullying, especially in his business life as a property dealer. A reporter who once started a probe into one of Wiley's transactions told me that when she returned after two days to the town hall, the relevant papers had vanished. Only two months before his death, Wiley had been engaged in a dubious property deal in his own constituency. He was Minister of the Environment from a city, Cape Town, which has been ruined over the last thirty years by property dealers and National Party ideologues, often the same people.

A big, powerful, handsome man at sixty, his age at death, Wiley
was an assiduous yachtsman, tennis player, socialite and gallant. The
Hollywood actress, Linda Christian, who has been married to Tyrone
Power among others, called Wiley the most attractive man she had ever
met. She painted his portrait while they were friends some years ago.
He made a point of talking to women at any gathering, I was told by
a woman who loathed him. If there was anything wrong with
Wiley's second marriage, the news had not reached either the Cape
Town press or rumour exchange. But Wiley's arrogance made him
the object of malice. He resembled a Hollywood villain: the western
rancher, driving the sheepmen out of a valley, or mine baron, starving
the poor Irish. Inevitably he was known, after the TV serial, as 'the
JR of the Cape'. Even Wiley's efforts as a conservationist had made
him enemies. A Cape Coloured from one of the fishing towns told me
of how they resented his preservation of seals: 'Didn't he know there
were fishermen starving? Just because he felt sorry for those cuddly,
baby seals.'

One political enemy, a bearded journalist from the *Cape Times*, had
actually thrown up his job to fight against Wiley as candidate of the
Progressive Federal Party, the liberal opposition. The day after Wiley's
death, the *Cape Times* printed a story that put into motion two highly
sensational rumours, neither with any foundation in fact. The article
showed that Wiley had been the acquaintance, according to one account
'a very close friend', of a Port Elizabeth businessman, David Allen, who
had committed suicide one month earlier. It so happened that Allen's
business interests lay in the sphere of Wiley's work as Conservation
Minister. He had the concession for guano off Bird Island, near Port
Elizabeth, as well as the franchise to breed oysters and mussels for sale
to the Far East. In his capacity as a Minister, Wiley had visited Allen's
commercial establishments. The *Cape Times* story of March 29th dis-
closed that Allen had shot himself on the beach at Port Elizabeth two
hours before he was due to appear in court on an unspecified charge. A
few days later the Sunday newspapers printed what had by then become
well known by rumour, that Allen was charged with acts of indecency
with young boys.

This stirred a miasma of innuendo. Although Wiley had never during
his lifetime come under public suspicion of homosexual leanings, nor
could he have done and kept his job in a puritanical government, the
rumours abounded after his death. The insinuations appeared in the
anti-government, English-language press. The Afrikaans press charac-

teristically came up with the story that Wiley's death had been foretold by the soothsayer, Gerald Burger in Stilfontein.

The memorial service for Wiley was held on April Fool's Day, 1987, which was also the fiftieth anniversary of the birth of Simon's Town's most famous and best loved resident, Just Nuisance, a Great Dane of outstanding size and intelligence, who became so popular during the Second World War with Royal Navy sailors that he was given the rank of Able Seaman. The memorabilia of this dog fill at least a third of the little museum at Simon's Town, which of course is naval in character. After seeing the relics and chatting to one of those cheerful ladies who keep museums in South Africa, I bought a copy of *Just Nuisance AB, His Full Story* by Terence Sisson, an Englishman who had served at the Cape as a Fleet Air Arm pilot, and met and befriended the legendary dog.

Just Nuisance came from pedigree stock, and he began life in 1937 under the grander name of The Pride of Rondebosch. Soon afterwards he became the property of a couple who ran the United Services Institute in Simon's Town, which provided comforts for men of all three services, but particularly for the Navy. He was remarkable for his huge physique, his intelligence and his appetite. He got through a quart of cream and three helpings of meat a day, plus special treats like a dozen thick slices of beef followed by spotted dick and custard. He was what they call in the Navy a 'gannet'. In his lavatory habits, he was 'as clean as a stoker', and liked to sleep under sheets on a bed.

Just Nuisance had an inverted snobbery about rank. According to Mr Sisson: 'It was apparent that he preferred the company of sailors who wore the famous "square rig" – that is, uniforms with bell-bottomed trousers, tight jumpers with a V-shaped front and a blue collar hanging over the back from the nape of the neck to below the shoulder blades.' He would tolerate officers, petty officers and ratings who wore the 'fore-and-aft' rig, but he made real friends only with tars. These were his 'oppos' or chums. He liked very much his encounters with Great Dane bitches but normally had little use for women. There were exceptions. At one social evening, a young woman jokingly asked for a dance, whereupon 'to everyone's amazement Nuisance reared up on his hind legs, placed his two front paws on each of her shoulders, and off they went in perfect time to the music.' Forty years later, his partner wrote to the *Cape Times*: 'I was only 5 ft 2 in in height and Nuisance towered over me, but we went in correct waltz time – 1, 2, 3 – and he even guided me by putting pressure on a shoulder to indicate which way he wanted me to turn. I was a ballroom dancer, but that waltz was one of the best I ever had . . . what a beautiful memory.'

Quite early in life, Just Nuisance acquired a passion for travelling on the train between Simon's Town and Cape Town. Sometimes his oppos or the civilian passengers would pay Nuisance's fare, but sometimes the ticket collectors bundled him off the train. At last South African Railways warned that if he continued to jump the train the dog would be put down. When the story appeared in the press, the C-in-C South Atlantic was inundated by letters from those who knew and liked the dog. This led to his formal appointment as Able Seaman, with all the privileges of the rank, including a pass for South African Railways.

By 1941, the Mediterranean had grown so hostile that ships bound for the Far East or even for Egypt were usually routed around South Africa. The fame of Just Nuisance spread through the Navy. There is a poignant photograph of him aboard the battleship *Prince of Wales*, not long before she was sunk by the Japanese. Just Nuisance appeared in fund-raising rallies. He learned to stand to attention for 'God Save the King'. But more than these formal occasions, Just Nuisance preferred an evening out with his oppos in Cape Town, visiting pubs and flopping out at one of the beds reserved for him at the Union Jack Club. He would stop first in Adderley Street at a pub called the Standard, but known to the fleet as the Texas Bar. The management gave him his first drink free, a quart of Lion lager poured into a brass bowl. He would accept another two quarts treated him by the sailors; then he would move upstairs to the balcony where he stood surveying the street, with his two front paws on the guard rail. When he saw dogs passing below he let out a bark that echoed down Adderley Street. Early on in his pub career, Just Nuisance over-imbibed and once collapsed in a corner. Later he knew how to space his drinks, and he enjoyed Navy rum as much as lager. He was expert at taking in hand those human oppos who grew 'three sheets to the wind'. In Cape Town he tugged them by the sleeve to the Union Jack Club. On returning to Simon's Town late in the evening he made sure that the drowsy sailors got off the train, and when it was necessary, pulled them past the guards. He could break up a fight by placing his great paws on the combatants.

Just Nuisance was sometimes in trouble. He once killed the mascot of a cruiser; he chased a conjuror off the stage of a music-hall; he pushed a Vice-Admiral into a swimming pool. The author, Mr Sisson, taught

Just Nuisance the joys of flying on anti-U-boat patrols. The sight of a school of porpoises drove him wild: 'Whether he thought they were canine oppos or potential enemies below, swimming in the waves, I'm not sure, but he was barking enthusiastically, his head swimming sideways, downwards and towards the pilot, who let him enjoy himself watching the aquatic mammals for a while then climbed back to 5,000 feet. The bombs and depth charges carried were for bigger fish than this – U-boats that had surfaced to recharge their batteries.'

When Just Nuisance took sick and had to be put down on his seventh birthday in 1944, some of his friends, like Mr Sisson, were inconsolable. In the course of doing research for his memoir, Mr Sisson encountered another oppo who had been present when Just Nuisance was shorn of an ingrowing toe-nail. Forty years later, Mr Sisson remarked that the piece of claw would fetch quite a sum in an auction in Cape Town, to which the ex-petty officer answered: 'Not for all the tea in China; that bit of Nuisance is going to be buried with me when I hit the deep six.' In a foreword to Mr Sisson's book, Vice-Admiral James Johnson of the South African Navy writes: 'Sadly the accents of Scouse, Yorkie, Geordie, Taffy, Jock and Shirer are no longer heard in the streets of Simon's Town. However, they will long be remembered with affection by South Africans, but none so much as the erstwhile shipmate of their forebears, Able Seaman Just Nuisance.'

A new generation of Cape Town British, in the university and cathedral for instance, would doubtless sneer at this book on Just Nuisance. The Royal Navy served British imperialism. Why should a dog eat beef and cream when African children are undernourished? It is clear from what has been left unsaid in the book that Just Nuisance did not have any non-white oppos. Nevertheless, I think that Admiral Johnson is right: that Just Nuisance should and will be remembered by many South Africans when they have long forgotten the politicians like Wiley.

As I was reading the story of Just Nuisance, I learned that a film had been made on another South African dog, *Jock of the Bushveld*, the immortal bull terrier of the old Transvaal. The author of this classic children's book, Sir Percy Fitzpatrick, had come to South Africa after the gold strike at Barberton, and he did the hard and dangerous work of driving the ox-wagons between the coast and the high veld, six thousand feet up on the berg. Like all the transport men, Fitzpatrick hunted game for the pot, and constantly used his gun against marauding lions, leopards, hyenas and that most bloodcurdling of enemies, the crocodile at the watering hole. His dog Jock was both a devoted friend in the bush and fearless in the pursuit of wounded game. The book is brim-full of excitement: the terror of drought, hailstorm and murderous flood, the tales of swashbuckling adventurers, of whom the most memorable is the big Zulu, Jim Makokel:

> Jock disliked black men. So did Jim. To Jim there were three big divisions of the human race – white men, Zulus and others. Zulu, old or young, was greeted by him as equal, friend and comrade – but the rest were trash. He cherished a most particular contempt for the Shangaans and Chopis, as a lot who were just about good enough for the job they did – that is, work in the mines. They could neither fight nor handle animals, and the sight of them stirred him to contempt and hostility. It was not long before Jim discovered this bond of sympathy between him and Jock.

On a previous trip to South Africa, five or so years back, I had bought a paperback *Jock of the Bushveld*, slightly abridged by Dolores Fleischer, though her changes had been approved by the Fitzpatrick family. On this visit, seeing that Jock was about to appear on film, I asked for a copy at various bookshops. It was difficult to find but at last I did manage to buy a paperback copy, but not the Dolores Fleischer edition. I soon sensed that something was badly wrong; I was brought up short by the words: ' . . . and before the second Rietbuck had gone 27 metres, Rocky toppled it over in its tracks.' Turning back to the start of the book, I found I had missed a note by the editor Linda Rosenberg: 'This South African classic among animal stories is published here in an edited version. For better understanding, the language has been modernised, the measurements have been metricated, and the glossary has been expanded. While the prejudicial racial references have been eliminated, the esoteric charm and innocent philosophical tone have been left scrupulously intact.'

After a long search through Cape Town, I found in Cranford's second-hand bookshop an unexpurgated copy. A comparison of the original with the bowdlerised or Rosenberged version suggests that the modern reader must not hear how people actually spoke one hundred years ago. Thus Fitzpatrick: 'There was only one kaffir whom Jock would take any notice of or would allow to touch him – a great big Zulu named Jim Makokel. Jim was one of the real Zulu breed . . .' Thus Rosenberg: 'The big Zulu wagon driver, Jim Makokel, took a real pride in Jock . . .' When Jock returns half dead from the chase, Jim, in the Fitzpatrick version 'worked himself up into a wild frenzy, it was the Zulu fighting blood on fire, and he "saw red" everywhere. I called for water. "Water!" roared Jim, "bring water", and glaring round he made a spring – stick in hand – at the nearest kaffir . . .' All this is Rosenberged.

Just as Jim is transformed from a blood-crazed fighting Zulu into a mild-mannered kennel attendant, so the white wagon-drivers are stripped of the bold pioneering pride that drove them to conquer the bush and build an empire. The impetuous Irishman, Fitzpatrick, was himself one of the leaders on the Witwatersrand who sought and helped to provoke the Boer War. The death of Jock, which generations of children have read with tears in their eyes but a glow of pride in their hearts, has been reduced to banality. At the end of the book Fitzpatrick has gone to work in one of the new mining cities, and Jock is left on a farm away from the danger of traffic. Before hearing the news of Jock's death in a shooting accident, Fitzpatrick had often wondered if it was fair to the gallant dog to let him fade away in domesticity, ill-health and feebleness:

> If on that last day of our hunting together he had got at the lioness and gone under in the hopeless fight, if the sable bull had caught and finished him with one of the scythe-like sweeps of the scimitar horns, if he could have died – like Nelson in the hour of victory! Would it not have been better for him – happier for me?

As Fitzpatrick intended, this splendid passage prepares the young readers for the impending news of Jock's death. It softens the blow. But in the Rosenberg version it is reduced to this: 'I had often thought that it might have been better had he died fighting.' So much for Nelson, who evidently is not now considered a suitable hero for children. In the preface to *Jock of the Bushveld*, Sir Percy Fitzpatrick explains how the book arose from the tales he told children, the little people, to use the whimsical phrase of Edwardian times. 'The story,' he wrote, 'belongs to the little people and their requirements were defined – "It must be all true! Don't leave out anything!" ' The plea of the little people has not been heard by those who now censor books in South Africa.

The bien-pensant South Africans of the academic world, the churches, the press and the publishing houses, are now as prudish on matters of race as Mrs Grundy was about sex. Not only is it forbidden to use words like 'kaffir', which was the normal way of saying what we call black; it is now taboo to suggest that people of different ethnic groups have different

characteristics or even foibles. Shakespeare's *Henry V* would be banned
for making fun of the Welsh; so would *The Tempest* which shows,
in Caliban, the plight of the savage confronted by civilisation. This
prudishness about race has overtaken a country that once erected racial
differences into a state ideology. Way back in the beginnings of the
anti-apartheid movement, it used to be claimed and believed that South
African censors had banned *Black Beauty*, imagining that its heroine was
a girl, not a horse. Certainly, at the time of the Immorality Amendment
Act, South Africa did censor books and films with explicit sexual acts
between people of different race, as indeed, between those of the same
race. Long after the *Lady Chatterley's Lover* trial in England, South Africa
stood by the ancient Christian principle that it is wrong to use pictures
or words to provoke lust. The South African government also imposed
a censorship on writings by those like Nelson Mandela, found guilty of
crimes against the state, and also on books that encouraged political
violence. Each month the newspapers published a list of the latest books
banned by the censor. One month in 1977, the list included: *The Legacy
of Che Guevara, Namibia Bulletin, Erection Specialist, Don't Scream When
You Feel a Prick, People's China* and *Sexual Options for Paraplegics and
Quadraplegics.*

South Africa has never permitted the sale of girlie magazines showing
total nudity, nor openly pornographic books, nor any promotion of
homosexual behaviour. One could not buy in a South African bookshop
the homosexual primers which British education authorities place in
school libraries. Perhaps coincidentally most of the few cases of Aids so
far reported here were whites who had lived in the United States, or
immigrant blacks from Central Africa.

One of the most popular novelists in South Africa is an Afrikaner,
André Brink. He wants total sanctions against South Africa, and recently
told West Germany's *Stern* magazine that he would like to be a freedom
fighter, but cannot be for domestic obligations. If Brink's political views
would once have made him unacceptable to the censor, so too would his
writings on multi-racial sex. Censorship would have stopped *An Instant
in the Wind*, set in the eighteenth-century Cape, where, in the words of
the blurb: 'A white woman and a black man are stranded in the wilderness
of the South African interior. She is an educated woman, totally helpless
in the wilds. He is a runaway slave, the lowest of the low in society's
eyes.' The first half of the book describes, in flashbacks, the cruelty of
effete whites to noble blacks such as Adam the hero. The second half
gets down to business: 'Meticulously, caressingly, she begins to wash

43

him, while he stands smiling, a restrained ritual of love, clasping his erection gently in both hands . . . his belly smooth, the dense seaweed of his love-hair. Miraculous life kindled in his penis.' If Mr Brink had not won the Martin Luther King Prize and twice been short-listed for the Booker, I might have thought that this novel was what is called in the publishing trade a 'slaver', one of those tales of plantation life in the old Southern United States, mingling sadism with sex over the colour line.

3

STELLENBOSCH

Beauty . . . and Colonial America . . . the Voortrekkers
. . . the Dutch Reformed Church

F OR MANY YEARS people had told me that Stellenbosch was one of
the loveliest towns in the world; and I was not disappointed. It lies
in a valley of vineyards, flanked by the mountains that follow the line of
the coast, and watered by brooks that gurgle pleasantly during the hot,
still summer days. The founder, Simon van der Stel, who gave his name
to the town in the 1680s, was said to have been a stiff Dutch bureaucrat,
but he loved trees, and planted the avenues of oak that have given
Stellenbosch its peculiar charm. The houses of Stellenbosch fully justify
Ruskin's remark that 'the only contribution to domestic architecture for
centuries was made by the Dutch at the Cape.' You can wander with
great enjoyment for hours among these buildings, some of which are
now museums, but they include a hotel, the Mother Church of the
Dutch Reformed Church, a general store and an art gallery. You can
stop at an outdoor café for orange juice or one of the local wines, and
lunch on crayfish. If you have a car, you can tour the vineyards and taste
the wines and admire the old farmhouses, straight from a painting by
Ruysdael or Hobbema. In the university terms there are frequent concerts
and plays, shown at what is the only theatre in the world which offers
free wine in the interval.

The Lanzerac Hotel was an eighteenth-century farmhouse, and guests
are lodged in the former out-buildings: my room and bathroom consisted
of half the fowl-house. The hotel is just outside town at the end of an
avenue of poplars, loud with the noise of doves and crickets. After a
swim in the pool, you sit on the verandah, watching the sun go down
over the mountains, drinking sekt, and hearing the students making
merry. These students are extraordinary, like something out of a Viennese
operetta. They laugh and sing and enjoy themselves. The boys and girls
hold hands and whisper sweet nothings. The couples look as though

they are really in love, rather than just 'shacked up together'. One of the townspeople told me: 'It's a good campus. You get the wild ones who drive on the pavement or pinch signs or chase a dog down the street, but there's no bad trouble like you hear about at the other universities.' Watching these students, I thought of a news item in the previous day's paper. The undergraduates at King's College, Cambridge, under pressure from feminists, had voted to buy a consignment of sanitary towels for the women guerillas of SWAPO, the left-wing guerillas who want to take over South West Africa, or Namibia. The newspaper made a joke of this: staunch support. Here at Stellenbosch, it did not seem quite so funny, since all of the young men have to go to the Army, and some will be killed fighting SWAPO, the Cubans and Russians.

Even Stellenbosch is not as serene as one thinks from a first impression. Among the ancient buildings there is a slave house, and some of the Coloureds here are full of resentment. Some of their grievances were expressed in a recent letter to *City Press*, a radical paper for non-whites. The correspondent attacked the Zulu political leader Chief Gatsha Buthelezi for having opened the Stellenbosch Connoisseurs Guild Food and Wine Festival:

> Every year Buthelezi also attends the Nederberg wine auction, where wine farmers make massive profits. I wonder if he is aware of the suffering, starvation and death in western Cape farms? According to a Stellenbosch academic, the average farm-worker gets R23.50 (£7.50) a month. One wonders what Buthelezi lives on in one week. On many farms, farmers spread alcoholism by paying workers by tots of wine. This continues today even although it has been made illegal . . . According to research by the London-based Anti-Slavery Society, during the harvesting season from December to April, one can find many children employed on cheap labour.

Rival statistics say that South African grape pickers are no worse off than those in Italy, Spain or even California, where many are illegal 'wetbacks' from Mexico. Whatever the truth of their grievances, many Cape Coloureds in Stellenbosch are angry and probably back radical groups such as the African National Congress rather than peaceful politicians like Chief Buthelezi.

Many Coloureds do quite well. For example, I fell into talk with a Coloured man who works at the university. He complained that he gets less pay than he would as a white. He then went on to talk about his two sons, in their twenties, who are teachers. How much do they earn? I asked, and he answered R2,000 a month which, at the official rate, is

£8,000 a year. But taking into account the cost of living and minimal tax, this is equivalent to at least £12,000 a year, which seems quite a lot for a teacher in his twenties, or even a freelance writer in his fifties. There was a news item the other day on a black youth who had set fire to a building because, he told the court, he wanted 'to kill the Boers'. He also told the court that at the age of seventeen he was earning R160 a week. When you think that one rand will pay for a bottle of beer or a packet of twenty cigarettes, the wages are not unreasonable.

At Stellenbosch, more than anywhere in the western Cape, I get a sense of America in the colonial age. There is the Dutch presence for one thing. They may not have left any mementoes in New York, the former New Amsterdam, but they are still strong in Pennsylvania. President Theodore Roosevelt was one of the Dutch Americans who understood and grieved over the conflict in South Africa. He was so upset by an article in the *Spectator* during the Boer War that he wrote to Frederick Selous, the big game hunter: 'Much of the pro-Boer feeling here is really anti-English. I have no sympathy with such manifestations . . . If the two races, Dutch and English, are not kept asunder by the intense antagonisms, surely they ought to amalgamate in South Africa as they have done here in North America, where I and all my fellows of Dutch blood are now mixed with English and other ancestry.'

Most of the British as well as the Dutch who settled in America up to the War of Independence were Calvinist in religion. Those who sailed on the *Mayflower* regarded themselves as political refugees from the tyranny of the Church of England; so did the Quakers who went to Pennsylvania; so did the Ulster Presbyterians, who suffered as much as the Catholics did from the penal laws on religion. Eleven Presidents were of Scots-Irish descent. Calvin himself was influenced by the discovery of America. He recognised that the opening of the New World and importation to Europe of tons of silver and gold had brought into existence a new money economy, based on investment, which later came to be known as capitalism. His doctrines found their most eager adherents in city states and countries like England and Holland which lived by overseas trade and speculation.

In his classic study of the Americans, de Tocqueville wrote: 'Men sacrifice for a religious opinion their friends, their family and their country; one can consider them devoted to the pursuit of intellectual goals which they care to purchase at so high a price. One sees them, however, seeking with almost equal eagerness, material wealth and moral satisfaction; heaven in the world beyond, and well-being and liberty in this.' The American sage, Benjamin Franklin, exalted the virtues of capitalism as well as Calvin: temperance, silence, order, resolution, frugality, industry, sincerity, justice, moderation, cleanliness, tranquillity, chastity and humility. As the North Americans prospered, their feelings of sin diminished. As God became less feared, so man was exalted. 'We hold these truths to be self-evident,' says the Declaration of Independence, 'that all men are created equal; that they are endowed by their creator with certain inalienable rights; that among these are life, liberty and the pursuit of happiness . . .' To quote de Tocqueville again: 'The people reign in the American political world as the Deity does in the Universe.' While losing the sense of sin and unworthiness, the Americans clung to Calvin's creed of divine destiny. A modern French writer, Alain Clement, says: 'This feeling of predestination and of self-wonder, served by unchanging rites and rhetoric has astonished even the most sympathetic observers of the American Republic from Alexis de Tocqueville to Sir Denis Brogan. The certainty that American institutions are the best in the world – even when some of their defects are acknowledged – expresses itself in an "American creed" and prolongs itself in an "American dream".'

The founding fathers of the United States could reconcile their high-flown principles with the practice of slavery. Before independence, there were as many slaves in the North as in the South. As late as 1790, only Massachusetts outlawed the institution of slavery, and Massachusetts grew rich from the shipment of slaves across the Atlantic. Even the noble Thomas Jefferson owned one hundred and fifty slaves, and he wrote: 'I advance it therefore as a suspicion only, that the blacks, whether originally a distinct race or made distinct by time and circumstance, are inferior to the whites in the endowments both of body and mind.' Such attitudes persisted till quite recent times. When I spent six months as a child in Virginia, Jefferson's own state, there was still a colour bar and the Jim Crow practice of voting for whites only. I can remember segregated buses and thinking, in a childish way, that this was unfair. The coloureds, as they were called then, played baseball at a field nearby, and I remember seeing a bloodthirsty scrap between two of the women spectators.

The Afrikaners are fully aware of what they have in common with the Americans. They are a settler people with just as much right to call themselves Africans (which is what Afrikaner means) as Americans or

48

Australians have to their names. Like the Americans, the Afrikaners fought for their independence against the British Crown. Like them, they took their wagons into the heart of a continent. Although most Afrikaners now live in the towns, they think of themselves as frontiers-men. They fought the indigenous blacks but did not try to wipe them out as, Afrikaners claim, the Americans wiped out the Indians. Because they are conscious of the resemblances, the Afrikaners hotly resent American critics of their society. They point out that American blacks have a high proportion of poverty, crime, drug addiction and broken homes. South African TV documentaries show that American cities divide into white suburbs and black, slum ghettoes.

Stellenbosch and the western Cape especially resemble America be-cause the Coloureds have a similar origin to American blacks. Most of the Cape Coloureds and all American blacks are the descendants of slaves. They have been deprived of their family names, their old religion, their language, their very ancestry. They cannot identify with the tribal Africans. For their part the Zulus, Xhosas, Tswanas and Sothos cannot accept the aspiration of the American blacks to some kind of common 'black consciousness'. The Back to Africa movement started by the Jamaican Marcus Garvey in the twenties, and now revived by groups such as the Rastafarians, has always resulted in farce and tragedy. The Africans will not accept their long-lost relatives. Liberia and Sierra Leone, which were founded by white philanthropists as a haven for freed slaves from America, are now two of the poorest and most corrupt states in West Africa; which really is saying something. The crime of transportation slavery left its curse on generations to come.

The early colonists at the Cape had the same Calvinist faith as those who went to America but they did not achieve the same economic and intellectual progress. The settlers in New England established factories, built ships and ran fishing and whaling fleets. In the South there were huge plantations of cotton and tobacco. The American colonists started the universities of Harvard, Princeton and Yale. American authors like Franklin and Jefferson not only imbibed the latest ideas from England and France but were themselves admired and studied in Europe. The intellectual ferment, as much as political grievance, led to the revolution of 1776 and the rise of what was indeed a New World.

There were no such developments at the Cape. The colony had been started as a victualling station for ships on the route to the East; it was two-thirds of the way to Java, and far more remote than America was from Europe. The East India Company which administered the Cape had no ambition to colonise southern Africa. People who wanted to emigrate from Europe naturally looked to the shorter route westward, and those few settlers at the Cape during the eighteenth century were for the most part German, discharged mercenaries from the Dutch army.

By the end of the eighteenth century, the Cape Dutch had produced no literature, music or painting. Even their fine domestic building was mostly the work of visiting architects, using slave labour. There was no Dutch university until the foundation at Stellenbosch in 1864. There was so little demand for higher education that a Latin (or high) school, started in 1714, had to close in 1742 for want of pupils. The parish clerks who taught in the elementary schools gave only a basic education. The one public library at the Cape had few books and was patronised mostly by foreigners. The social life of the Afrikaners was simple and rough to the point of crudity. English visitors early on started to make the joke of writing the word 'boer', the Dutch for farmer, as 'boor'. Here are two anecdotes from George Thompson's *Travels and Adventure in Southern Africa*, written soon after the British occupation. At Struys Bay, in 1822, he attended a party of farmers who had been to a sale of goods from a shipwreck:

> An ox was killed and the carcase, mangled in a most disgusting manner, was cut up, and part, yet warm from the blood, thrown into a pot and boiled to rags: this was heaped upon the table in huge pewter plates; and at the same time about 100 pounds of boiled rice was served up to the company, who consisted of about 30 men with their wives and daughters. The men seated themselves round the table, and with their hunting knives fell voraciously upon the viands, each helping himself as he could without either offering a seat to the females, or inviting them to partake, until their own hunger was satisfied. After dinner the boors drank raw brandy until they were half tipsy, and then commenced dancing, which they carried on amidst loud talking, vulgar jesting, and obstreperous laughter, the whole night long.

On another occasion, after a long, taxing ride, George Thompson had to endure a more painful example of Afrikaner vrolikheid, or frolicking. 'At about one o'clock in the morning, the company sat down to a splendid and luxurious party; after which the wine again circulated freely among the male guests.' Squibs and other fireworks were scattered among the dancers. At five a.m. the author attempted to sneak away to an outhouse but was brought back by his host. He escaped again and lay down to rest. His host and his friends would not allow it: 'They got hold of an old cannon which happened to be about the place, loaded it with wet straw, and then fired it into the room where we were just sinking into sleep, breaking with the concussion all the windows to shivers, and very nearly shaking down the roof about our ears.'

The more adventurous Boers headed east towards the territory of the nearest blacks, the Xhosas. From there, in 1836, they headed north on the Great Trek to the Orange Free State, Natal, the Transvaal and even further, to what are now the black independent states of Africa. These Voortrekkers tended to look with disdain on those who remained in the peace and security of the Cape, under the rule of the British. With the discovery of diamonds at Kimberley, in 1867, and gold on the Witwatersrand, in 1886, the Voortrekkers found themselves once more threatened by British imperialism. The mining financier Cecil Rhodes, who also became Prime Minister of the Cape, had conquered a territory to the north which he named after himself, Rhodesia. He posed a threat to the Orange Free State and the Transvaal Republic.

But in this dispute between Rhodes and the two Boer republics, the Cape Dutch, as they still were called, did not all side with their fellow-countrymen in the north. Early in his parliamentary life, Rhodes went out of his way to gain the support of the Afrikaner Bond, the only political party in the Cape. In 1886 he joined with the Bond in voting against the Cape government over separate religious schools, taxation for Africans, the excise, irrigation, and opposition to Sunday trams. Above all, he opposed the extension of voting rights for the blacks. He asked rhetorically, in a speech in 1887: 'Does this house think it is right that man in a state of pure barbarism should have the franchise? The natives do not want it. For myself I tell the "Bond" that if I cannot retain my position in the House on the European vote, I wish to be cleared out, for I am above going to the native vote for support.'

The Bond and the Cape Dutch gave Rhodes their support for his venture in 1890, across the Limpopo River. They supported him when, in the same year, he became Prime Minister of the Cape. He repaid their support with a series of sweeping and most successful reforms of the colony's agriculture. He introduced tariffs, and shopped round the world for the latest scientific improvements: new methods of packaging, Angora goats from Turkey, pesticide for the orange groves, and Californian vine roots, free of phylloxera. He removed all disabilities from speakers of Dutch. Above all he took the side of the Bond on the 'native question'. His Glen Grey Act in 1894 prevented Africans getting a title to land in contended areas. He raised, from £25 to £75 a year, the property qualification for having the franchise. The Act had the effect of disenfranchising 3,348 non-white voters and adding 4,506 whites to the electoral roll. Rhodes even supported what came to be known as the Strop Bill, permitting the use of the whip on disobedient African labourers. The feminist and progressive Olive Schreiner, the author of *The Story of an African Farm*, had formerly been an admirer of Rhodes, and perhaps was in love with him. At one dinner party during the Strop Bill debate she grew so angry at Rhodes that she started to bang her head on the table.

Rhodes's popularity with the Cape Dutch ended abruptly after the Jameson Raid in 1896, an abortive coup d'état against the Transvaal Republic. The future imperial statesman and Field Marshal, Jan Smuts, was twenty-six at the time:

> How shall I describe the sensations with which I received the news on New Year's Day of 1896 of that fatal and perfidious venture? . . . It became so clear to me that the British connection was harmful to SA's best interests that I feared my future position as a Cape politician would be a false one. I therefore left the old colony for good . . .

In the three years between the Jameson Raid and the Boer War, the British paid small regard to the sentiment of the Cape Dutch. Her Majesty's High Commissioner in South Africa, the cold and authoritarian Alfred, Lord Milner, was met at Graaff-Reinet in 1898 by a group of the Bond, who gave him assurances of their loyalty to the Empire. 'I am glad to be assured that any section of Her Majesty's subjects are loyal,' this prig replied. 'I would be much more glad to be allowed to take that for granted. Why should I not? . . . Well gentlemen, of course you are loyal. It would be monstrous if you were not. And now, if I have one wish, it is that I may never again have to deal at any length with the topic.'

The Cape Dutch had stayed aloof from the Voortrekkers. They offered their sympathy but not their men as soldiers during the Boer War. Yet it was here in the Cape, above all at Stellenbosch, that there arose during the 1930s the new radical Afrikaner nationalism, whose most famous expression was the apartheid system. The Boer War had been ruinous to the Afrikaner farmers up in the Transvaal and the Orange Free State. They came back from prison camp to find their homesteads burnt and deserted, their cattle gone, their families stricken by death and disease in British concentration camps. Everywhere British immigrants had arrived to take the Boer land. Everywhere burgers, the citizen farmers, were forced to become squatters, or bywoners. The poor Afrikaners looked for a livelihood in the new mining towns such as Johannesburg. Often unable to speak English, and ignorant of the new technology, they fought to maintain a standard of living higher than that of the blacks. To safeguard their wages, these Afrikaners made common cause with the English-speaking miners and other trade unionists, most of whom were socialists. They joined in a strike which was almost a revolution, in 1922, on the Witwatersrand, under the slogan, 'Workers of the World Unite for a White South Africa'. The government used planes and field artillery to suppress the insurrection, in which hundreds were killed. The strike leaders afterwards went to the gallows, chanting the 'Red Flag'.

Two years later, an Afrikaner/Labour government came into power. It nationalised the railways, giving most of the jobs to Afrikaners. It created the iron and steel industry, based on the great reserves of coal and iron ore. It brought in a Mines and Works Act (1926) whose purpose, clear from its popular title, was the Colour Bar Act. The Prime Minister, J. B. M. Hertzog, one of the Boer War heroes, defended such acts as measures to guard the poor whites against the capitalists who wanted to bring in scab black labour. There was not yet an ideology of apartheid, as can be seen from Hertzog's attitude to the Coloureds. He said of these people in 1925: 'They came about and exist in our midst . . . They know no other civilisation . . . They use the languages of the whites . . . There can be no question of segregation.'

The ideology of apartheid sprang not from the conflicts of the Witwatersrand but from the cafés of Cape Town and tranquil Stellenbosch. The founding fathers of the apartheid movement were neither of Voortrekker nor country stock; even those who were old enough had not fought in the Boer War; they were middle-class, urban intellectuals almost all from the Cape. The foremost of these, and the first Prime Minister of a National Party government, was the politician and clergyman, Dr D. F. Malan: these Nationalists have a liking for using their initials in the Dutch custom rather than Christian names. Although Malan was of military age, he prudently spent the Boer War reading theology at Stellenbosch and at Leiden in Holland. After becoming a doctor of divinity and a dominee in the Dutch Reformed Church, Malan was editor of *Die Burger*, and went into politics, joining the Cabinet of the Afrikaner/Labour Pact in 1924. Malan's disciples at Cape Town koffiehuise and in the classrooms of Stellenbosch were men of a similar background: N. J. van der Merwe, T. E. Donges, Eric Louw, C. R. Swart, J. G. Strijdom and H. F. Verwoerd. All were urban Cape intellectuals except Dr Verwoerd, who had been born in the Netherlands.

These Cape intellectuals started off as a theoretical ginger group within Hertzog's National Party after the end of the Afrikaner/Labour alliance. They transformed the Broederbond from a kind of Afrikaner Rotary Club, or perhaps freemasonry, into a secret society, sworn to achieve power for the volk. They attacked Hertzog for compromising with Smuts, the Boer War hero who had become a friend of Britain. According to W. A. De Klerk, the decent Hertzog had no time for these intellectual critics:

> What did these politician parvenus know about principles when they libelled a man of the stature of Smuts in the way they did? . . . What had these 'super-nationalists' ever done for their country to warrant their fantastic claims? All they ever seemed to do, he might have thought, was to gather in koffiehuise in Cape Town. There they sat, morning after morning, listening to the pronouncements of a man who had watched the Anglo-Boer War from the comfort of the Netherlands.

These remote Stellenbosch intellectuals nevertheless dreamed up a pageant that was to inflame Afrikaner nationalism. This was the ox-wagon trek of 1938 to mark the centenary of the Great Trek. As the procession moved north through dorps, towns and cities, hundreds of thousands of Afrikaners attended to cheer, to pray and to touch the lumbering wagons. The centenary trek, with its folksiness, its pride of race and aggressive nationalism, was no doubt under the influence of the Nazis. The Ossewabrandwag (Ox-wagon firewatch) went in for blood oaths and torchlight rallies. The Afrikaner Stormjaers modelled themselves on Hitler's Stormtroopers.

Some of the National Party ideologues were anti-semitic, but it is misleading to lump together Hitler's loathing of Jews with Dr Malan's apartheid theory, first presented under the name in 1935. Hitler's anti-semitic fury was only the latest and maddest manifestation of a dislike for a people who, though few in numbers, have played a powerful role in Europe's economic and cultural life. It represented the jealousy felt by the poor for the rich, by the ignorant for the clever. The racial theories of Dr Malan concerned the utterly different problem of how a few million educated and civilised whites could live with tens of millions of tribal Africans. These are two different, indeed opposite, problems.

Because Naziism and the apartheid theory are both concerned with questions of race, they are stamped with the same brand of 'racism', a modern and very ambiguous term. The term is especially confusing in South Africa where until fifty years ago the 'racial problem' was taken to mean the enmity between English and Afrikaner. Whether or not Dr Malan shared Hitler's hostility to the Jews, he certainly did not look on the Africans in the same light as Jews. Far from wanting to punish, expel or exterminate Africans, Dr Malan regarded them with paternal care: '... it is the Christian duty of the white to act as guardians over the non-white races until such time as they have reached that level where they can look after their own affairs.'

Whatever they thought of modern Jews, such as the capitalists of Johannesburg, the Afrikaners likened themselves to the Jews of their sacred book, the Old Testament. The Voortrekkers, heading north, identified with the Children of Israel, seeking the Promised Land. Many a tiny stream in the Orange Free State or the Transvaal was named by them, hopefully, as the Nile. The Thirst Trekkers who found in Angola plentiful cattle and wild bees quite naturally called it 'the land flowing with milk and honey'. The Afrikaner intellectuals followed the revolutionary, Messianic tradition of those seeking the Kingdom of Heaven on earth – from the Jews themselves, the Calvinists of the Reformation, the American and the French revolutionaries, to Marx, with his dream of a 'classless society'. These revolutionary leaders regarded themselves as controllers of destiny, the Chosen Race, the Children of God, the Saints, the Will of the Revolution, the Proletarian Vanguard, which in a Marxist Messianic phrase is 'on the side of history'. Predestination, the theory which Calvin applied to individual souls, was taken up and transformed by power-hungry demagogues like Robespierre, Napoleon, Lenin, Hitler and Mao Tse Tung.

The Messianic vision was clear to the one undisputed genius of the apartheid ideologues, H. F. Verwoerd, who was both a psychiatrist and a sociologist, in some ways a mad professor out of a children's comic book. Here is some of his rhetoric, chosen almost at random:

> Perhaps it was intended that we should have been planted here at the southern point within the crisis area so that from the resistance might emanate the victory whereby all that has been built up since the days of Christ may be maintained for the good of all mankind. We have been planted here, we believe, with a destiny – destiny not for the sake of a selfishness of a nation, but for the sake of the service of a nation to the world of which it forms a part, and the service of a nation to the Deity in which it believes.

Fifty years have passed since Dr Verwoerd lectured in sociology here in Stellenbosch. Sociology is still one of the most popular subjects on the campus, though now, I would guess, it appeals more to radicals of the left. One hears sociological chit-chat everywhere: 'The people who matter are Freud and Weber. It's amazing when you get to the States and find how many Weberians there are. South Africa is a typical Weberian society. Whites at the top.' At the time of the general election in 1987, I called at the offices of the Independent candidate who was standing against the National Party. One of the party workers, an Afrikaner engaged in the wine business, said they were making progress but 'politics-wise, we're on a learning curve'.

The Independent of Stellenbosch, an Afrikaner businesswoman, did not do as well at the polls as Denis Worrall, the former Ambassador at the Court of St James, who stood for the neighbouring seat of Helderberg. There are more English-speakers in Helderberg. Some said it was brave for an Afrikaner to challenge the National Party here in the very birthplace of the apartheid ideology. It should not surprise. The Afrikaners of Stellenbosch prosper in farming, the wine industry, academic life, or commuting to Cape Town. They face no immediate threat from the blacks to their jobs, their schools or their suburbs. These well-to-do Afrikaners are much more liberal than the workers in the industrial belt of the Transvaal and Orange Free State, or in the poor districts of cities like Cape Town, where Coloureds and blacks are moving into areas designated as white. Among the Afrikaners as well as the English-speakers, the liberal left wing are found in the monied classes; the working class are less tolerant. The same thing is found all over the world. In London or Birmingham it is the people that read the *Guardian* who champion the non-white immigrants. The poor whites feel threatened. In South Africa, in the 1987 election, the Independents won only a wealthy Afrikaner suburb of North Johannesburg. The proletarian Afrikaners moved to the right-wing Conservative Party.

One Sunday morning in 1986, the Afrikaans paper *Rapport* devoted most of its first two pages to the, for them, sensational news of a split within the Dutch Reformed Church, the NGK, the spiritual leaders of Afrikanerdom. The rebellion had been expected since the October Synod made the historic ruling that the apartheid system was not justified by the Bible. Now, a group of protesters, led by Professor Willi Lubbe, the former editor of the Church's journal, had formed an action committee and called for another, extraordinary Synod, which had already been rejected by the Moderator, Professor Johan Heyns. Although Professor Lubbe had claimed that his standpoint was based on the Bible, having 'nothing to do with racial feelings', his own supporters belong to the right-wing or verkrampte side in politics, as in religion. The leader of the Conservative Party, Andreas Treurnicht, another former clerical journalist, had compared the Moderator, Heyns, with Archbishop Tutu.

This quarrel reopened arguments that had split the Dutch Reformed Church in the fifties and sixties. Theologians of apartheid such as Verwoerd and Treurnicht claimed that God had ordained a multiplicity of nations, citing the Tower of Babel and Acts 17:26. A large part of the NGK – including the Transvaal Moderator – argued that no one should be excluded from any Church on grounds of colour, and went on to denounce the social effects of apartheid. As in politics, so in religion, the application of the apartheid system affected the Coloureds far more than the blacks. The General Synod of the NG Mission Church wrote a report on the hurts and hardship caused by the Group Areas Act to Christians in District Six and other ancestral Coloured areas:

> Proclamations have already declared the church buildings of more than fifty congregations to be affected property. These buildings are mostly of great historical value. There is e.g. the SA Gestig in Long Street, Cape Town, which is equivalent to the Mission Church of the Groote Kerk. There is also the Sionskerk at Paarl, the Rhenish Church at Stellenbosch, the church at Worcester, Beaufort West, George and Upington, and many others. The Coloured people simply have to abandon these and bid farewell. This is suffering, almost too deep to understand. The Church shares this pain with its members. Their heritage is no longer theirs.

A Coloured Christian told me of how he had tried to get support to restore a Moravian Church, abandoned in District Six, and now almost derelict. He said that the new churches provided at Cape Flats had no feeling of sanctity: 'It's like trying to pray in a box,' he said.

Now, twenty years after the devastation wrought on the Mission Church of the Coloureds, the Dutch Reformed Church is trying to make amends. On the Sunday that the *Rapport* story appeared, I was in Stellenbosch, so I went to the morning service at the Mother Church of a sect which has earned the opprobrium of the whole Christian world. The arguments of the Synod had not spoilt the tranquillity of a late spring morning in this incomparable town. As I walked over the university meadows, I heard the toot of a horn; it was a motor-bike policeman greeting a friend. Small children were paddling in the brook that runs beside an avenue of oak trees. Bigger children, spotlessly dressed, went off smiling to Sunday School, as cheerful and well-behaved as the youngsters you see in some West Indian islands like Barbados and Grenada. The grown-ups go to the Mother Church, where there has been a congregation since 1684. The present building, begun in 1715 and renovated during the nineteenth century, now has a peculiar boomerang shape, so that if you are sitting near one of the entrance doors you cannot see or hear what is going on at the other side.

The congregation who filled the church were impeccably dressed, the men in coats and ties, the women in summer dresses of normal length at the arms and legs, instead of the seventeenth-century garb one tends to associate with Calvinism. There were no Puritan bonnets, and few hats. The congregation has little to do except sing the metrical psalms out of the book they carry to church. The prayers are said, not chanted, by the dominee, who devotes much if not most of the service to his sermon. In form and spirit, the service reminded me of the Presbyterian Church of Scotland. This Sunday, a stirring one for the Dutch Reformed Church, the minister read out the Synod's ruling against apartheid, and justified it at length from scripture. As far as I grasped with my minimal Afrikaans, he kept making the point that Christ offered salvation to Jews and gentiles, men and women, freemen and slaves alike.

The service would normally finish after the last psalm, but on this historic Sunday, another preacher got up and said he wanted just five minutes to get back to the subject of apartheid, then spoke for ten. After that, a woman who sounded cross said something I could not hear from the other side of the Mother Church. A man stood up on my side of the church, and when he began to speak there was much exchange of smiles and whispers, and some of the congregation walked out, then stood in the doorway, chattering noisily, perhaps in a pointed fashion. Perhaps they just needed a cigarette. Never before, in this nation of chain-smokers, have I observed so many people go so long without lighting up. From the fact that most of the people who got up to speak were old, and most of those who walked out were young, it was obvious that the latter belonged to the enlightened, verligte tendency.

Stellenbosch is not only the Oxford and Cambridge of Afrikanerdom; it has the one seminary of the Dutch Reformed Church. I read in *Die Burger* that one of the graduates of this seminary was an Englishman, Lewis Prockter who, like myself, had read history at Cambridge. I rang him up and we met for lunch. There are so many jokes about dominees in what the English South Africans call 'the Dutch Deformed Church', that I half expected Mr Prockter to fit the caricature of a stern, ranting Puritan. He turned out to be a quiet, scholarly man in his forties, with tinted spectacles and flecks of grey in his beard; he enjoyed good food and wine and discourse ranging around all kinds of subject. He was born in Sussex and brought up as an Anglican but he had lost his Christian faith by the time he went up to Christ's, Cambridge, during the sixties. He and his wife went in 1973 to teach in Rhodesia, but found the country was living in the imperial past. They came down to South Africa, which seemed to Mr Prockter more of a real nation. It was here that he and his wife became Christians. I did not ask Mr Prockter what had converted him, taking the old-fashioned view that Englishmen do not discuss their private religion or sexual life.

When he enrolled at the Stellenbosch seminary, Mr Prockter did not speak much Afrikaans, but found everyone helpful once they discovered he wanted to learn. He also had to learn Hebrew and Greek, a task that brought the rich reward of reading Homer in the original. He also says that Calvin is a 'tremendous' writer. 'He starts by saying that man is nothing without God. He rejects any idea that man is perfectible. The English can't really believe that man is completely sinful. They like to think that so-and-so is a nice chap and probably has some good in him.' I mentioned that nowadays the Church of Scotland, which used to regard itself as Calvinist, was very permissive on matters such as abortion. 'Our Church is against abortion,' Mr Prockter said, 'and we're completely against homosexuality too.'

Knowing almost nothing about theology, I asked Mr Prockter if it was true that the Dutch Reformed Church put most of its emphasis on St Paul's version of Christianity. Yes, Calvinism derived from Pauline teaching but still more from St Augustine. By contrast, the Roman Catholics look more to Thomas Aquinas and Aristotle. Unlike our Northern Irish Calvinists, Mr Prockter expresses a high regard for the Roman Catholic Church, and especially for the present Pope. His differences with the Roman, as with the Orthodox, Church are purely theological. But Mr Prockter has no respect at all for the poor old Church of England: 'When I was an agnostic, I talked to Anglican priests and I despised them, because they didn't seem to believe in what they were teaching . . . Bishop Robinson (John Robinson, author of *Honest to God*) had read the modern German theologians but he wasn't intelligent enough to understand them . . . Tutu? He's witty.'

The Dutch Reformed Church has seven English-speaking parishes but it remains the national church of the Afrikaners. Had it been hard for Mr Prockter to understand these peculiar people? He reassured me by saying that he too regarded W. A. De Klerk's *The Puritans in Africa* as indispensable reading. He had no time for the popular theory that Cape Afrikaners are more verligte or liberal than are their fellow countrymen in the north. He made a different distinction:

> Contrary to what most people think, there is more money here in the Cape than in Johannesburg. It's old money from land, handed down from generation to generation. In the Transvaal people make quick fortunes and gamble them away. Often the children don't inherit. In a way it's like Jane Austen's England, with a division between the landed class and the people in business in the city.

Just as Cape Afrikaners formed the koffiehuis set – men like Malan, Verwoerd and Strijdom – so Cape Afrikaners maintained the apartheid system. The last State President, B. J. Vorster, was raised in the eastern Cape and studied sociology here in Stellenbosch, under Verwoerd. The current State President, P. W. Botha, comes from the west Cape town of George, which some Afrikaners insist on trying to pronounce with guttural aitches for the gees, so that it sounds like the hee-haw bray of an ass. The whites of George are proud of their famous son, and the George Museum has a room of Botha memorabilia such as the gifts presented him on travels abroad: a dagger from Israel, a flag made of butterfly wings from Taiwan, and a medallion from the head of Chile's military intelligence. Yet it cannot be said that Botha is either more liberal or refined than fellow Afrikaners in the Transvaal or Orange Free State.

According to Peter Younghusband in *Inside South Africa*:

> When he was in his early teens, State President Pieter Botha had a pony called Tieckie, which he saddled one day and rode off to visit a neighbouring farm. When he got there, he rode his horse straight in the front door, through the living room, down the passage, through the back door, without exchanging any greetings with the startled occupants. The family who suffered the intrusion felt insulted and complained to the boy's parents about young Piet's arrogance and bad manners . . . His recollections of early days as a National Party organiser abound with stories of punch-ups, some of them chortlingly recounted by P. W. himself . . . Pushing his way through a group of hecklers at a meeting of his home constituency of George, in the days when he was a Minister of Defence, P.W. slapped the nearest offender in the face. He later denied that he had deliberately slapped the man. He said he had merely

dismissed him with a gesture of contempt, and the heckler had got in the way.

If Botha now hobnobs with Chinese, Israelis and South Americans, it is from necessity rather than wide cultural interests. This was obvious from the press and TV reports of Mr and Mrs Botha's trip to Madeira. The Afrikaners used to regard the Portuguese in Mozambique and Angola as Papists who went to bed with the blacks. Since those two countries got independence, and fell under the influence of the Soviet Union, South Africa has given a welcome to the expelled Portuguese colonists and to immigrants from Portugal itself. Half the inhabitants of Madeira now live in South Africa, whose Portuguese speakers now number almost a million. During his visit there, President Botha made some jokes: 'If this is a private reception,' we heard him say on TV, 'I should like to see what the public reception is like . . . The President [of Madeira] has said I should come on a holiday with my family. I think I should come without my family.' We saw him dance with his wife, but not the moment described by a *Sunday Times* reporter: 'As Madeira folk musicians flayed and humped medieval musical instruments, the State President knelt on the shawl of a Bailinho dancer and kissed the olive-haired beauty twice.'

4

PORT ELIZABETH

Necklace City . . . Turbulent history . . .
Nelson Mandela . . . Steve Biko

T HE EDWARD HOTEL stands on the crest of the hill that rises steeply out of the sea at Port Elizabeth. On its left, looking down at the green that covers the hillside, there is the Anglican church built by the settlers who founded the city in 1820. On the right is another reminder of home, the Up The Khyber Curry House. On the east side of the green, on Donkin Street, a terrace of houses plunges down to the business centre, as steep as Edinburgh or Bristol. The old town is so reminiscent of Britain that I was taken aback by a brass name plate for H. Minnaar, Sielkundige, which is the Afrikaans for psychiatrist. On the street descending the other side of the green, I passed the theatre, showing a play from England about 'a homosexual boxer and his friend, a rapist'. The director is quoted as saying that scenes of full frontal nudity were essential to the play. In Port Elizabeth I discovered something like an English pub, the Grand. The landlord talked of England; perhaps he wanted to make me feel at home: 'I went to the UK once, on a package tour to the international ballroom dancing at the Albert Hall. That used to be my game. My partner was from the UK, and of course most of the adjudicators were UK. We won several South African championship titles, starting with the tango, and then the quick and the slow.'

In spite of such reassuring hints of home, I soon found Port Elizabeth sinister, if not scary. It is a city gripped by a mighty fear. The first thing you notice, coming from somewhere else in South Africa, is the curious absence of blacks. They are not in the pubs, as they are everywhere in Johannesburg. They are not in the shops, as they used to be even during the heyday of apartheid. Those blacks you do meet, like hotel servants, do not return a smile on greeting. And what you read in their faces is not hatred but fear.

Port Elizabeth is the largest town of the Xhosas, pronounced roughly cosa, with an initial click if you can manage it. They are one of the largest African nations, whose territory comprehends all the eastern Cape as well as Transkei and Ciskei, two of the 'homelands' recognised as independent states by South Africa but by no one else. The Xhosas, who have produced such politicians as Nelson Mandela, Oliver Tambo and Steve Biko, have always been the most militant of the black opponents of the Pretoria government. Outside the two homelands, the Xhosas tend to be under the sway of the African National Congress and its ally, the South African Communist Party. When the latest troubles began in 1985, the followers of the ANC went into action all over the eastern Cape. They rioted; they attacked black policemen, officials and their families; they closed the schools; they boycotted all white-owned shops; and they instituted a reign of terror, whose now notorious instrument was the burning of people alive in a tyre filled with petrol. The word necklace no longer requires inverted commas.

The 'comrades', teenage boys and girls, took control of most of the African townships around Port Elizabeth. Having themselves dropped out of school, they forced all the other children to do the same, on pain of a necklace. Not one black child over the age of eight got any education for eighteen months. The effect of this boycott has been disastrous for the whole Xhosa nation. In South Africa, as in all black Africa, with its rapidly growing population and shortage of jobs, success in life depends especially on the matric exam, the equivalent of our O-levels. A black South African with matric may be able to get a well-paid job on leaving school, with the possibility of advancement in business or the professions. Without matric, the young South African is condemned to life as a shanty dweller. Matric, for the individual, is a passport into the middle classes. Education is for the blacks in general the only means of winning equality with the whites. The boycott of education has put the Xhosas years behind the Zulus, Tswanas and Sothos.

At the end of 1986, there were one thousand four hundred Port Elizabeth Africans in detention under emergency law. Yet those who remained at large still ran the townships by terror. The 'comrades' have challenged and almost usurped the authority of their tribal elders, teachers, parents and ministers of religion, both Christian and those of the sects such as the Zionists. Young Xhosas apparently no longer go through the circumcision rite. The 'comrades' have brought in a crude taxation on people at work. A nurse, for example, has to pay R50 (£15) a month. They have not won control of the black, middle-class suburb of New Brighton, which is now ringed by a barbed-wire fence.

The power of the 'comrades' is seen in the way they enforce the boycott of white-owned shops. Few Port Elizabeth blacks would talk to an unknown white man, let alone tell him about the 'comrades', but various whites have told me of how the boycott is run:

> A man had gone to a white shop and bought a supply of groceries for the family for some days ahead. The comrades stopped him and made him eat the whole lot himself, on the spot . . . They make people drink cooking oil . . . A woman who works for me and a friend of hers were carrying parcels, not from a white shop. But a group of youths trashed the parcels and then gave them both a beating. They went to complain to the street committee but they were all in prison . . . There's an African in our office who badly wanted a carpet. I gave him one from my flat but when he took it home they burned it.

The 'comrades' deal out justice in kangaroo courts, or what are called by the sociologists of the ANC, 'the established street structures'. For those found guilty of any form of co-operation with the authorities, the lightest punishment is a flogging with wire rope. Grave offenders receive the necklace. Before coming to Port Elizabeth, I had not realised that the necklace often involves not only physical pain but prolonged psychological torture. The ritual was explained to me by a Port Elizabeth journalist who grew up among Xhosas and speaks their language. He was describing not the spontaneous lynching of somebody caught by a rioting mob, but what might be called a judicial necklace. On being sentenced, the victim is told to present himself at ten the following day at the place of execution out in the bush. He is not kept physically under arrest but a number of comrades are detailed to watch him, in case he tries to escape, as two people succeeded in doing. After a night of anticipation, whose horror is scarcely imaginable, the victim goes voluntarily to his place of death, perhaps out of fatalism, perhaps from a sense of tribal obedience. Before execution, the victim is ordered to pay a R1 (30p) 'burial fee'. He is then given a joint of dagga (pronounced dah-ha, the local marijuana) to calm his nerves. The tyre filled with petrol is put round his shoulders and he is handed a box of matches to light his own last cigarette. Striking the first match sometimes ignites the necklace. If not the victim can enjoy his dagga. Then he is made to light the petrol. He has become his own executioner. The crowd laugh and jeer at him as he burns to death.

'Together hand-in-hand, with our boxes of matches and our necklaces, we shall liberate this country.' This was the boast of Winnie Mandela, quoted in the *Daily Mail*, April 14th, 1986, whose husband Nelson Mandela has always refused to condemn the necklaces and other atrocities. When two men were hanged in 1987 for taking part in political killings, including the necklace, Mrs Mandela saluted them: 'I greet you in the name of Umkhonto we Sizwe. We have come to terms with the fact that an enemy has declared war. We accept the challenge. The blood of the comrades has not flowed in vain.' (*The Independent*, September 2nd, 1987.)

The former long-time head of Umkhonto we Sizwe [the ANC's military wing], who was also chairman of the South African Communist Party, Joe Slovo, a lawyer born in Lithuania, complains that the whites have not so far suffered as much as the blacks. In an interview with the British Communist magazine *Marxism Today* (December 1986), Mr Slovo expounded his grandiose military plans:

> Another aspect of the armed struggle is the need for combat to become ever more visible not only in the black areas but also in the white areas. This is not a policy of attacks against civilians. But the average white has been completely unaware of the conflict which has been taking place in the black areas. The white soldiers go back after having done their dirty work to their white areas. It is important that people who have been the backbone of support for the regime and who have lived in relative security and safety in South Africa, should now begin to fear what the future holds for them . . . In the past we have been inhibited by the possibility that civilians might be injured as a result of an attack on a military target, and we are becoming less and less inhibited by this factor. In other words, we are not allowing the presence of civilians in the vicinity necessarily to prevent us from embarking upon an action against a genuine military installation, or against a target which it is legitimate for us to attack as an armed force of a liberation movement . . .

The arrogant and pretentious military jargon of 'armed struggle', 'legitimate targets' and 'liberation movements', is all too familiar to those who have suffered over the last forty years from bombing and murder by terrorists. The ANC are exceptional only because they have the support abroad of politicians and bishops who ought to know better. The paramilitary language of Mr Slovo does not convey the human consequence of his attacks: the children burnt alive for daring to go to school; the women hideously maimed by a bomb in a supermarket; the miners

65

hacked to death for defying their union leaders. Blacks suffer more because there are more of them. A bomb in a shop or bar is likely to kill more blacks than whites. As far as I could establish, only three Port Elizabeth whites have suffered the necklace. One of these was a West German folk musician who liked to play with African bands. He had a black girlfriend; he used to give lifts to blacks, and, in spite of the warning of friends, he drove at night into African townships. After a year or so, his luck ran out. His charred remains, mingled with rubber, were found one day in a used car dump.

Port Elizabeth saw the first real test of economic sanctions against South Africa. In the summer of 1986, the Congress of the United States made it illegal for companies to invest in or trade with South Africa until the government of Pretoria released Nelson Mandela and did away with apartheid. After Kodak and IBM had announced they would disinvest, the giant car company, General Motors, said it would sell its Port Elizabeth plant, employing six thousand people. When the news broke all the assembly-line workers, whites as well as Coloureds and blacks, started a sit-down strike, apparently in a protest against disinvestment. However, it soon became clear that the general secretary of the National Automobile and Allied Workers Union, Freddie Sauls, wanted to turn the crisis into a demonstration against the South African government. He demanded severance pay and a refund of pension payments for all his members, most of whom are, like Mr Sauls, Coloureds, or blacks. The management sacked 567 strikers, then advertised for replacements. The general manager, George Stegman, said: 'If Mr Sauls was quoted accurately in this morning's newspapers, he has finally found the courage to state publicly what he said privately two weeks ago, and that is that he would like to see GM shut down.' He called it unfortunate that 'a large number of loyal GM workers had been caught up in the ideological beliefs of an elected union official whose actions posed a question as to any real concern on his part for the interests of GM's employees or their families.'

The union replied with scarcely disguised threats against General Motors vehicles and the 'scabs' who continued to make them. 'If we do not succeed,' said Mr Sauls, 'then we will have to look at GM products and it will be up to the workers to decide if they are willing to tolerate the presence of GM cars in their areas.' A newspaper reported that the response by the union to the management, 'had been to turn to the community for help. It has begun organising street committees in black and Coloured areas to identify scab labour and to try to prevent such labour from applying for jobs. Mr Sauls and other union officials and members confidently predicted that not one black worker and very few Coloured workers would apply for work at General Motors.'

The very report that 'street committees' were out to identify 'scabs' must constitute, in the atmosphere of Port Elizabeth, the threat of a necklace. A year later, after the unsuccessful strike of the gold and coal miners, thirty-five men who had stayed at work were eventually murdered, most of them hacked to death on leaving their hostels. That was in the Transvaal and the Orange Free State, where the ANC is not nearly so strong as at Port Elizabeth. Yet General Motors was overwhelmed by applicants for the jobs, including a high proportion of those who had first been sacked for striking. As many as five hundred men at a time assembled outside General Motors, passing their application forms through the wire. Even the whites were anxious not to be interviewed and the blacks implored journalists not to take their pictures. The scene at Port Elizabeth was striking proof that a large number of the blacks, as well as the whites and Coloureds, oppose economic sanctions.

A Coloured man said to me: 'Where I live, in Kensington, nobody wants this strike. Sauls must be just a politician. He likes to appear on TV. And he's not a car worker. The Coloured people are desperate for work. Some people haven't worked more than six weeks this year.' It was November 1986. Port Elizabeth used to be known as both the Northampton and Coventry of South Africa. It still makes shoes but some of the car manufacture has already moved north to the Transvaal where there is plentiful iron ore and coal, as well as a big market for cars. The ANC's campaign of disruption has wrecked the economy of the whole eastern Cape. Unemployment is running at sixty per cent. Investment is moving to more peaceful areas, such as Natal and the eastern Transvaal. With factories closing, and most of the schools shut, the most advanced and successful Africans, the Xhosas, are slipping back into poverty and ignorance.

It was here in the eastern Cape that the whites in South Africa first encountered the blacks; and here that relations between the races have long been poorest. Nobody knows exactly when the blacks arrived in this part of Africa. Archaeology is fraught with political passion. All we know is that many hundreds of years ago, a people calling themselves the Nguni moved from the region of Lake Victoria into the south-east of

Africa. The Zulus, who were to be the most powerful of the Nguni clans, have long resided in present Zululand, in northern Natal. The Xhosas, during the sixteenth to the nineteenth centuries, moved south and west along the coast, driving their cattle into the temperate region as far as the Fish River.

The Nguni first encountered the whites when ships were wrecked on the coast in the sixteenth century. In 1705, an expedition sent to Natal to cut timber discovered an Englishman living with African wives in such contentment that two of the sailors jumped ship to join him. Two survivors of a shipwreck founded a clan in Pondoland which is still known as the Lungu, or whites. From about the start of the eighteenth century, the Dutch in Stellenbosch used to trade with the Nguni people. The whites wanted ivory, and the Xhosas wanted metal bands, blankets, brandy, tobacco, above all muskets and horses. Although the distance between the whites and the Xhosas was, at the start, enormous, the absence of tsetse fly made it easy to go on horse or by wagon, instead of the train of porters required in tropical Africa.

In the course of the eighteenth century, white farmers settled ever nearer the Xhosas, who were in their turn moving westward. Often the whites went with Bushmen or Hottentots on trading visits, some of whom knew the Xhosa language. All four peoples raided each other's cattle and quarrelled. The whites and the blacks often clashed but there was also mutual attraction. The whites valued the Xhosas as herdsmen; the Xhosas wanted money in wages. As one historian put it, the two races also travelled for pleasure: 'Adventure beckoned. Young burghers rode eastward, exploring, hunting, love-making, raiding. Xhosas walked westward as far as Cape Town, viewing the marvels of a strange culture and visiting their friends in the employment of farmers.'

By the start of the nineteenth century, with Britain now the colonial ruler, the eastern Cape saw constant skirmishing over land and cattle. At one time the Hottentots and the Bushmen took the side of the Xhosas against the Trekboere, as the Dutch farmers now came to be called. Then, in 1815, the Boers were up in arms against the British who had hanged five of their number for killing a Coloured. The Boers had compounded this offence by seeking to make alliance with the Xhosas. The martyrdom of the five at Slagtersnek (Butcher Pass), was one of the grievances of the Boers who started the Great Trek north in 1836; it still forms part of Afrikaner mythology.

For nearly three centuries there has been argument over who occupied what land in the eastern Cape. The Hottentots (khoikhois) and Bushmen

(San) gradually lost their separate identities and came to be lumped under the designation of Coloureds. The Xhosas stuck to their language, their monarchy and their rituals, like circumcision; however the whites were increasingly dominant. The Boers took the grazing land. The missionaries challenged traditional faith. There was also a constant rise in the Xhosa population, partly due to the introduction of maize. The discontent of the Xhosa erupted in 1819, when one of their military leaders, Makanda, led nine thousand warriors in a futile attack on Grahamstown, the first in a long line of what came to be called the 'Xhosa Wars' or 'Kaffir Wars'.

The attack on Grahamstown encouraged the British government to build a new settlement in the eastern Cape province. The Westminster parliament voted money to ship and supply an expedition, for which there were many candidates in the lean years after the wars with France. Among the four thousand, who came to be known as the 1820 Settlers, was Thomas Pringle, a poet with an adventurous spirit, though crippled since childhood. He had the support of his famous countryman Sir Walter Scott. Although few of us now read Pringle's verse, or his *Narrative of a Residence in South Africa*, he merits a place in South African history as the first white liberal, or kaffirboetie (kaffir-lover) to use a less flattering Afrikaans term.

Within days of landing at Port Elizabeth, Pringle saw the arrest of a Xhosa woman who had illegally crossed the frontier near Uitenhage. For this offence, she and her children were sent in servitude to a colonist. Pringle witnessed her speech of complaint:

> Though I did not understand a single word she uttered, I have seldom been more struck with surprise and admiration. The language, to which she appeared to give full and forcible intonation, was highly musical and sonorous; her gestures were natural, graceful and impressive, and her large dark eyes and handsome bronze countenance were full of elegant expression. Sometimes she raised her tones aloud, and shook her clenched hand, as if she denounced our injustice, and threatened us with the vengeance of her tribe ... For my own part I was not a little struck by the scene, and could not help beginning to suspect that my European countrymen, who thus made captives of harmless women and children, were in reality greater barbarians than the savage natives of Caffraria.

Pringle condemned the Dutch-African colonists who wanted revenge for their comrades, hanged at Slagtersnek. He recalls that 'great excesses of inebriety' took place by the graves of what he sarcastically calls the 'colonial patriots'. He was full of praise for the Xhosas: 'The Caffers are a tall, athletic and handsome race of men with features often approaching to the European or Asiatic model . . . Their colour is a clear, dark brown. Their address is frank, cheerful and manly.' The Xhosa custom of circumcision, 'universally practised among them without any vestige of Islam', suggested to Pringle that they derived from 'a people of much higher civilisation'.

Pringle championed the Xhosa leader Makanda who led the attack on Grahamstown in 1819. His account of Makanda's treatment bears an uncanny resemblance to what some of our modern white liberals say of Nelson Mandela. Indeed our white liberals often compare the two men. Here is Pringle, writing one hundred and fifty years ago:

> By the order of the Colonial Government, he was forwarded by sea from Algoa Bay to Cape Town; there confined as a prisoner in the common gaol; and finally with others of his countrymen, guilty of no other offence than fighting for their native land against its civilised invaders, he was condemned to be imprisoned for life on Robben Island – the Botany Bay of the Cape – a spot appropriated for the custody of convicted felons, rebellious slaves and other malefactors, doomed to work in irons in the slave quarters.

After a year on Robben Island, Makanda and some of his fellow-prisoners got hold of a boat and made for the shore. The boat capsized and Makanda was drowned, but according to Pringle: 'Several of his companions who escaped relate that Makanda clung for some time to a rock, and that his deep sonorous voice was heard loudly cheering on those who were struggling with the billows, until he was swept off and engulfed by the raging surf.'

What little we know of Makanda does not suggest a wise or worthy political leader. According to Pringle's own account, Makanda promised his soldiers that he would turn the white men's bullets to rain. He said that when the whites had been driven into the sea, 'we will sit down and eat honey'. His massive attack on Grahamstown failed to subdue its small band of defenders. Yet Pringle says this of him, as so many liberal whites have said of more recent African rebels:

> As regards to the chief Makanda, it is melancholy to reflect how valuable an instrument for promoting the civilisation of the Caffer tribes was apparently lost by the nefarious treatment and indirect destruction of that extraordinary barbarian, whom a wiser and more generous policy might have rendered a grateful ally to the colony, and a permanent benefactor to his own countrymen.

When Pringle returned from South Africa, he went to work for the Anti-Slavery Society. He had already written an article on slavery at the Cape in the *New Monthly Magazine* for 1826. Coming from such a champion of the non-white races, the article is moderate in tone:

> The mildness of Slavery at the Cape has been much dwelt upon by certain travellers, whose opinions on the subject, being echoed by the *Quarterly Review*, and similar publications, seem to be generally admitted in England as perfectly just and incontrovertible . . . The general condition of slaves in this colony . . . may be less deplorable [than for instance the Ile de France, Mauritius] . . . but slavery at the Cape is assuredly a bitter and baleful draught.

He goes on to say that slaves could not marry without their master's consent; they could not purchase their freedom, and that in Cape Town it was 'as notorious as noon-day that the rearing and educating of handsome female slaves, as objects of licentious traffic with the Europeans, and especially with the rich Indian residents, is extensively practised among slave-holders.'

Pringle claimed to have witnessed the cruel treatment of slaves: 'I have even known ladies, born and educated in England, charitable and benevolent in their general character, yet capable of standing over their female slaves when they were flogged, and afterwards ordering salt and pepper to be rubbed into their lacerated flesh.' This kind of detail appeared with rather suspicious frequency in the anti-slavery literature, as it does in modern 'slaver' novels. Yet even Pringle concludes that: 'If the African Colonists, as a body, are notwithstanding all this, less corrupted than the mass of slave-holders in some other countries, they owe it chiefly to the comparatively limited extent of their slave population, and to the early marriages, and simpler and purer manners, of the majority of the country's inhabitants.' It is interesting to discover that the South Africans were once regarded as better than other whites in their treatment of non-white people.

Thomas Pringle might have remarked on two other differences between slavery at the Cape and in the Americas. The blacks of the United States and the Caribbean had been transported against their will across the Atlantic. Those who survived the journey lost their African names, their families and their ancestral customs. Few of them knew from which part of Africa they or their forefathers had come. The great majority of American slaves were made to toil on plantations of sugar, tobacco or cotton, in gangs, under the threat of the lash. Of the slaves in South Africa, only the Javanese had been brought from another continent, and many of them were able to keep their names and Islamic religion. By the nineteenth century, most of the slaves at the Cape had at least an admixture of Bushman or Hottentot blood, as well as Asian or European. They were by now Coloureds, belonging to Africa. There were no plantations, and even the slaves who worked in the vineyards lived better than those in America. In the eastern Cape, most of the slaves were farm-hands or household servants, similar to the house slaves in black Africa. Their state was nearer to that of a serf or bondman in medieval Europe. If conditions became too harsh they could, and frequently did, escape to the north to join one of the bands of freemen, known by such names as Baster or Griqua.

Yet when slavery was abolished in 1833, throughout the British Empire, it was here in the eastern Cape that the owners were most upset. The frontier Boers had long been fretting against the British. They had not forgotten the hanging of five of their fellows at Slagtersnek. They resented the spread of English at the expense of Dutch, or their own argot, Afrikaans. They had suffered from drought and everlasting Xhosa wars. They disliked the sanctimonious Anglo-Saxon missionaries. Emancipation seemed to the Boers a crowning insult, especially because they were offered small compensation and the decree came into force at harvest time. The abolition of slavery was the immediate cause of the Great Trek, from the eastern Cape, that gathered momentum during the 1830s.

The departure of so many Trekkers did not reduce the pressure on grazing land, especially since there were now thousands of refugees from the terror unleashed in the north by the Zulu chief, Shaka Zulu. The sixth Xhosa War of 1834-5 put all the frontier territory in a panic. As early as 1846, Port Elizabeth suffered the first recorded strike in South African history. There was at that time a boom in the world price of wool, especially that from the sheep of the eastern Cape, so the beach labourers asked for and won an extra sixpence a day to carry the bales to waiting ships.

In the 1840s, a young Xhosa orator called Mlanjeni had made a name for himself as a witch-doctor and prophet. He told his people to rid themselves of the British by making a sacrifice, as a penance, of all the dun- and cream-coloured cattle in Xhosa territory. Some ten years later, in 1856, another seer and politician, Mhlakaza, told his people to make an even greater sacrifice. According to one of the missionaries, John A.

Chalmers, the prophecy included the coming back from the dead of all the Xhosa heroes: Mhlakaza told the people: 'as a pledge of their belief and as a means of hastening the arrival of the golden age of liberty and prosperity, that there must be the utter extermination of all cattle, great and small – horses and dogs being the only animals excepted, also that every grain of corn or cafir maize should be sold or thrown away.' According to Chalmers, the rebels talked 'of armies arriving on sea; others sailing in umbrellas; thousands of cattle were heard knocking their horns together and bellowing in caverns, impatient to rise, only waiting until all their fellows who still walked the earth were slain.' The seers told them that when this sacrifice had been offered, 'the choicest of English cattle would fill the byres; the grain pits would overflow; wagons, clothes, guns and ammunition would appear in abundance; and a great wind would sweep the whites into the sea.'

On the instruction of their prophets, the Xhosas slaughtered between 150,000 and 200,000 cattle. By February 1857 the countryside was starving. According to Chalmers: 'The point was now reached in the deeply laid plot, so cunningly calculated by its originators. Upwards of 100,000 wild kaffirs – stung by the pangs of hunger, and the deeper pangs of disappointment, driven to despair, their cattle recklessly killed and nothing found in their stead – were now ready, like a pack of wolves, to commit all possible mischief.' But the revolt collapsed. The government and the colonists provided soup kitchens to feed the starving Xhosas. As Chalmers smugly remarked: 'The very nation, whose destruction was so secretly sought by this perfidious tragedy, became the saviour of many hundreds of kaffirs.'

Just as Mhlakaza made the Xhosas destroy their cattle and grain, so the ANC leaders make them close their factories and their schools. Once again the Xhosas have ruined themselves in the name of liberation. There is another curious parallel between the Xhosas, one hundred and thirty years ago, and those who follow the lead of people like Joe Slovo. According to Chalmers, rumours about the Crimean War were current in Xhosa country from 1854: '. . . the remark was frequently made "The Russians are black like ourselves, and they are coming to assist us to drive the English into the sea . . ." ' A Xhosa councillor, early in 1856, said he had met a delegation of black people, including a brother some years dead: 'He was told by their people that they had come from across the water; that they were the people – the Russians – who had been fighting against the English, with whom they would wage perpetual warfare; and they had now come to aid the kaffirs, but before anything could be done for them, they were to put away witchcraft, and as they would have abundance of cattle at the coming resurrection, those now in their possession were to be destroyed.'

A similar cult arose in the Transkei in 1921, though now the rebels looked to the Marcus Garvey 'Back to Africa' movement, which claimed to have a black Air Force. The Xhosa leaders told the people to kill all pigs and white fowls, after which they would soon be saved by American aeroplanes, flown by blacks.

Few people outside South Africa have heard of those nineteenth-century rebels: Makanda, Mlanjeni and Mhlakaza. A modern Xhosa revolution-ary, Nelson Mandela, became the most famous prisoner of the twentieth century, perhaps of all time. A statue has been erected to him in London, and it has been suggested, seriously, that the monument in Trafalgar Square should be re-cast, and renamed Nelson Mandela's Column. A constantly growing number of streets, squares, parks, junior common rooms, bars and racehorses now bear his name. He has been given the Nehru Award by the Indian government; an honorary law degree by Lesotho, and freedom of countless cities. The blacks of Boston, Massa-chusetts, are agitating to form a separate city out of their enclave, named Mandela. In May 1973, three scientists at Leeds University discovered a new nuclear particle and called it the Mandela Particle. The name of Nelson Mandela is so familiar, and so much regard is felt for his evident bravery and intelligence, that almost nobody now remembers why he was sent to prison or why he stayed so long, refusing all offers of pardon because he would not renounce the use of violence. I found that my own memory of his case was sketchy, even though I try to keep up with affairs in South Africa; even though I was actually in this country during that southern winter of 1964 when Mandela was sentenced, with others, at the Rivonia trial.

The Rivonia trial was so called because the accused had plotted at a house in the Rivonia suburb of Johannesburg, where some of them were arrested during a raid on July 11th, 1963. The Rivonia trial occurred in between the Treason Trial of 1956–60, in which all the accused were acquitted, and the trial in 1965 of Bram Fischer, an Afrikaner and head of the South African Communist Party, who had been the defending counsel in both the Treason and the Rivonia trials. Reading about those distant events, here in the public library of Port Elizabeth, I was amazed to realise that not only were Nelson Mandela and Fischer rightly and justly sentenced, but that the Rivonia plot, launched twenty-five years ago, has proved a triumphant success.

It was at Lilliesleaf, a house in Rivonia, that the South African Communist Party, and its allied organisation, the ANC, drew up a plan for the overthrow of the South African government. This would start by a campaign of violence, first using sabotage, then by an armed insurrection backed by an outside force. Police repression and the imprisonment of ANC activists would stir up feelings against South Africa in the Western world, leading eventually to an economic boycott. This boycott was stated to be the supreme objective of the South African Communist Party. Documents, explaining the plot and giving specific requirements of arms and explosives, were found in the raid on Lilliesleaf. The authenticity of these documents was not denied by those found guilty at the Rivonia trial.

While Mandela remained in gaol, becoming each year a more famous and useful martyr, the ANC kept up its campaign for a boycott of South African sporting tours, South African fruit and wine, and companies such as Barclays Bank, which dealt with South Africa. When the Communists took Angola and Mozambique, and later had the co-operation of independent Zimbabwe, the ANC's military wing, Umkhonto we Sizwe, run by the Communist leader Joe Slovo, was able to mount attacks along the South African border, as well as supplying guns and bombs to its followers inside the country. After the riots of 1976, and still worse turmoil starting in 1985, all of it shown on western TV, the ANC won ever increasing support for a boycott, and even a vote for sanctions by the United States Congress. Thus the greatest power in the Western world had fallen in line with the plan devised by the tiny South African Communist Party, in a Rivonia farmhouse, a quarter century earlier. It sounds like a grotesque political thriller, written by someone obsessed by the red menace. Yet it is all recorded history. Far from denying the plot at Rivonia, the SACP now boasts of its achievement.

The story of the Rivonia plot and of Nelson Mandela must start with the founding of ANC in 1912. This was two years after the Act of Union, in which the British had tried to placate the defeated Boers by taking away the few political rights of Africans. The Act of Union most affected the Xhosas of the Cape. After a century of British rule, the Xhosas were far more advanced than the Zulus of Natal, most of whom had not come under British rule until 1879. The British in the Cape had always been more sympathetic to African aspirations than were the Boers of the Transvaal and the Orange Free State. A high proportion of Xhosa children, girls as much as boys, had received an education. Even before the foundation of Fort Hare College for blacks in 1916, many Xhosas went to a university, and took a profession. The British colonial government allowed and even encouraged the Xhosas to own the farm land. And here in the Cape, some of the blacks had the vote, until the Act of Union.

When the founding fathers of ANC assembled at Bloemfontein, as the most central town in South Africa, the Xhosas were prominent. A Xhosa musician, Enoch Sontonga, had written the noble anthem 'Nkosi Skelel i-Afrika' – Lord Bless Africa – here sung for the first time at a gathering of politicians, but now familiar to countless millions of television viewers all over the world. In her book *The Struggle for a Birthright*, Mary Benson says of that first meeting at Bloemfontein:

> When it came to the election of a President-General, it would have been obvious for a distinguished Xhosa to be chosen as they had been the first to be educated and their outstanding representative, the Rev Walter Rubusana, teacher and author, and the only African ever to be elected to the Cape Provincial Council, was present. But the Xhosa delegates at the conference decided that the Cape should take a back seat in order to unite people from the other provinces who besides suffered under greater restrictions. A renowned Zulu was elected: the Rev John Langalibele ('the bright sun') Dube.

Unlike its later rival, the Pan African Congress (PAC), the ANC has always accepted whites, Asians and Coloureds as equal members. It has always claimed to rise above tribal differences. In particular, it has tried not to appear a party of Xhosas against the Zulus. Apologists for the ANC always remind their critics that Dube, the first President-General, was Zulu, as was another distinguished leader, the Nobel Peace Prize winner, Chief Albert Luthuli. In rather the same way, Hindu Indians point out that their first two Presidents after independence were Muslims; and Irish Roman Catholics point out that the first two Presidents of the Republic were Protestants. The fact remains that the ANC has always received its most fervent support from Xhosas, particularly in the eastern Cape. The first university for the Africans, Fort Hare in the eastern Cape, has always been an ANC stronghold.

The Fort Hare freshmen of 1938 included two young Xhosa men from the Transkei, Oliver Tambo and Nelson Mandela, one of the Thembe royal family. Mandela left Fort Hare in a hurry, having taken part in a boycott against the reduction in power of the student body. He started work as a mines policeman, then went on to take an external arts degree and to study law at the University of Witwatersrand, which then was a hotbed of left-wing views, like our own London School of Economics. In 1944, Mandela and others founded the National Congress Youth League. When the National Party came to power in 1948 and started to introduce or tighten up the practice of apartheid, the ANC became increasingly desperate. More and more channels of protest, like strikes and demonstrations, were closed; more and more activists were imprisoned. After the riots of 1960, and the gunning down of a crowd at Sharpeville, the government banned the ANC, which by then had formed an alliance with the Communists.

The Soviet Communist Party first got its eye on South Africa in 1921, soon after winning power in Russia. A special committee, chaired by Leon Trotsky, met in Odessa to plan a strategy for the African continent. The committee resolved to use American black Communists to infiltrate the British and French African colonies. In South Africa, it was planned to organise the white working class. There was an economic depression and much discontent in the gold mines, where owners were bringing in African labour to undercut the whites. A strike in Johannesburg in 1922 led to an armed revolt under the banner, 'Workers of the World Unite for a White South Africa'. The rebels killed many innocent blacks before they were crushed by planes and artillery of the South African Army.

After this failure, the miners turned for an ally to the Afrikaners, still smarting from their defeat in the Boer War. The white working class from then on supported the National Party, or one of the groups on the far right. However, the South African Communist Party had some support among intellectuals and professional people, especially among the Jews who had fled persecution in Tsarist Russia or in the Kaiser's Germany. Many formed an idealised view of the new Soviet Union, which appeared still more admirable after the rise to power of Hitler in Germany. After the Second World War, intellectuals in the United States and in Western Europe came to see that Stalin's Russia was quite as cruel, aggressive and totalitarian as Hitler's Germany had been; moreover, Stalin revealed himself as an anti-semite. Perhaps because of their great distance from Russia, South African Communists did not become disillusioned. Besides, there had come to power in 1948 the South African National Party, many of whose leaders had been pro-German during the war.

The government, in 1950, outlawed the South African Communist Party, and later put on trial some of its leading ex-members, charged with treason, including Joe Slovo, who was at that time a Johannesburg lawyer. In the treason trial which lasted from 1956 to 1960 all the accused were found not guilty, largely thanks to their outstanding advocate, Bram Fischer, who was, in secret, the general secretary of the South African Communist Party. Born to a distinguished Afrikaans family in the Orange Free State, Fischer had gone as a Rhodes scholar to Oxford and then to the LSE during the thirties. He visited and admired the Soviet Union. Like most South African Communists, Fischer appears to have been an inflexible Stalinist. There was not much searching of souls about the invasion of Hungary, the revelations of Khrushchev about the behaviour of Stalin, or Solzhenitsyn's exposé of the Gulag Archipelago. It seems that Fischer was genuine in his freedom from racial prejudice. The black comrades returned his liking and trust. It was probably due to Fischer and to Mandela that, in 1960, the ANC and the SACP joined forces. Of course there were still many whites in the ANC who were not SACP members or sympathisers. But the SACP still had an influence on the ANC and other radical movements disproportionate to its own numbers.

The creation in 1961 of Umkhonto we Sizwe marked the decision by ANC to wage a campaign of violence. Like most terrorist groups, they started with sabotage against such 'economic' targets as power installations, bridges and railways. At this time, the early sixties, Angola and Mozambique were still under Portuguese rule, so that the ANC had no easy access to Soviet weapons. They had to rely for explosives on dynamite pinched from the gold mines. The leaders of both the ANC and the SACP led perilous lives. Some, like Ruth First, the estranged wife of Joe Slovo, were put in prison under a law permitting ninety days' detention, later extended to two years, without trial. Because of apartheid, it had become dangerous for people of different races to mingle socially. I can remember a coffee party where, at every knock on the door, an African woman guest put on an apron, pretending to be the maid. As a precaution, the Communists organised their cells by race. Their one safe house was Lilliesleaf, in the almost country suburb of Rivonia, where there were no inquisitive neighbours to watch who came in and out. Nelson Mandela used this as a safe house when he came back illegally to the country. In the end he was caught and was already in prison on a charge of illegal entry when the police descended on Lilliesleaf. Most of the white Rivonia plotters, including Joe Slovo, were out of the country or made their escape soon after the raid. There was only one white among those who stood trial the following year, 1964, in Pretoria.

Among the two hundred and fifty documents found at Rivonia was one called 'Mayibuye', setting out the long-term strategy for the overthrow of the state. At the top of the list was: 'Complete enforcement of a South African boycott'. The 'Mayibuye' document also contained some homely political maxims, such as: 'Shamelessly attack the weak, and shamelessly flee from the strong.' Among the other documents was one detailing, 'Production requirements: 210,000 hand-grenades; 48,000 anti-personnel mines; 1,500 time devices for bombs; 144 tons of ammonium nitrate; 21.6 tons of aluminium powder and 15 tons of black powder.' That document leads one to doubt the avowal by Mandela that human beings were not to become targets, or not till other means failed. The later success of the Marxist guerillas in Mozambique and Angola was largely due to the use of mines and anti-personnel bombs against the Portuguese. Hundreds of young Portuguese conscripts died or had their legs and genitals blown away by these fearsome weapons. The Communists in El Salvador call them the 'limb removers'.

No defendant at the Rivonia trial denied the truth of the documents that convicted him. All except one man, who was cleared, admitted to charges of planning or having already committed sabotage. Nelson Mandela admitted that he had trained in weaponry and had studied the revolution in Indonesia, Malaysia and Algeria: 'I acknowledge that I made these studies to equip myself for the role which I might have to play if the struggle drifted into guerilla warfare. I also made arrangements for our recruits to undergo military training.'

In his long and now very famous speech to the dock, Mandela evaded the question of whether he was or was not a Communist Party member:

> It is perhaps difficult for white South Africans with an ingrained prejudice against Communists to understand why experienced African politicians so readily accept Communists as their friends. But to us the reason is obvious. Theoretical differences amongst those fighting against oppression is a luxury we cannot afford at this stage. What is more, for many decades Communists were the only political group in South Africa who were prepared to treat Africans as human beings and their equals; who were prepared to eat with us, talk with us, live with us and work with us.

The speech from the dock made a huge impression on British liberal opinion when it was published afterwards in the London *Observer*.

There was no suggestion at the time, nor has there been since, that the Rivonia trial was unfair. The only criticism came from government supporters such as a judge, H. H. W. de Villiers, who said the defendants should have been charged with the more serious crime of high treason. The *Rand Daily Mail*, which then was the main voice of resistance to the apartheid government, said in an editorial (June 17th, 1964):

> The sentences pronounced by Mr Justice De Wet in Pretoria yesterday at the conclusion of the Rivonia trial were both wise and just. The law is seen at its best when there is justice tinged with mercy, and this was the case yesterday. The sentences could not have been less severe than those passed. The men found guilty had organised sabotage on a wide scale and had plotted armed revolution. As the judge pointed out, the crime of which they were found guilty was essentially high treason.

A few weeks after the trial, I was in Johannesburg and had many talks with liberal whites. This was what I wrote in a book published in 1965:

> The laws of South Africa may be odious, but the law men have not been corrupted. There could be no better example of this than the Rivonia trial last year of Nelson Mandela and others, both white and black, who had conspired to use violence against the state. Outside liberal opinion presented the trial as a conspiracy against freedom. Yet liberals inside South Africa regarded it as a victory. Many of them no doubt agree with Mandela that the time has come to use violence as well as agitation to overthrow the regime, but they were not shocked by the sentences. One liberal summed up his feelings: 'There was no doubt that the plotters were guilty. In fact, what really annoyed us about the case was the way they allowed themselves to get caught red-handed and all in a bunch. What really surprised us was the judge, who's a fanatical Nat, and was appointed only recently by Verwoerd. On the first day of the trial, the prosecuting counsel made a speech in which he kept referring to the accused men as the guilty men. The judge came down on him like a stone and said he wasn't to use that kind of talk in his court . . . It was a scrupulously fair trial.'

That was written in 1964, when we were all rather naive about 'violence against the state'. It was before the age of the Birmingham pub bombings, the Black September massacre at the Olympic Games, or the car bombs of Beirut. Nor did I know at the time of the all-important role in the Rivonia plot of the South African Communist Party. Soon after my stay there, Johannesburg got a taste of what the Rivonia plotters intended. On July 24th, 1964, a white Communist, John Harris, planted a bomb in Johannesburg Central Station. It killed one person and burnt and maimed many others. The police arrested and beat a confession out of Harris, who later was hanged. Then the following year, the police arrested Bram Fischer and charged him with being a member of the illegal Communist Party. He came back from England to face the charge but then discovered that the police had two unshakeable witnesses to his guilt. He skipped bail but was caught, tried and sentenced to prison. He contracted cancer and died after his release. In *South Africa, A Modern History*, Professor T. R. H. Davenport, from the Rhodes University of Grahamstown, calls Fischer 'a Marxist for whom treason, patriotism and humanity were synonymous in the South African context.'

The discovery of the Rivonia plot was a triumph for John Vorster, the Justice Minister, and for Hendrik van den Bergh, the head of the Security Police. They went on to become, in the next decade, the two most powerful men in South Africa, with Vorster as Premier, and Van den Bergh as head of the Bureau of State Security, generally known as BOSS. There is no doubt that the 'Tall Man', the huge and formidable Van den Bergh, was a dedicated and sometimes inspired policeman. In dealing with black opponents of the regime, 'Long Hendrik' as he was also called, was able to use a tried combination of bribery and brutality, corruption and terror. His greatest success and personal innovation was the employment of spies inside the white liberal or left-wing opposition. He specialised in recruiting journalists on the English-language newspapers – as many as twenty-five at the time of Rivonia. Two of these journalists, Gordon Winter and Gerard Ludi, took part in the uncovering of the plot, and have since written books about their experiences.

At the beginning of *Inside BOSS*, Winter says candidly that he came to South Africa in 1960 'not as an ordinary immigrant but as a burglar with three convictions and a twenty-one-month jail sentence behind me in London'. He got a job on the Johannesburg *Sunday Express*, appropriately as a crime reporter. Soon after this, Winter learned that his girlfriend was lending her flat for trysts between a white woman student and a black journalist. Winter did not hesitate: 'I passed the information about Pamela and Joe's love affair on to a high-ranking CID officer. I had nothing personal against either of the lovers. It was just that I needed to make some high-level contacts in the police force if I was going to succeed as a crime reporter.' When Joe and Pamela later escaped from South Africa, Winter got their exclusive story, thus boosting his reputation as a crusading, liberal journalist.

One day Winter went to interview John Vorster, 'the only man I have ever met with a square pot belly'. Apparently Vorster understood that Winter was not a run-of-the-mill, guilt-ridden, liberal Englishman, for he supplied him with several good stories. In return, Winter gave Vorster information about the anti-apartheid activists. In 1963, Winter was summoned to meet the 'Tall Man', Van den Bergh, who had just been appointed head of the Security Police. 'He was so relaxed and charming,' Winter recalls, 'that I found it difficult to believe that he had also been a Nazi sympathiser, and was interned with Vorster during the war.' He also noticed that Van den Bergh was 'highly intelligent, devious and cunning'. Soon after his appointment in 1963, Van den Bergh started the forerunner of BOSS, known as 'Republic Intelligence', whose specific aim was recruitment of journalists from the English-language press.

Although Winter was early involved in spying on left-wing enemies of Pretoria, he has to concede that 'my part in the capture of Bram Fischer was insignificant compared with the role played by Gerard Ludi.' The chief prosecution witness, Ludi testified that he had been in the same Communist Party cell as Fischer. He revealed himself as not only a journalist with the *Rand Daily Mail*, but a police Warrant Officer, detailed to infiltrate plots against the regime. Some years later, Ludi published two short and rather evasive books about his experiences: *The Amazing Mr Fischer* (with Blaar Grobbelaar) and *Operation Q-018* which he said was his code number.

Ludi was twenty-six at the time of the Fischer trial, a tall, dark man with a goatee beard, born of German immigrants but now fluent in English and Afrikaans. As a schoolboy staying in Germany after the war, he formed 'an abhorrence of Communism'. At the University of the Witwatersrand, where he studied political science, Ludi says that he drank, and raced fast cars. He annoyed his parents by pretending to be a leftist, and he annoyed fellow-students by pretending to be a rightist. His own political hero, he says, was John Stuart Mill, the Victorian liberal. While at university, he grew to detest the Communists: 'As I became more and more interested in their antics, I also became increasingly annoyed with Communism.' A friend's father, who worked in the Security Police, suggested that he enrol, to infiltrate the Communist Party.

On leaving university, Ludi got a job on the *Rand Daily Mail*, whose editor, Lawrence Gandar, was a fearless and upright critic of the regime. Ludi joined the Congress of Democrats. He attended left-wing parties where there was naked bathing and 'married white women made overtures to non-white men'. He was one of the few South Africans to attend an international youth congress in Russia in 1962, taking elaborate precautions not to be seen getting his visa in London. His Russian hosts found Ludi a troublesome delegate:

> I joined the queue eating my ice-cream. It was not long before a little middle-aged man with a red arm-band stopped next to me. First he glared at me. I turned my back on him. Then he began to remonstrate with me loudly in Russian. I knew it was about the ice-cream as he repeated the word morushne (Russian for ice-cream) with unfailing regularity. I still ignored him. Then he became really angry. He knocked the ice-cream out of my hand. I stared at him, trying very hard to keep my temper from flaring. He kept on shouting at me. That did it. Simultaneously I kicked him on the shin and thumped him on the nose.

This nekulturny behaviour was not held against Ludi, who joined the Communist Party soon after getting back to South Africa. He attended Marxist study groups and committees. He was beaten up by police at a left-wing rally. At last came the moment of triumph and revelation:

> On May 22nd, 1963 – the evening of my twenty-fifth birthday – I attended my second Communist Party meeting. Jean, a tall, throaty-voiced blonde in her early thirties, prepared coffee in the kitchenette of a small modern bachelor flat while Flo, a brunette with a good figure, and I discussed recent developments in our organisation. There was a knock at the door and Jan, another member of our cell, entered quietly. My eyes popped when I saw who Jan was. It was none other than the grey-haired advocate Bram Fischer.

Then came the Rivonia trial and the arrests of many left-wing sympathisers, some of them on the liberal newspapers. On July 24th, Ludi went to the *Rand Daily Mail* for the evening shift as a crime reporter – he was a rival of Winter: '. . . My telephone jangled. It was a contact. "There has just been a terrific explosion at the station," he shouted. "People are dying all over the place." ' A woman gave a description of the man who had left the petrol bomb. Ludi put two and two together: John Harris was of medium height, blue eyes and had sparse blond hair. He also wore a dark coat during the summer (sic). I knew John Harris well. We had served on many committees together and he and I had been fellow-students in the politics honours class.' Ludi tipped off the police who arrested Harris immediately.

Already Ludi believed that the Communists knew of his double role. He says shots were fired at him outside the office. He was called to a meeting at Fordsburg to find a painted slogan, 'Death To All Police Stooges'. The editor, Lawrence Gandar, questioned him on the rumours that he was tied up with Special Branch. Then he was told he would have to appear as a witness in State v Fischer. His cover was blown. He had fulfilled the mission bestowed on him at the start of Operation Q-018: 'Join the Communist Party. It exists somewhere and somehow, we don't know where and who the office bearers are. Find them, even if it takes years.'

But when exactly was the start of Operation Q-018? Ludi conveys the impression, but does not exactly state, that it was somewhere around 1959, when he was still at university. According to Winter, this was all hogwash: 'The less palatable truth is that Ludi was a traitor who betrayed his closest friends to save his own skin when the police caught him in bed with an Indian woman.' The accusation of treachery comes ill from Winter, who admits having betrayed two friends just to further his journalistic career. There seems to have been no love lost between Winter and Ludi, both crime reporters, both agents of Van den Bergh. Winter says that in June 1963, Ludi was 'caught having a lunch-time sex session with a petite Indian girl who lived in Mooi Street'. Ludi begged the arresting police to drop the charges under the Immorality Act because his right-wing father 'would beat the hell out of him, quite apart from the shame he would bring on his entire family'. To avoid arrest, he offered to trade information about the Communist Party. According to Winter, Ludi told Van den Bergh that he 'had only joined the Communist Party to further his career as a liberal reporter. He said he was really a staunch government supporter like his father . . .' When Ludi asked if he could go on seeing his Indian girlfriend, Van den Bergh replied that 'he could have babies by the girl for all he cared'.

Reading of Winter, Ludi and Van den Bergh, I thought of Joseph Conrad's novels, *The Secret Agent* and *Under Western Eyes*. They are concerned with the efforts of Tsarist Russian secret police to spy on exiled revolutionaries. The revolutionaries come from the upper and middle class they want to abolish. They care no more for the Russian peasantry than do South African liberals for the blacks. They project on to politics their own personal anger and guilt. If their revolution succeeds, they will force on Russia a despotism far more cruel than that of the Tsar.

In Johannesburg in July 1964 a freak snowfall had given the city another suggestion of Russia. In the pubs, I met many journalists from the liberal newspapers, perhaps even Winter and Ludi. They all chattered about the police raids on themselves and colleagues. There was an atmosphere of alarm, not unmixed with pleasurable excitement and even vainglory, for if you were white and not an actual Communist, you had little to fear but a few days in prison, and then the glamorous role of political refugee in London. Even the genuine revolutionaries survive in South Africa, as they did in Tsarist Russia. When Lenin was in Siberia he got a whole sheep each week. Nelson Mandela remains in prison because he refuses to forswear violence. Meanwhile he enjoys the world-wide praise and attention which are to a politician as sweet as freedom or even as power.

South Africa might be compared with Tsarist Russia but not with the monstrous tyranny of the Soviet Union. While Nelson Mandela, convicted of planning political terror, basks in the praise of the Western world, hundreds of thousands of innocent, unknown Russians toil in the Gulag Archipelago.

If you want a drink at Warwick University, you go to the Nelson Mandela Hall and ask for the Steve Biko Bar. The two famous Xhosas are now inextricably linked in left-wing hagiography as fellow-victims of the apartheid system. The comparison does an injustice to Biko, the young man done to death by policemen here at Port Elizabeth, in the Sanlam insurance building. Nelson Mandela was, if not a Communist Party member, a conscious and eager collaborator. He took part in a plot to overthrow the South African state. Neither he nor anyone else disputed the legality of his trial or conviction.

Steve Biko was not a Communist and he did not advocate terrorism. In an interview with the *New York Times*, he did predict that 'blacks are going to move out of the townships into white suburbs, destroying and burning there.' He said that this was inevitable. He did not think it desirable. Although Biko had many disciples around King William's Town in the eastern Cape, he was not a political organiser. At the university in Durban, he led a breakaway from the National Union of South African Students (NUSAS) to found the non-white South African Students Organisation (SASO) and later was prominent in the Black People's Convention (BPC). But these were talking shops rather than parties with plans of action.

Biko was not so much a political activist as a teacher. He was a Gandhi more than a Nehru. He taught the Africans to take a pride in their race and culture. The same idea had been preached in the 1930s by French-speaking West Indians and West Africans, such as the Senegalese poet, Leopold Senghor. They called it 'negritude'. American blacks in the sixties called it 'black consciousness', which is the term that Biko preferred.

This is no place to debate the merits of negritude or black consciousness, which its opponents call black fascism. One should take note of some of the special problems arising in the South African context. For instance, where does black consciousness leave the Coloureds? In the United States, the black consciousness movement often appeals most to people of mixed race, some of them more European than African. As a Senegalese once said to me, referring to one such American: 'Black is beautiful to those who are not really black.' Although the Jamaican Marcus Garvey was coal black, and detested mulattos, many modern West Indians of a lighter hue subscribe to black consciousness. The South African Coloureds, with their mixture of Dutch, Malay, Bushman and Hottentot blood, can hardly identify with the blacks, such as Steve Biko. The Indians of Natal have good reason to fear the black consciousness movement. They do not get on well with the Zulus. They know what happened to Indians in Uganda when Idi Amin exalted the black race. Yet oddly enough, some Indians belonged to the Black People's Convention.

Like its rival, the ANC, the black consciousness movement says that the different tribal groups such as Xhosas and Zulus will make common cause in the interest of their race. Experience of the rest of Africa does not support this faith. And here in South Africa one is bound to ask: why should there be black consciousness when there is still no white consciousness? The English-speaking South Africans and the Afrikaners are similar in appearance, at any rate to a foreigner. Their languages are as close as, say, Xhosa and Zulu. They follow the same religion. They share a belief in parliamentary democracy (for themselves), the rule of law and freedom of speech. They both feel threatened, as whites outnumbered by Africans. Yet less than a hundred years ago the English and Afrikaners were fighting each other. They seldom mix socially; they live in separate suburbs and their children go to different schools.

If you cannot agree with Steve Biko's opinions, you have to admire the lucidity, verve and humour with which he expressed them. One good example is Biko's testimony at the trial of nine young blacks for alleged subversion by intent. The state tried to establish that the philosophy of SASO and BPC was an incitement to racial confrontation. Although Biko was not on trial, he was called as witness for the defence, and he soon became engaged in a kind of Socratic debate with the advocates and Judge Boshoff. Here is one verbal exchange:

DEFENCE COUNSEL SOGGOTT: When you have phrases such as 'black is beautiful', now would that sort of phrase fit in with the black consciousness approach?

BIKO: Yes.

SOGGOTT: What is the idea of such a slogan?

BIKO: That slogan serves a very important aspect of our attempt to get at humanity. It challenges the very roots of the black man's belief about himself. When you say 'black is beautiful', what in fact you are saying to him is: 'Man, you are okay as you are. Begin to look upon yourself as a human being.' Now, in African life especially, it also relates to the way women prepare themselves for viewing by society. The way they dress, the way they make up and so on, tends to be a negation of their true state, and, in a sense, a running away from their colour. They use skin-lightening creams; they use straightening devices for their hair, and so on. They sort of believe, I think, that their natural state, which is a black state, is not synonymous with beauty . . .

THE JUDGE: Mr Biko, why do you people then pick on the word 'black'? I mean 'black' is really an innocent reference which has been arrived at over the years, the same as 'white'. Snow is regarded as white, and snow is regarded as the purest form of water and so it symbolises purity. So 'white' there has got nothing to do with the white man?

BIKO: Right.

THE JUDGE: But now, why do you refer to you people as blacks? Why not brown people? I mean you people are more brown than black.

BIKO: In the same way as I think white people are more pink than white. (Laughter.)

THE JUDGE: Quite. But why do you not use the word 'brown' then?

This trial is yet another example of the South African enigma: that a state can be at the same time brutally oppressive (all nine accused were sent to prison) and almost absurdly outspoken. Can one imagine such an exchange in open court in a Communist country, or even in England?

Much of the posthumous fame of Biko is due to his friend and biographer, the East London journalist Donald Woods. Some of Biko's present disciples, and still more his enemies in the ANC, have tried to suggest that Biko and Woods were not really friends. Perhaps Woods did not know Biko as well or as long as he sometimes suggested; however he knew and greatly admired him. Just as editor of the *Daily Dispatch*, Woods must have made it his business to know one of the most influential men in his circulation area, especially since most of his readers were black. And Biko was fortunate to have a friend and biographer who appreciated what he was trying to do. An ancestor of Woods was one of the 1820 settlers. He is in the tradition of Thomas Pringle, the first white liberal South African.

The inquest on Biko, held in the handsome old synagogue in Pretoria, was yet another instance of the South African mystery. A state which had allowed its policemen to batter a man on the skull, and drive him, chained and naked, up to Pretoria where he died, then placed these men in the witness box to answer questions in front of the world. It was a gruesome and fascinating spectacle even if the men were not subsequently charged with murder. The Polish authorities recently tried some secret policemen for killing a priest, but nobody in the Soviet Union has ever been charged for one of the twenty or thirty million deaths in the Gulag Archipelago.

There is no point in repeating the story of why and how Biko was murdered. It has been well and fully told by Woods. Ten years later, all one can do is inquire if there has been any improvement in police behaviour. The murder of Biko occurred in the heyday of Vorster, then Prime Minister, and Van den Bergh, then head of BOSS and the whole security apparatus. Their heads were swollen by years in power. Far from heeding black grievances, Vorster insisted on bringing in the teaching of Afrikaans in township schools, provoking riot in Soweto. These were crushed by one of South Africa's most feared policemen, T. J. 'Rooi Russ' Swanepoel. 'Long Hendrik' van den Bergh commanded a huge apparatus of espionage and suppression, but he still took a detailed interest in the personal and political lives of thousands of people who might be a threat to South Africa. I once wrote an article on why the Afrikaners would not fight for a state called Rhodesia, any more than the Irish would fight for a state called Cromwellia. A few weeks later, a friend of mine happened to meet Van den Bergh, who said to him: 'That was a good article by Richard West. How extraordinary that he should have the same name as that dreadful communistic Richard West.'

Van den Bergh's network of agents stretched to Britain. His favourite journalist Gordon Winter had run into trouble when he was visited in Johannesburg by two people out of his old East End criminal past. A few days later, Winter's gun was used in a murder. Van den Bergh put Winter in custody for his own safety, then sent him to London, ostensibly under a deportation order, in fact as a spy for BOSS. While in London, Winter became involved in the BOSS attempt to publicise the relationship between Jeremy Thorpe, the Liberal Party leader, and Norman Scott, a homosexual male model.

Soon after the Biko murder, a National Party politician, Robert Smit, and his wife, were found shot dead at their home in the Transvaal. It soon became known that Smit, a financial expert, had recently made inquiries about the transfer of government funds to a private Swiss bank account. There was talk of corruption in very high places. A journalist I know was given the task of visiting Van den Bergh on his farm to question him on the Smit affair. The journalist found 'Long Hendrik' poking a stick into the tank of his tractor. After a few innocuous questions, to which there was no reply, the journalist summoned up the courage to ask if Van den Bergh had anything to do with the Smit murder. The 'Tall Man' took the stick out of the tractor, drew himself up to his full six feet five inches, and bellowed 'f— off!' Here again, it has to be pointed out that there are not many countries in the world where a reporter could call on the chief of the secret police at his farm and ask, in effect, had he murdered anyone recently, and live to tell the tale.

Soon after the Biko murder, stories started to leak to the press about what came to be called the Information scandal. Public money was being secretly used to buy South Africa a better 'image'. The government had funded the new English-language newspaper *The Citizen* in Johannes-burg. It had tried to purchase a paper in Washington DC, apparently unaware that most of its readers were black. It had made payments to some obscure Norwegian political party. Much of the secret fund went on jaunts and luxuries for senior politicians and civil servants. The first senior politician to fall was Connie Mulder, the Information Minister. Then Vorster was moved upstairs to the presidency, before that post was combined with the premiership. Then Van den Bergh was obliged to retire. Another journalist went to the farm and found 'Long Hendrik' perched on top of his tractor. The interview was short and sharp:

'Who are you?'

'I'm a reporter from the *Star*.'

'You are the devil!'

According to Winter, most of the Information scandal was leaked to the press by the then Defence Minister, P. W. Botha, now the State President. It is also said that Botha has downgraded the whole police and security apparatus, giving more power to the armed forces. Vorster is dead, and most of his former cronies have moved from the National Party to its more right-wing rival, the Conservative Party. The former Justice Minister Jimmy Kruger, who said that the death of Biko 'leaves me cold', became a Conservative before he died. General Van den Bergh stood as parliamentary candidate for the same party. The former police chief Swanepoel stood as Conservative candidate against R. F. 'Pik'

Botha, the Foreign Minister. Another occasional candidate in the same constituency is Pieter-Dirk Uys, a comic actor and left-wing political satirist, who specialises in playing a Cabinet Minister's wife in drag.

The three members of the Security Police who held Steve Biko when he was killed were never formally reprimanded or charged. They were not dismissed from the service. According to Donald Woods, one was promoted, one was sent to a small town in the sticks, and a third has become an alcoholic. Police brutality no doubt continues. Since Biko's death, there have been an unpardonable number of deaths in detention and allegations of torture. Two members of the police force have been sentenced to death for murdering a prisoner. That is the paradox of South Africa, about which I wrote ten years ago in an earlier book. Let me repeat it.

Soon after Biko's death, a friend took me to see what he promised to be an 'interesting' exhibition of sculpture in a gallery over the Market Theatre, one of the few 'multi-racial' establishments in Johannesburg. And interesting it turned out to be. Climbing the stairs to the gallery you discovered a life-size, white figure sprawled head-down with a broken neck in your path. The bar of soap on the top step indicated that this was the Asian political leader who died in Cape Town in the custody of the police after 'slipping and falling down stairs'. The four other sculptures by Paul Stopforth showed a man on tiptoe leaning on finger-tips on a wall; a man slung by the knees from a pole suspended between two tables; a man strangled by a sheet and a man tied naked on a bottomless chair to be whipped on the testicles with a fly-swat – which also was shown. This blood-curdling exhibition needed no catalogue to explain itself to South African art-lovers, but how can one convey to non-South African readers the character of a country that not only allows its police to torture and murder detainees but allows these crimes to be shown in an art gallery? How can one ever explain what is at the same time a tyranny and a free country?

5
DURBAN

Town planning . . . Hindu, Muslim and Christian . . .
Conscription . . . a Literary Partnership in the 1920s

T HERE IS A JOKE in Durban about the visitor to a seaside hotel who
asks the Asian head porter: 'Is that the Indian Ocean out there?'
'No, sir,' comes the polite reply, 'that is the White Ocean. The Indian
Ocean is further down the beach.' This 'petty apartheid' lingers still on
the beaches, perhaps because white men fear having their womenfolk
seen in a state of undress by men of another race. There are still signs
to say what parts of the beach are reserved for whites, though the law
is seldom enforced and often deliberately broken by anti-apartheid
protesters. I have not seen any Asians on what the head porter described
as the Indian Ocean; but there are Coloured anglers who cast from a
breakwater into the surf. On the beaches south of the city, during the
Christmas holiday, the local Zulus sometimes brawl with the Afrikaner
lads from the north. A cartoon in *Die Beeld* showed a caravan with a
pennant 'Up the Transvaal!' and beside it an old man clutching a beer
can and watching the mêlée. 'Look, old girl,' he says to his wife in delight,
'it's just like home.'

Some of the trouble on Durban beach has nothing to do with racial
politics. The Afrikaner actress Amanda Strydom, who says something
outrageous almost every week, has told how a life-saver ordered her off
the beach at Durban:

I started crying . . . I started leaving the beach and an old woman said I was
disgusting. I was wearing a red tanga and I told her I was covered. All the
parts that need to be covered were covered. I told her I had more sense than
to walk around without clothes on. I said to her, 'Don't scream at me, it's
people like you that cause all the trouble we're having.' The woman went
crazy but I turned around and showed her my bum and said, 'God made that
too, isn't it beautiful?'

The Indian Ocean really begins at the Cape Peninsula, but it is not till Natal that you get a feeling of India and the damp, warm, spicy East. The Mediterranean atmosphere of the Cape has changed to balmy, sub-tropical languor. Whereas at the Cape you look south at an empty ocean, stretching towards Antarctica, at Durban you look north and east towards Asia. In the late nineteenth century, tens of thousands of Indians came to Natal as indentured labourers on the sugar plantations. They stayed and multiplied and fought for their rights under the leadership of Mahatma Gandhi. Their presence made Durban more aware of its ties with India. Ships from as far as Japan called regularly at the port. Durban was a staging post for troopships bound for India during the Second World War, and those who rested here for a few weeks talk of it still with gratitude and affection.

After the independence of India and Pakistan in 1947, some of the former imperial rulers came to live in Natal, or Argentina, rather than start a new life in cold, socialist Britain. The Natal British are patriots of a country that no longer exists. There are comic mugs and T-shirts depicting Natal as 'the last outpost of Empire'. In the last two decades there have been more arrivals from former African colonies such as Kenya and later Rhodesia. The 'Rhodies' as they are known, or the 'whenwes' (from 'when we were in Rhodesia') are not always popular with the English-speaking South Africans. They complain loudly about the presence of blacks in bars and public places. The 'whenwes' tend to believe that because they have been in a civil war they understand Africans. Two recent graduates of the Cape Town University told me that 'Rhodie' students beat up those they called 'lefties'. The last outpost of Empire regards the Rhodesians as common.

The architectural historian, Gavin Stamp, once remarked to me that you see in South African cities like Cape Town and Durban the full destruction and ugliness that might have occurred in Britain, had there been no constraints at all on the developers and town planners. It may have been Gavin Stamp who first pointed out to me that South African town planners and ideologues of apartheid share a common motive, interest and mentality. The unholy alliance achieved its worst result in Cape Town, with a gigantic motorway cutting the city off from the sea, and the Coloured community driven from District Six to their far locations. It was certainly Gavin Stamp who first pointed out to me that most of the townships for blacks, Coloureds and Asians were built on the principle of an English garden suburb, with streets laid out to a tidy pattern. To say that the blacks and Coloureds do not want to live in one of these garden suburbs does not reflect on their sense of culture: the Cape Coloureds felt more at home in the narrow alleys of District Six. They dislike these housing estates for the same good reason that Belfast people hated the Divis Flats, and Liverpudlians did not want to be moved to Kirkby New Town, or to the Piggeries.

The chief town planner of Durban was William, Lord Holford, whose name is infamous in the annals of architecture. He was responsible for Paternoster Square and other visual obscenities next to St Paul's Cathedral. Sir Christopher Wren's obituary inside the church would equally well serve for Lord Holford's, if it were sprayed in aerosol on one of the walls in Paternoster Square: *Si monumentum requiris, circumspice* ['If you want a monument, look around you.']. Lord Holford was born in Johannesburg and educated in Cape Town, before moving to Liverpool, then a great city, but now largely wrecked by the town planning profession. He was called in by Durban to draw up a master plan that would at the same time 'develop' the city centre, and push the Asians into the new suburbs allotted them by the apartheid theorists. Some old buildings were saved, including the town hall and the railway station. A group of conservationists also managed to stop the developers knocking down the railway workshops, a fine brick building. This has now been turned into a shopping centre of beauty and charm. At one end is a food emporium. Shops on two levels surround the wide and airy plaza on which there are carts, laden with clothes, trinkets, toys, ribbons and packets of herbs, attended by pretty Zulu salesgirls in grey trouser-suits, butcher's aprons and straw hats. Although by nature hostile to shopping centres, I took to this place in Durban. The people who ran the boutiques were eager to gossip. I learned about karakul rugs and the sheep that provide the wool. In the shop selling antique fire-arms, an elderly Zulu told me about the rival merits of different guns, unfortunately in his own tongue, so that I understood only the words 'three-O-three'. One day a Zulu film star came to promote the wares of a ladies' boutique.

After Port Elizabeth it is good to see Africans not only thronging the shops, but well-dressed, friendly and cheerful. There is a price to pay for this. Because the ANC does not control the Zulus, still less the Indians, and cannot enforce a boycott of white-owned shops, it makes its presence felt by terrorist bombing. A bomb went off in a supermarket just before Christmas 1985 killing and maiming many people, most of them black women. Another bomb killed three of the customers at the Magoo beachfront café. Some of the perpetrators were caught and have gone on trial. Others are now in England as political refugees. As long as we shelter terrorists from South Africa, we cannot complain when America shelters the IRA bombers.

Thanks to Lord Holford's town planning and the apartheid system, the centre of Durban has lost its Indian flavour. You do not hear the plaintive twang of the theme song from the latest Bombay movie; most of the Indian women wear European clothes instead of the sari; I could not discover a curry house. The Indians here (a term which includes those whose ancestors came from what are now Pakistan and Bangladesh) as in London or Birmingham, have blended into a drab environment; yet they prosper. The taxi-driver who brought me in from the airport gave me a spiel he has no doubt practised on every passenger: 'I have nothing against this government. We can live very well here. We have everything, diamonds, gold and the black gold of coal, here in Natal Midlands. You don't have trouble and crime here, like in Johannesburg and Cape Town. People are very friendly. You can talk to anyone. It's not like Washington and New York and those places. And people are well off. They use a loaf of bread for a football, there is so much food here.'

A local newspaper carries a special supplement for Divali, with articles to explain its religious meaning, and greetings from advertisers: 'In most Hindu homes all over Natal, many little clay lamps will decorate window sills and doorways tomorrow night, reminding Hindus of the great cultural heritage they possess, and of their religious duty to keep the "language of truth" alive and untainted by evil and untruth.' An article on the Glory of Hinduism by Sri Swami Sivananda claims that 'Jesus who lived as an ascetic in Kashmir and Benares, imbibed the teachings and principles of Hinduism and brought forth a religion to suit the fishermen of Palestine.'

The advertisements cover the spectrum of business involvement. Raj Naidoo, consultant for the Old Mutual insurance company, wishes a very happy Divali to all his Hindu clients and friends, especially in the South African police, and the Posts and Telecommunications. Similar wishes come from M. K. Naidoo Travel Agency; the Troika Township and Property Developers; the Umhlali Saw Mills; Union Flour Mills, Manufacturers of Blue Ribbon Cake Flour, Nyali Super Maize Meal; Govan Mani, the largest audio-visual hi-fi specialists; Eston Goat Farm Wholesalers, 'contact us for prayer goats, sheep, poultry'; Kit Kat café; Mobeni Super Save Supermarket; Atlas battery centre; Mr Clutch; Mr Tyre and Mr X-haust. Not all the well-wishers are Hindu. The Wainstein

Group of Companies, manufacturers of Tastie and Aunt Carolina Rice, 'are privileged to be associated with the Hindu Community'; and the McCarthy Car Bar, 'used cars you can rely on', wishes its Hindu customers, staff and friends, 'a happy Divali and a prosperous New Year'.

Alas, this Divali festival ended in Durban with fifty knife attacks, one of them fatal. Long residence in South Africa has bred in many a Muslim and Hindu a weakness for alcohol. But they prosper. Whatever the slights of apartheid, the Indians here suffer no economic constraints. They do not meet from white South Africans the jealousy and resentment that Indians face in Uganda, Kenya, Sri Lanka and Fiji. Many Indian university students, though only a few of their elders, take an ideological stance against the South African government. The majority are prepared to forswear politics for the sake of prosperity. Because of their international family networks, the Indians find it easier than the whites to get money out of South Africa. They often journey to London, and to Bombay, where I have heard them compare South Africa, to its advantage, with India. In the struggle for power in Natal between the Zulus, the Afrikaners, the English and the Asians, the latter will argue and bargain for their interests; but in the long run, it is the Zulus they see as the danger. Quite apart from the lesson of Idi Amin, Indians here have suffered attack and looting from Zulu mobs, one of which recently burned down Gandhi's old house.

Here in Durban, the Hindu and Muslim Indians get on well with each other, but Muslims especially are quick to defend their faith from outsiders. The editor of the *Daily News*, Michael Green, tells me that when he publishes stories on floggings and amputation of limbs in Saudi Arabia, Muslim readers threaten him with the curse of Allah. All South African Muslims were enraged when the Dutch Reformed Church, having at last rejected apartheid, described Islam as 'a false religion'. There was a riot in Cape Town. Sheikh Najaar, President of the Islamic Council of South Africa, said that the Dutch Reformed Church must 'stop living in the Middle Ages, when they fostered or encouraged religious strife'. Pedants might argue that Calvin was not a medieval man; moreover the Muslims are not averse to doctrinal strife between the Sunni and Shiite factions, as we see in the Lebanon and the Gulf. The Asian students in Durban and Johannesburg have come to blows with the Jewish students, and recently smashed an exhibition on Israel.

Here in Natal, the Church of England is still the most popular version of Christianity. On Sunday, All Souls Day, I went to the eight o'clock service at St Paul's, the oldest church in Natal. As usual when venturing into a strange Anglican church, I prepared myself for the shock of some hideous, newspeak liturgy and a sermon full of politics. What I found was an Anglican service of fifty or even a hundred years ago. The liturgy came from the 1662 Prayer Book. The lessons were read from the King James' Bible. The preacher, the Rev Ernest Pugsley, a naval chaplain attached to the South African forces, talked about death, and the need to avoid sins of omission, as well as those of commission, such as adultery. Did we visit the sick and prisoners? Did we refuse to give money to African children, to pay for their school books, just because we suspect that they spend the money on sweets? Did we cross the road to avoid an old lady who wanted to bend our ears with her aches and pains? Did we despise the alcoholics and tramps who come down to Durban when it is cold in the Transvaal, and congregate here at St Paul's, the most central church?

Our prayers were asked for the Anglican Church in the West Indies and its members, especially that they might have a more stable family life. In the Anglican Church in England, it would not be thinkable to suggest that some of the problems and unhappiness of West Indians come from their feckless attitude towards marriage and child-rearing, rather than outside causes like unemployment, inner city deprivation, racism, 'the cuts' and, of course, Margaret Thatcher. A prayer was said for peace in South Africa, 'for those young people who face violence and suffer violence'; 'for the children, that the Holy Angels may guard them'.

There were some hundred people at the service, including a few Indians but no Zulus, who live far away in separate areas and go to services in their own language. Some of the congregation were old ladies, as it has always been, even when the Anglican Church was strong and assured. Perhaps some of these old ladies had been those girls I have heard and read about from soldiers who stopped here during the war; those patriotic or flighty English girls who served high tea to the other ranks, and afterwards danced and fell in love with the officers at the Yacht Club or the Edward Hotel. It was all very English and old-fashioned. As the congregation rose to one of the grandest hymns, 'For all the saints, who from their labours rest', it was pleasing to think back to the days when the English still took a pride in themselves, and their Church, and their role in Africa:

From earth's wide bounds, from ocean's farthest coast,
Through gates of pearl streams in the countless host,
Saying to Father, Son and Holy Ghost, Alleluia! Alleluia!

Two white students, a boy and a girl, are standing on West Street in yellow T-shirts that read: 'Take the troops out of townships and schools'. They hand me one of the leaflets of the End Conscription Campaign. It relates how, in 1984, the security forces were called into the Transvaal townships after a boycott of increased rents, and how when the riots got worse reserves were brought in to help the regulars: 'These call-ups affect mainly "campers" who are being pushed out of their normal lives for two months every year and thrown into a civil conflict not necessarily of their choosing. Growing numbers of conscripts are living on the run from the Army or fleeing the country.'

It is true that the civil conflict was not of the choosing of the reserves, or indeed of the regular Army, the government, the white population, or the vast majority of the Asians, Coloureds and blacks. The civil conflict was quite openly of the choosing of the South African Communist Party. Civil conflict, followed by global sanctions against South Africa and then by military intervention, were all part of the strategy drawn up twenty-five years ago by Slovo, Mandela and other plotters at the Rivonia farmhouse. The civil conflict of two or three years ago was more of a threat to South Africa than it would have been at the time of Rivonia, not because there is more social unrest, but because the South African forces are facing a military threat from abroad. A Russian general in Angola now leads an army of thirty thousand Cuban troops and at least twenty thousand Africans, supported by tanks, artillery and the latest war-planes. South African troops are on the alert against armed intruders along the whole of the northern frontier sometimes crossing into Angola.

Many South African Army reservists dislike riot control more than combat. It involves the use of tear gas, whips, batons and even bullets against civilians, including women and children – especially children, since they enjoy the riots. The police and soldiers who quell the riots appear to the outside world as bully-boys of a racist regime. The liberal, English-speaking reservists may find themselves standing alongside police and regular soldiers whose attitude to the blacks is harsh and contemptuous, if not brutal. Those young, white South Africans who depart the country rather than do their 'camper' service regard themselves as people of principle.

It is not for me, an outsider, to judge whether South Africans should serve in the Army. But it has to be said that if all white South Africans refused to police the townships, it is the blacks themselves who would suffer. In the eastern Cape, and in some of the Transvaal townships, the soldiers have intervened to guard the lives and property of black officials and middle-class families; they have kept open the schools for those who wanted to study; they have caught and put on trial some of the necklace murderers. In the western Cape they have separated the rival mobs of ANC and the vigilante groups, such as the 'white cloths'. Here in Natal, the white troops and police have intervened to protect Indians, tribal minorities such as the Xhosas, and even the ANC, from murderous gangs of Zulus. The white troops and police have seldom had to defend white lives or property, though of course the need might arise in the future.

It is not just the English-speaking and liberal whites who want to take the troops out of the townships and schools. In Port Elizabeth, I fell into talk with a young Afrikaner accountant, of interesting and original political views. For instance, he had deduced from reading Tolstoy and Dostoevsky that Russia now has a Communist government because its people have always revelled in despotism. He was well disposed towards Africans, and learning Xhosa as well as the native languages of his home in the Transvaal. He was horrified by the necklaces and the terror around Port Elizabeth. Then he remarked almost casually: 'There are people who say we should just let the blacks get on with it and kill each other and not send troops to protect them ... and I am one of those people.'

The English equivalents of the End Conscription Campaign are those who cry 'Brits out of Ireland'. But there are millions of Englishmen who are not left-wing ideologues yet nevertheless believe that the Ulstermen 'should be left to get on with it', and to 'sort it out amongst themselves'. This was a constant refrain at the end of the British Empire, especially from conscript soldiers ordered to hold the peace between Hindus and Muslims in India, Jews and Arabs in Palestine, or Greeks and Turks in Cyprus. During my own military service in Trieste, I had to police civil conflicts, not of my own choosing, between Italian and Yugoslav nationalists, between supporters of Stalin and Tito.

We have all seen what happened in other parts of the continent when former colonial powers like Britain left the Africans to 'get on with it'. The result has often been tribal war, as in the Congo (Zaire), Nigeria, Chad, Sudan, Uganda, Rwanda and Burundi; or tribal wars, combined with Soviet intervention, as in Mozambique, Angola, Eritrea and Somalia. Those white South Africans who want to take troops out of the townships and schools should think very hard about who will replace them. They should study not only the black-ruled African states, but other parts of the world confronted by terrorist revolutionaries such as

Ireland, the Middle East, El Salvador and Peru, Sri Lanka, the Philippines and Indo-China.

The English-speakers of Durban are still as provincial in outlook as they were sixty years ago, when three young men founded a magazine, *Voorslag*, intended to shock them from their complacency. Although it was short-lived, *Voorslag* created a stink in Natal and all South Africa by its forthright attacks on institutions such as the colour bar. The story of *Voorslag* is also remarkable for the partnership of its brilliant and heterogeneous editors: William Plomer, Roy Campbell and Laurens van der Post. Though all three were born in South Africa, they belonged to different histories and traditions: Plomer, the rebel son of an English servant of Empire; Campbell, the Scots-Irish descendant of early Natal settlers; and van der Post, the Afrikaner lad from the backveld, the Orange Free State. Their early lives, their editorship of *Voorslag*, and their subsequent, very diverse careers, have much to tell us about South Africa.

The least well-known of the trio, William Plomer (pronounced 'Ploomer') described himself at times as an 'Anglo-African-Asian' because he had lived for years in Japan as well as his native South Africa and ancestral England. He also coined the expression 'Anglikaner' for whites who regarded themselves as Africans but were not Boers. He was actually born in 1903 at the very Boer town of Pietersburg in the northern Transvaal, where his father then worked as itinerant tax-collector and magistrate with the Department of Native Affairs. Charles Plomer sounds to have been an easy-going chap. After almost a decade of wandering as a trader, soldier, policeman, hotel manager and odd-job-man, Charles Plomer became a journalist in Pretoria, where he made friends with President Kruger. He even persuaded the old man to visit the local swimming club of which he was both the secretary and the star performer. 'Charles did a high dive,' wrote William Plomer about his father, 'and then swam round the bath under water, picking up as he went twenty-four plates, which he gratefully deposited at the President's feet. "Machtig" said Kruger. "*Die kerel swemt net als een visch*" ("Good God! The fellow swims just like a fish").' As well as getting on with the Boers, Charles Plomer liked and respected Africans, acquiring a negrophil reputation, which did not help in government service.

William Plomer had most of his education at English boarding schools before and during the First World War. Like so many literary men of his generation, Plomer rebelled against his teachers, the war, the Empire, compulsory games, religion and the family. In Plomer's autobiography, published after his death in 1973, we read of an uncle born at Poona, 'that byword for the limitations of the Anglo-Indian'. Plomer's father had gone to Westward Ho!, 'the school about which Kipling wrote *Stalky and Co*, which I have no wish to read'. He detested cricket which had been 'inflated from a rustic game into the "done thing" and even into a kind of mystic-patriotic cult bound up with notions of English racial superiority.' After the dreary round of lessons, games and church, the young Plomer enjoyed a rare escape to the theatre, where Maeterlinck's *Blue Bird* 'spirited me away into a vivid dream-world . . .' He discovered the *New Statesman*, 'written without peevishness, bigotry or conceit,' and Havelock Ellis's *The Psychology of Sex*: 'There were still stupid adults capable of asking one if one had read *Ivanhoe* or *Westward Ho!*, not knowing that one was already being geared to the permissive future.'

At the end of the First World War, Plomer returned to South Africa and a school in Johannesburg, but he refused to go on to Oxford. Instead he took a job on a sheep farm in the eastern Cape, where he was comforted by the thought of two earlier writers who lived there, Olive Schreiner and Thomas Pringle, 'that rare thing, a good man'. Plomer then went to join his parents in running a shop, perhaps more of a trading post, at Entumeni, in Zululand, in the north of Natal. It was here that Plomer's adolescent indignation fastened upon the treatment handed out to the Zulus by crass and ignorant whites.

The Zulus enchanted Plomer: 'Zulu voices are euphonious and finely produced, and they know all the arts of oratory and conversation – the skilful maintenance of tension in leading up to a point, the vivid description, the harangue, the formal speech, the quick repartee, the dry and ironical comment, the perfect metaphor, mimicry and so on.' He also remarked on the physical beauty of Zulus: 'Many of them went about all but naked, and their presence was to me deeply and agreeably disturbing.' This could have been a reference to the 'well-developed girls', but since Plomer in later life was exclusively homosexual in his tastes, he was no doubt thinking about 'the young bucks, descendants of Chaka's braves, ornamented with a few beads and little else, and moving with superb grace and upright carriage . . .'

While he was trading at Entumeni, Plomer made the acquaintance of John L. Dube, the first President-General of the ANC. Indeed Plomer's first published poem appeared in *Ilanga lase Natal*, the Zulu-language newspaper which Dube edited. Plomer also made friends with Mahatma Gandhi's son, Manilal, who was his own age, nineteen. From his daily experience of Zulu life, and from his interest in racial politics, Plomer began to write his first novel, *Turbott Wolfe*, which he sent in pencil manuscript to the Hogarth Press in London. The husband and wife publishers, Leonard and Virginia Woolf, not only read this chronicle of a Zulu trading station, but gladly agreed to publish it. When the novel appeared in 1926, it was acclaimed by Desmond MacCarthy and most respected critics in London and New York. The South African newspapers said the novel was nasty, obscene and ought to be burned. One Durban editor was found with 'his teeth chattering with rage', after perusing *Turbott Wolfe*. The book was afterwards kept under lock and key in Durban public library. The critics accused the book of pornography but what they really disliked was Plomer's championship of the Zulus and disrespect for the whites. The book is indeed intemperate and, to me, unreadable. In a short story written about the same time, Plomer described an Afrikaner at prayer as 'a blood-faced, hell-handed, witless, loveless, many-acred, stone-squeezing, leather-bellied blockhead'.

One of the few South Africans to applaud *Turbott Wolfe* was Roy Campbell, whose long poem, *The Flaming Terrapin*, had just been published in London. He and Plomer had first met at Twine's Hotel on the Esplanade in Durban: 'nowadays crammed with traffic but quiet enough in June 1925 for the passing jingle of a rickshaw puller's ornaments to be audible'. The two young men became friends over lunch and afterwards walked for hours on the beach, Plomer telling his hopes for *Turbott Wolfe*, which was then at the printers, and Campbell describing his plans for a literary magazine, called *Voorslag*, the forward crack of an ox-driver's whip. Plomer gladly agreed to become an editor.

In spite of his shocking novel, Plomer was still a gauche and virginal English adolescent, rebellious against his parents and society. Roy Campbell was older by more than his two years. He was bearded, aggressive and cocksure. He had brought back from England a beautiful and high-spirited wife, Mary. The rage and contempt he felt for the whites of Natal came not from any particular sympathy for the blacks but a kind of Byronic arrogance. Unlike Plomer, an Englishman who chanced to be born in Pietersburg, Campbell was third-generation Scots-Irish South African. His grandfather had built some of the public buildings of Durban, and also the North Pier, 'that great breakwater . . . recalling the thrills of fishing for sharks, kingfish, barracuda, musselcracker, rock-cod, garrick and other big fish'. Campbell claimed to have spent much of his youth at sea, on merchant vessels and whalers, or galloping in the hills with Amazon girlfriends.

While plans were going ahead for the publication of *Voorslag*, Plomer went to stay at the Campbells' borrowed house on the coast at Sezela. Plomer recalls that 'Campbell wrote at night, slept in the morning, and appeared at lunch-time . . . He sometimes went fishing or flew a kite from a fishing rod and he liked making a bonfire at night on the rocks near the sea, which seemed to me the sort of thing that Shelley might have done – not that he took after Shelley. He was much under the influence of Nietzsche and somewhat under that of the French Symbolists.'

Early on in their friendship, Plomer was startled to hear Campbell use the word 'Bloomsbury' as a term of contempt. Whatever he thought of the publishers, Leonard and Virginia Woolf, Campbell sang the praise of *Turbott Wolfe* when it appeared in 1926, just before *Voorslag*. Campbell delighted in the abuse received by Plomer, who later tartly remarked: 'I think a romantic idea of himself as a wronged and persecuted hero had already recurred in his writings, and perhaps he didn't quite like the idea of my drawing *all* the fire, so in his *Poets in Africa*, we appeared as "twin Sebastians", each in his "uniform of darts".'

Both Campbell and Plomer received a barrage of darts after the first number of *Voorslag*. When Campbell conceived the project and raised the money from friends, he had in mind a South African version of *Blast* and *The Tyro*, two London magazines produced by his friend, the author and artist Wyndham Lewis. A bound volume of *Voorslag* is now on sale in South Africa, but it does not stand up to the test of time. Who, for that matter, now reads *Blast* or *The Tyro*? It deserves praise for attacking the colour prejudice of the time. It especially annoyed the English-speaking South Africans, who were anyway angry against the Afrikaner-Socialist government, which had nationalised some of the basic industries, and threatened the dominance of the English language and flag. To Campbell, at least, it was fine and proper that those who had so long exploited the blacks should suffer the persecution of men like Tielman Roos, the militant Afrikaner politician:

> Now do you groan when Tielman flays your back
> You, who condone the bondage of the black?
> Is it the sign of a 'superior race'
> To whine to have 'the nigger kept in place'?

Sixty years later, *Voorslag* is best remembered because it published the early writings of Laurens van der Post. Whereas Plomer is largely forgotten outside South Africa, and Campbell is underrated because of his fascist political views, Sir Laurens is still alive, and writing better than ever. Because of his natural wisdom and vast experience and learning, he has become one of the most respected teachers of this century, a world figure, comparable with Solzhenitsyn. So great is his eminence and his age that we find it hard to recognise in Sir Laurens the cub reporter discovered by Plomer and Campbell at Durban in 1926. Sir Laurens has himself recounted this episode in his rich and enthralling memoir *Yet Being Someone Else*, published in 1982. The passage reveals the difference in outlook between van der Post and his two young colleagues; it also captures the feeling of Durban sixty years ago.

Laurens van der Post was just seventeen when he got a job as reporter on the *Natal Advertiser*. Apart from holidays at the Cape, he had spent his life on a farm in the Orange Free State. Although his father, a lawyer, had built up a library, and the van der Posts spoke English and German as well as Dutch and of course Afrikaans, Laurens was conscious of being a Boer from the backveld when he applied for a job on an English-language newspaper. In those days, almost all journalists on the English newspapers came from Britain, and made it a term of employment that they returned for six months' home leave every two years at the paper's expense. Van der Post was the first South African, let alone the first Afrikaner, to get a job on the *Advertiser*, whose staff, as he mildly puts it, 'had a Kiplingesque sense of empire and its mission'. They did not take kindly to his recruitment.

The new journalist so quickly mastered the tricks of the trade, and wrote so well in his second language, that he was given the job of reporting the visit to Durban of Edward, the Prince of Wales, the great-uncle of Charles, Prince of Wales, to whom van der Post is now the friend and philosopher, like Aristotle to Alexander. After this journalistic triumph, van der Post was appointed shipping reporter, a job that indulged and encouraged his childhood love of the sea. His accounts of journeys in cargo boats, whalers and Union Castle liners are all the more fascinating because it is now so hard to travel by ship. Love of the sea led inevitably to living in foreign countries, especially the East. But even before he had left South Africa, van der Post discovered next to his newspaper office a foretaste of India:

In fact the fruit and vegetable part of the Indian Market, in the light of an early sub-tropical morning, with piles of polished fruit in pyramids, would glow like treasure and never ceased to delight and excite my eyes ... The variety, brilliance and totally un-African colour of the scene would be reinforced by the saris of the Indian women, the silk trousers and tunics of their Moslem fellow-countrymen, who now pass under the name of Pakistani. From the smallest child to the oldest man or woman, I rarely saw a single being who was not comely or of the most marked beauty.

The memory would remain with van der Post when he had served for years as an officer with the old Indian Army.

When *Voorslag* appeared in 1926, van der Post wrote to offer a contribution in Afrikaans. Plomer went to see him in Durban, and soon van der Post was taking the train each Saturday night to Sezela, and walking four miles in the dark to the beach house to help in editing the magazine. Scarcely had van der Post started to work on *Voorslag* when it developed 'internal problems of personalities and management of a disastrous potential'. The public vilification worried financial backers. 'Even my brother George,' wrote Campbell, 'who had disagreed with most of the opinions expressed in it, but had generously helped us with money when I resigned from the editorship, lost more than half his medical practice because he was my brother.' The end of the paper mattered less to Plomer, who had no family obligations: 'We had derived a great deal of amusement from the enterprise and perhaps, like twentieth-century Bushmen, had left a few vivid paintings on the walls of that dark cave, the mind of the white South African.'

Oddly enough it was van der Post, the youngest and last arrival on *Voorslag*, who felt most worried by its collapse. As the only one left with a paid job, he invited Plomer and both the Campbells to share his flat in Durban. And having invited them, he felt apprehensive when he was offered the chance of a great adventure abroad. Before he started to work on *Voorslag*, van der Post had spent his Saturdays playing hockey, and one weekend went to a match in Pretoria. In a café, he heard the manageress insult and refuse to serve two Asian men. He rebuked her and asked the strangers to sit at his table. They turned out to be Japanese journalists. As a result of this chance act of courtesy, van der Post later received an invitation to sail to Japan and spend a few months there as guest of a shipping line. He told the Japanese about Plomer, the highly acclaimed young novelist, and he too was offered a berth. But what of the Campbells, who now would have nowhere to stay in Durban? Van der Post had been over-delicate. Although Roy Campbell talked of starting another magazine, he and his wife were really eager to get back to London and to the literary scene. They would not hear of van der Post and Plomer refusing the chance to go to Japan. Years later Campbell wrote:

> When others jumped the liner for Japan
> I stayed and faced the music like a man . . .

but by then, he had quarrelled with Plomer.

The trip to Japan was momentous for both Plomer and van der Post. Plomer spent two years there and wrote a successful novel about the country. When van der Post was taken prisoner by the Japanese in the Second World War, his knowledge of their language and thinking helped him and the whole camp to survive. All three of the *Voorslag* editors came to live for a time in London, but only Plomer settled there. He made friends with the Bloomsbury set and literary dames such as Lady Ottoline Morrell and Vita Sackville-West. He grew ashamed of his raw colonial background, and later apologised to Leonard Woolf for the savage, intolerant tone of some of his early letters from Zululand. He went on writing poems and literary criticism and worked as a 'taster' for Jonathan Cape. He did Cape proud by spotting the first James Bond novel; he did me proud by recommending my first book on Africa.

Soon after leaving Durban, Roy Campbell published a poem, 'Wayzgoose', mocking the white South Africans and all they held dear:

> Even the animals had scented fun,
> Jock from the Bushveld all the way had run,

to which Campbell added: 'Footnote on Jock of the Bushveld, one of the national heroes of South Africa – which further illustrates my remark on the national bonds between colonials and dogs. He occurs in a sentimental novel which displays the usual train-window insight into "native psychology" which is so dear to colonials; and the usual animal-lover sloppiness which is popular everywhere. Jock was a big-game hunting dog, he had soulful eyes and always tried to bite niggers – a typical colonial.'

The poem, published in 1928, pays handsome tribute to Plomer:

> Plomer, twas you, although a boy in age,
> Awoke a sleepy continent to rage,

Who dared alone to thrash a craven race
And hold a mirror to its dirty face.

However, the friendship between the two men had been sorely tried when they were still in South Africa. In an unpublished 'Note on Campbell', dated October 7th, 1931, Plomer describes Campbell's bad eating habits, his mania for brewing undrinkable ginger beer, and his lack of skill as a cook and angler. He accused Campbell of breaking secrets, an accusation that Campbell returned. Campbell wrote to a friend: 'As for Plomer, I don't know what has come over him, he writes like an Anglican parson – and I have treated him like one accordingly. He has become a proper Bloomsbury.' Later he wrote a poem on Plomer called 'Creeping Jesus':

For his friends' actions, with unerring snout,
He always foxed his own low motive out.

The cause of the quarrel was sex, and specifically Havelock Ellis's book, *The Psychology of Sex*. The young William Plomer, as he records in his autobiography, had read Havelock Ellis, and no doubt found in his teachings some relief from the homosexual guilt which drove him almost to suicide. Whatever Ellis intended by his *Psychology of Sex*, it had the effect on men and women between the wars of making them come to terms with their sexual preferences. It was therefore blamed by people like Campbell for proselytising homosexual liaisons. Campbell was furious when his own wife Mary went to bed with Vita Sackville-West, whose other literary lovers included Virginia Woolf, doyenne of the 'Bloomsberries'. Twenty years later, Campbell still raged against Ellis, Bloomsbury and lesbian authoresses:

Dante rightly puts the gloomy, despairing and ungrateful people in one of the lowest circles of hell – and that is where all the more tearful female disciples of the dismal humourless Havelock Ellis should be with their caterwauling sonnets, the Dusty Answers and Wells of Loneliness.

Campbell hated Bloomsbury as much for its left-wing politics as its perverted sexuality. He went to live in Spain, became a Roman Catholic and took the side of Franco when the civil war began. He lampooned the left-wing poets like Auden, Spender, MacNeice and Day Lewis, lumping them all together under the name 'MacSpaunday'. His friend George Orwell was one of the few who recognised that Campbell wrote excellent poems, whatever his nasty politics.

When Laurens van der Post arrived in London, after Japan, he remained aloof from the squabbles of England's literati. He was not, after all, an Englishman. Although aghast at the rise of Nazi Germany, van der Post was never attracted by socialism in any form. His first novel he later described as, 'among other things, a rejection of the lure and blasphemy of Communism'. He agreed with Goethe's sentiments, 'I hate any revolution because as much good as bad is destroyed thereby. I hate those who cause revolutions as much as those who make them.'

When van der Post went to work for a spell on the *Cape Times*, he solicited contributions from Campbell and Plomer, in order to keep up the struggle against the colour bar. 'They also both needed the money,' he said. Although van der Post maintained his friendship with Plomer up to the latter's death in 1973, he never was very close to Campbell. The three of them had little in common except for their love of literature and South Africa.

Campbell came back here once on a troopship in 1944, and spent an agreeable three weeks' leave. He harked back to his big game fishing, and rides in the mountains, but his macho fantasies were now directed to Europe: 'This year,' he wrote in 1951, 'Domingo Ortega, the greatest matador in the world, has invited me to act as his picador . . . Although I cannot walk properly, I can still ride with my left strap shortened three inches.' He was killed in a car crash six years later.

Plomer returned to South Africa in 1956, to lecture at the University of the Witwatersrand. He took an interest in South African writers and, therefore, inevitably in the racial politics of the country. Although he of course abhorred apartheid, his attitude to the whites had mellowed since *Voorslag* days: 'It is easy enough to remember the wrongs of Europe's incursions into Africa – the slave trade, commercial exploitation, racial contempt, and social injustice: but it is still well to remember that the wrongs done to Africans by Africans, out of greed, cruelty, callousness, superstition and ignorance, are beyond computing.'

Sir Laurens van der Post has written so much on Asia, Europe, exploration, the sea, Carl Gustav Jung, war, peace and mankind's future, that we sometimes forget he is also an Afrikaner, supremely fitted to give his views on South Africa. Oddly enough, the press and television seldom inquire from van der Post his views on, for instance, sanctions – he is against them – preferring to canvas comments from shallow and ignorant politicians and clergymen. Yet almost everything that Sir Laurens says on South Africa seems to me wise and worth attention. He condemns all forms of racial discrimination, as he has done since *Voorslag* days but also perceives that the South African government is moving away from apartheid. He condemns in the strongest possible terms the revolutionary terrorists who want to remove the government by force. Sixty years ago, van der Post attacked those in the West who glorified Stalin's Russia. Today he condemns the equally foolish liberals and socialists in the West who want revolution in Asia and Africa. He says of them in *A Walk with a White Bushman*:

> They give people an ideological and not a real idea of what life should be about, and this is immoral. They project onto other societies and countries solutions for problems they do not have to live themselves and this is obscene. They feel good by being highly moral about other people's lives, and this is immoral ... I think any 'ism' is a poison. They should look at the consequences since the war of their preaching, their pharisaical stancing, and the way, when the logical casualties of their philosophies lie bleeding and dying in millions on their way, they pass by on the other side.

6

PIETERMARITZBURG

Strife among the Zulus ... Shaka Zulu
on television

T EN YEARS HAVE gone by since I was last in Pietermaritzburg, and it
is good to find it as handsome as ever, a British imperial garrison
town with broad, shaded streets and wrought-iron balconies. There is
still a statue of Queen Victoria, and the Victoria Club, which raises the
Union Jack each morning. The church still stands where Bishop Colenso
preached in defence of the Zulu nation, and then caused greater scandal
by casting doubt on the Book of Genesis. Pietermaritzburg was for a
time the focus of two great debates: between the Imperialists and the
Little Englanders, and between the Scripturalists and the Evolutionists.
Once again I stayed at the Imperial Hotel, so called after the Prince
Napoleon who died fighting for Britain against the Zulus in 1879. Other
guests have included Rhodes, Mark Twain, Conan Doyle, George
Bernard Shaw and Trollope, who praised the courtyard, where 'vine
leaves trailed over red brick walls and oranges hung within tempting
distance.' There are no oranges now, but many Indians and Zulus,
chattering over their beer.

In spite of its placid appearance, its croquet, golf and numerous
English boarding schools, this part of Natal has a bloodstained past and
some of the worst contemporary troubles: 'Boy, ten, beheaded in township . . . forty-two die in faction fight.' The Zulus, British and Afrikaners
have killed each other around here. The Church of the Vow, with its
statue of Piet Retief and Gert Maritz, recalls the Battle of Blood River
on December 16th, 1836, the most solemn date in the history of the
Afrikaners. This victory over the Zulus is marked each year by oratory,
and sometimes by bombs, for December 16th, 1961 was chosen by ANC
to launch its military wing Umkhonto we Sizwe, ('Spear of the Nation').
The Spear has made its presence felt in Maritzburg with bomb attacks
on each of the three buildings of the Supreme Court. During my stay

there was huge security, including police snipers so I was told, for the trial of several people accused of bomb attacks in Durban against a shopping centre, a girls' school and the Magoo café.

Pietermaritzburg has a very good newspaper, *The Natal Witness*, founded in 1846 and still not owned by the Anglo-American Corporation. Its editor in 1926 was alone in supporting *Voorslag*, and later commissioned William Plomer to write for him from Japan. The present incumbent, Richard Steyn, was educated at Stellenbosch and practised law in London before he was asked to try editing. It is a tough job, anywhere in South Africa, and most of all in Natal, where the whites, Asians and blacks divide on politics and religion as much as on race.

It is painful to witness how thoughtful South Africans brood over their country, and over its reputation abroad. For instance Steyn told me of how he had recently gone for a year to Harvard, taking his wife and their children, who joined the nearby state school and enjoyed it. The American academics in these married quarters would not use this school because of the high proportion of blacks, and yet they lectured the Steyns on the wrongs of South Africa. Among Steyn's colleagues at lunch in the old Victoria Club was David Robbins, the author of *Inside the Last Outpost*. He started to talk about Shiva Naipaul and Shiva's theory that Kurtz, in Conrad's story about the Congo, *Heart of Darkness*, was typical of the white man in Africa. The whites in Africa are obsessed with Kurtz. I have been myself, since reading the book in the Congo in 1964. Later I wrote an article on the Congo and a certain journalist who told me he could not get up in the morning till he had read some pages of *Heart of Darkness*. Afterwards, two other journalists thought I referred to them.

The obsession with politics may be worse in Natal because it extends to the blacks as well. A third *Witness* journalist, Khaba Mkhize, was with us for curry at the Victoria Club, which now admits African guests, provided of course that they wear a jacket and tie. In the Cape or the Transvaal, the blacks either support the UDF (United Democratic Front) or stand aside from politics. Here in Natal, as in the homelands like Transkei and Bophuthatswana, blacks are involved in the politics of government. The Zulus divide into those who support the UDF and those who support Chief Gatsha Buthelezi's Inkatha movement, which rules the KwaZulu homeland and claims the loyalty of a great many of the Zulus outside. Inkatha, which says it has one and a half million members, is not as well-known abroad as the ANC, but in terms of manpower, discipline and potential military strength, the Zulu nation is formidable.

The last black people to lose independence, the Zulus have suffered the most from white domination. The Zulus are chiefly remembered now for the military genius which made them masters over the other blacks and capable of destroying a British expedition armed with the latest machine-guns. Generations of movie-goers have thrilled at the sight of the impis rising over the crest of the hill, and the muffled thunder of thousands of feet advancing into the charge. The Zulus are known by people who could not tell you the name of another African people, or even find Africa on the map. I read in the paper the other day that a gang of Birmingham football hooligans march under the title of Zulu Warriors. And you see the words 'Zulu Warriors' scrawled by aerosol in the streets of Belgrade whose football hooligans follow the English fashion. The Zulus were more than a conquering army such as the Goths and Huns coming to Europe from Asia. They were a nation state, with a system of law and government, savage and cruel though it appears to us. The Zulus did not have even the barest attributes of what we call civilisation. They could not write their language. They did not build in stone. There was no private property in land or cattle; and there was no money. The Zulus made steel but had not discovered wheel transport or boat building. In these and other respects, the Zulus were still at a lower level of civilisation than Britain before the Romans came. What they did have was pride and a sense of identity.

After beating the Zulus in battle, the British determined to humble their pride. They did this by letting white settlers on to the Zulu land. In other regions, the British had set up Crown Colonies in which the blacks were guaranteed ownership of the land, and protection from settlers. Thus a large proportion of Sothos, Tswanas and Swazis maintained their traditions under benign British rule in what are now Lesotho, Botswana and Swaziland. And, as we have seen, the Xhosas had farming rights, good education and even a limited franchise in most of the eastern Cape.

The British gave no such advantages to the defeated Zulus. 'The English and Dutch are conspiring together to finally crush out the Zulu and divide the spoils,' wrote Harriet Colenso, the daughter of the pugnacious bishop. She went on to prophesy: 'And if the Zulu make an attempt to stand for their liberty, they will be mercilessly butchered by either or both of these civilised and Christian nations. And I want you to understand the real nature of the transaction, and the cruel injustice of thus wiping out the national existence of the Zulu people, by robbing them of their country.' Those words were written in 1886, the year which saw the discovery of the gold on the Witwatersrand. By the end of the nineteenth century, white settlers had taken most of the good land in Zulu country. The province government imposed a tax on huts intended to force the Zulus into the labour market on white-owned farms or the mines. The American writer Negley Farson heard a Zulu saying in 1939: 'Once the white men had the Bible and we had the land. Now we have the Bible and they have the land.' As late as the 1970s, tens of thousands of Zulus were driven off their ancestral ground to make way for mining and large-scale agriculture.

It has to be said that capitalistic farming and mines have helped to create South Africa's wealth, of which only a proportion goes to the blacks. Had it been left to subsistence farming, Zululand would now be even poorer than it now is. All the same, the Zulus have some of the problems of Mozambique and Zimbabwe: huge population growth, deforestation, crop failure, and civil strife. The breakdown of traditional methods of population control – notably warfare – accounts for most of the trouble. Too many people fight for space, with spears, clubs and, increasingly, guns. The decline of the Zulus over the last hundred years is seen in their very physique. The tall, athletic warrior race are now poor specimens, nearer to five foot than six foot tall. The whites, by contrast, have grown. A friend of mine who lives in a Cape farmhouse built in the eighteenth century, says that he, his family and his friends all have to stoop to get through the doorways. An anthropologist at the University of Potchefstroom claims to have found, by measurement of the local population, that South African citizens (i.e., Afrikaners) are one inch taller than the Americans.

A Zulu revolt at the start of the present century was crushed, and its leaders hanged. A Zulu, the Rev John L. Dube, was President-General of the ANC; another, Chief Albert Luthuli, was ANC head when he was given the Nobel Peace Prize in 1961. But about that time, the ANC joined up with the Communist Party and founded Umkhonto we Sizwe. Its leadership was increasingly Xhosa, white, Asian and Coloured. The Inkatha movement grew as an expression of Zulu nationhood and tradition, to which has been added over the last hundred years a strong religious commitment. Many Zulus are Anglicans like Chief Gatsha Buthelezi. Millions follow such semi-Christian cults as the Zionists. The Inkatha movement is strongly opposed, in theory at least, to terrorism and armed insurrection. Chief Buthelezi has made it clear that 'no member of any organisation that supported necklacing would be tolerated as an employee of the KwaZulu government.' In the same address to a group of nurses, Buthelezi claimed that the General Secretary of the ANC, Mr Alfred Nzo, 'had given the ANC's official blessing to necklacing'. He added that 'we in the KwaZulu government have been the butt of many strictures because we have refused to take into our employ people who are committed to these ghastly methods of sorting out differences.'

Chief Buthelezi has always demanded the freeing of Nelson Mandela, and says he would serve under him, if the people so wished. This course of events would depend on Mandela renouncing the necklace and, in effect, the ANC. The Zulu King, Goodwill Zwelthini, has spoken of other differences between his people and Nelson Mandela's ANC. In a speech in November 1986, King Goodwill 'hit out at those using Nelson Mandela's royal [Xhosa] background to sow trouble between Zulu and Xhosa royal families'. King Goodwill went on: 'We all respect Mandela as one of the people's leaders and a member of the Thembe royal family. It is quite clear how explosive the situation is likely to be if Mandela is used, as a scion of another royal house, to denigrate us as members of our own royal house.'

In the same speech, King Goodwill brought out the utter divergence between Inkatha and ANC on the question of sanctions. The Rivonia plotters made sanctions their number one aim. The United States and all the Commonwealth countries, with the exception of Britain, want sanctions against South Africa. They also believe that the black South Africans want sanctions. In fact it is the ANC and its front organisations that call for sanctions. Chief Buthelezi opposes sanctions. So does King Goodwill, who told the men at Hlobane Colliery that people would soon know a South Africa in which even mine managers and engineers would be black ... He urged blacks to be diligent and seek promotion, as in the new South Africa there would be total equality and their positions would be determined by what they did now. Workers throughout the country did not want their mines and factories to close. But because of the disinvestment campaign, thousands were going to lose their jobs, either through closures or retrenchment. Inkatha has set up its own trade unions in opposition to the COSATU backed by the ANC. Whereas COSATU is, almost overtly, trying to wreck the economy of South Africa, the Inkatha union wants to create employment. In the short run, this means that Inkatha is less demanding on wages and terms of work.

In the long run it means an enormous shift of jobs and industry from places like Port Elizabeth, run by the ANC, to places like Durban, run by Inkatha. It means a shift of wealth and therefore of power from Xhosas to Zulus. And because Inkatha has kept open the schools, while ANC has succeeded in closing them, the Zulus are now more advanced in education.

If Nelson Mandela is Russia's favourite South African, Buthelezi is Uncle Sam's. In his dealings with the Pretoria government, Buthelezi is tough but polite. He managed to knock on the head a plan to surrender part of Zululand in order to give the land-locked Swazis a corridor to the sea. He probably thinks that Pretoria needs his friendship more than he needs Pretoria's.

The enemies of Inkatha in Natal are the UDF, the 'black consciousness movement' and most of the Xhosa minority. All for different reasons dislike Zulu nationalism. A high proportion of Zulu university graduates, professional people and teachers are sympathetic to ANC, as are some who dislike Buthelezi for clan or family reasons. There is a small but active support for the ANC among Asians, Coloureds and whites, particularly in the NUSAS student union. When Brendon Barry of NUSAS described participants in Indaba as 'elite and undemocratic', the acting chief of Inkatha, Dr Oscar Dhlomo said he was sick and tired of such arrogance: 'Rich, comfort-loving, white students who claim to work for the black man's progress are nothing but an elite of two-faced jackals. What can Mr Barry tell us about elitism, when he and his fellow students went to the top white schools, live in the best white suburbs, and go to the best white universities?' He said that many of these white liberal champions of the black man, after they left college, turned into greedy capitalists and police informers. (*Die Burger*, December 3rd, 1986.)

Black enemies of Inkatha have suffered more than verbal abuse. Supporters of the United Democratic Front find it increasingly hard to live in townships round Durban and Pietermaritzburg. Newspapers carry censored and therefore obscure accounts of stabbings and beatings. 'The seven stabbed to death were seen handing out advertising flyers for an electrical repair shop. The vigilantes – many of whom cannot read – may have mistaken the tracts for political tracts of the UDF . . . An Inkatha Youth Brigade member who allegedly took part in the abduction and disruption of the funeral was stoned to death.'

One township I went to near Maritzburg would not allow Inkatha members. In most, the UDF is getting the worst of it. 'The Inkatha

Youth Brigade once were called the cissies of the struggle,' Chief Buthelezi proclaimed, but now had become 'the warriors for freedom'. Much of the new-found militancy of the Zulus comes from, of all things, television.

Pietermaritzburg was the setting of *The Dingleys*, the first and surely the worst South African TV soap opera. The beginning of each instalment showed the statue of Queen Victoria and a number of old ladies taking their constitutional. The Dingley paterfamilias was a pompous bookshop owner who wanted to be the mayor, and the actual mayor took part in the film. One of the two instalments I saw concerned the visit to Maritzburg of 'The Rabbit', a heavy underground rock group.

When I saw *The Dingleys* in 1976, the one TV channel then operating showed only five hours of programmes a day; a set cost £775, and the licence fee was £25 per annum. The viewing public were anyway ill-disposed towards SABC (South African Broadcasting Corporation), and took it out on *The Dingleys*. Page after page of the new TV supplements in the press were taken up with readers' complaints. 'If *The Dingleys* is supposed to show typical family life, we must be a nation of morons . . . Five minutes were enough to leave me stunned . . . The first time I saw *The Dingleys* on TV I nearly died,' were some of the comments printed by the *Rand Daily Mail*.

Pietermaritzburg gave the series a cold reception. The manager of the bookshop on which *The Dingleys* was based, and the mayor who appeared in the last two instalments, claimed that they did not possess a TV set, while those who had watched *The Dingleys* complained of factual anomalies such as Johannesburg milk bottles and newspapers at breakfast. Those who commented on the quality of the serial called it 'weak' or 'it makes out that Pietermaritzburg is olde world with lots of little old ladies.' One resident asked: 'Is the aim of the series to illustrate the utter inanity and spinelessness of the English-speaking South African female?' Here the overt suspicion was mooted that television, like everything else in South Africa, had become caught up in the ancient rivalry between English and Afrikaners. Many probably thought that *The Dingleys*, produced by a man with an Afrikaans name, was part of a plot by the National Party government to do down the English-speakers and the United Party, of which Mr Dingley was clearly a stalwart. Probably some Afrikaners do distrust the loyalty of a town like Pietermaritzburg, where the Union Jack is raised each morning.

South African television has grown out of its Dingley phase. There are now four channels, including one in an African language. The two-hour, early morning programme of news and current affairs, presented by two men and a woman, bilingual in English and Afrikaans, is pleasant, informative and inoffensive. Critics accuse it of bland Pretoria propaganda. You do not see riots, nor interviews with extremist leaders, white or black. I think this is sensible. We would not now have such trouble in Ireland had we kept the terrorists off the screen.

If SABC is cautious about the news, it does not shirk the tough aspects of South African history. There was an excellent drama serial, so I am told, about the 1922 strike, when white Johannesburg miners rose in protest against the recruitment of cheap black labour. There was another series, called *Heroes*, again I am told it was very well done, concerning the enmity between English and Afrikaners during the Second World War. Whereas ten years ago the vilification of SABC came almost entirely from white viewers, it now comes also from the blacks. In the townships round Maritzburg, every third family has a TV set, and those who do not view with the neighbours. Some complaints against SABC appear to be aimed at the government in Pretoria. For example Khaba Mkhize, the editor of the *Witness* weekend supplement, published the story that 'soccer fans may kick back at TV' by refusing to pay their licence fees. Black viewers certainly had a grievance about the coverage of Sunday football. A semi-final between the Moroko Swallows and Mamelodi Sundowns had reached its most exciting moment when SABC interrupted the match to show a documentary film on the architectural wonders of Malta, with commentary in Afrikaans. The following Sunday, SABC again interrupted a match to show the same documentary, this time with a Zulu commentary. The *Witness* quoted football fans who called this behaviour 'sheer cruelty to the entertainment-starved public'. But even the row over football did not produce excitement and fury comparable with that over the television series on *Shaka Zulu*.

Some ten years ago, I voiced the suggestion that, should danger threaten South Africa, the Afrikaners might ally themselves with the Zulus; I called it a 'prospect full of menace'. It now looks as though Chief Buthelezi's Inkatha movement, with or without the blessing of Pretoria, is locked in battle with the ANC in Natal. On the day I write this (October 26th, 1987) the *Daily Telegraph* reports: 'The black townships of Pietermaritzburg have become war zones, as the two rival black groups fight for political control of the region. Unofficial reports say that up to fifty black corpses are passing through the city's mortuaries each week ... There are persistent allegations, voiced by both rival factions, that the South African police are "standing by", as the feuding continues.'

Historians of the future may see more clearly than we can how much of this new-found fighting spirit was due to the bloodthirsty TV serial, *Shaka Zulu* first shown in English and Zulu versions during the southern summer of 1986–87. This extraordinary and at times magnificent drama not only chronicles but exalts the first King Shaka, the black Napoleon, whose armies spread terror and death through Africa one hundred and seventy years ago. A Hollywood film company backed and produced the ten-part series but its director, William Faure, is a white South African, and of course it was shown on the state TV network, SABC. Black South Africans play the Zulus, and British actors play the parts of their fellow-countrymen. Although *Shaka Zulu* was televised in America and Australia, in most countries of Western Europe and even in Poland, it could not be shown in Britain because of a ban by the television trade unions. The British public missed an instructive as well as a thrilling experience. Whereas recent films on Nelson Mandela and Steve Biko were played by American actors, and aimed at American audiences, *Shaka Zulu* was made by and aimed at South Africans, white and black. It shows Africa in its sombre and savage truth, stripped of glamour and sentimentality. I saw the film first in a Johannesburg viewing theatre, then as it came out in weekly instalments, and once again in an edited, video version in London. The more I see it, the greater becomes my admiration, and also unease. For Shaka was not just a military genius – he was a monster. The film, which has helped to revive a feeling of Zulu pride and nationhood, may also have roused the old Zulu bloodlust.

The director, Faure, had the support in making the film of Chief Buthelezi, King Goodwill and Zulu historians. He and his scriptwriters also have studied the white historians, Donald R. Morris, who wrote *The Washing of the Spears*, and E. A. Ritter, who grew up among Zulus, and based his biography, *Shaka Zulu*, on stories handed down from generation to generation. The film is a drama and not a documentary, so that, as Faure told me: 'We had to change the story line a bit, as you would in a film about Caesar or Napoleon.' The film contains anachronisms and errors of detail on African social life. Limitations of budget meant that Faure could not assemble the multitudinous armies that feature in Hollywood versions of Zulu history. It is nevertheless the only film I have seen about Africa that really conveys what the place is like.

The first instalment sets out to explain the importance of Shaka and of the Zulu nation in British imperial history. It begins in 1882, three years after the Zulu War, when King Cetshwayo is brought to England to meet and plead with his conquerors. The King, huge and magnificent in a frock coat, is coldly received by Queen Victoria, played as a querulous china doll. Aristocratic and arrogant statesmen talk of him, in his hearing, as a savage, until Cetshwayo confounds the Queen and her courtiers by making a speech in impeccable English. He is then dismissed into servitude. In fact Cetshwayo's visit to England was not like that. He and his retinue took a house in Kensington, where admiring crowds gathered to see him. All traffic was stopped when he went to shop. He got on famously with the Queen at what was described as 'a hugely successful lunch' in her home at Osborne. For reasons that will become apparent, the TV *Shaka* is just as hostile towards the English as it is favourable to the Zulus.

From Queen Victoria, the film jumps back sixty years to the reign of George IV. The Earl Bathurst, the Secretary of State for War and the Colonies, has just had an urgent letter from Lord Charles Somerset at the Cape, advising him of the menace of Shaka. The alarmed Lord Bathurst hies to the royal palace, where George is still in bed with two of his doxies. The King, here played by Roy Dotrice, rebukes Lord Bathurst for interrupting his levee, then shares his breakfast with one of the girls, each chewing an end of the same sausage. When George is at last made aware of the danger from Africa, he warns his Colonial Secretary: 'Tend to the Zulu, Bathurst, or it will be my hard task to find someone who can.'

At this time, 1822, Lord Bathurst had probably never heard of the Zulus, and certainly would not have bothered the King with such an outlandish matter. Lord Charles Somerset, the Governor at the Cape, was opposed to annexing territory in Natal, though he favoured the establishment of a trading station. To that end, he gave his support to Francis Farwell and Henry Fynn, played in the film by Edward Fox and Robert Powell. A former naval lieutenant, Farwell is shown as a greedy and cynical hooray-henry who, in his own words, would not miss a chance to serve his king and collect the ivory. Fynn, who is remembered still for a tribe of half-caste descendants, is shown as a pious and gentle Irish physician. He does not stand for 'God Save the King'. At about this point in the film it dawned on me that Faure, the Afrikaner director, shares with the Irish an atavistic hostility to the British Crown and Empire.

The film *Shaka Zulu* does not really take off until Farwell and Fynn arrive in Natal, near what is now Durban. A Zulu regiment meets them and takes them to see the King at his kraal named KwaBulawayo, the Place of Killing. The film acquires a new dimension on the appearance of Shaka, played with stupendous force and conviction by Henry Cele, a former boxer and footballer. Like the original Shaka, Cele is well over six foot tall, and possessed of kingly grace, the power to command and a deep, sonorous speaking voice. With his intense, burning and pitiless stare, his occasional bitter smile in a face stretched taut over the cheek-bones, Cele conveys by his very appearance the will that drove Shaka to conquer Africa. The narrator, Fynn, says, 'it was clear that he knew enough about the Cape Colony and the whites to make him suspicious of our motives.' He is not impressed by the mirror and other trinkets of Western science. When he learns that Fynn has used his medical knowledge to bring a young woman out of a coma, he promptly orders her speared to death. There is a good scene where Shaka inspects the horse of one of the Europeans. He strokes its head and flank, and sniffs its sweat on his hand, then mounts the beast to canter around the kraal. 'By proving that he can tame the animal,' Farwell says, 'he's trying to prove he can tame us.'

After this meeting, the film goes back to 1786, to tell of Shaka's conception, birth, childhood and rise to power. This part of the film is interesting because it portrays an Africa still untouched by the outside world; yet the drama is played by people who speak the same language and know the events from oral tradition. Here is a modern film, set in pre-history. The finest directors and the most learned scholars could not hope to portray life in Boadicea's England. Modern Mexicans and Peruvians have only the dimmest awareness of life under the Aztecs and Incas. The Zulus are still fresh out of Eden.

Shaka's father, Senzangakona, a junior chieftain of the then small Zulu clan, discovers the beautiful Nandi taking a bathe in a forest stream. He asks if she will join with him in ama hlay endlela, literally 'fun of the roads', a form of supposedly safe sexual intercourse, in which the woman closes her thighs tight, and the man holds back from full penetration. But on this occasion, Nandi loses control of herself, and conceives. The pregnancy is the more unfortunate because Nandi's mother belongs to a clan which is too near to the Zulus for marriage. When Nandi's family charges Senzangakona with having fathered the baby, the Zulus reply: 'Impossible. Go back home and inform them the girl is but harbouring I-Shaka' – a beetle thought to interfere with the menstrual cycle. When Nandi gave birth in 1787, she called the boy U-Shaka, and went to live in shame and disgrace as an unwanted wife of Senzangakona.

Scenes like that of 'the fun of the roads' inspired one headline writer to call the series 'Starker Zulu'. But there is nothing prurient in the film. The Zulus take a robust and frank delight in sex, and discuss it without embarrassment. Witchcraft, not sex, is the dark and fearful influence on the Zulu mind, and it guides Shaka's destiny in the film. Witches scream and prophesy; lightning forks; and devil hyenas guffaw, as the blood-red infant Shaka is wrenched out of Nandi's womb.

Senzangakona took Nandi and Shaka into his kraal but did not give them the love or care accorded his other wives and children. Shaka's childhood was blighted by the disgrace and unhappiness of his mother, whom he adored. When Nandi was turned out of the Zulu kraal, she went to live with her own E-Langeni people, twenty miles away. The E-Langeni scorned and rejected Nandi because she had first conceived while taking 'the fun of the roads', and had then been expelled from her husband's kraal. The children tormented Nandi and burnt her hut. They beat and teased the friendless Shaka. According to Ritter, 'we may trace Shaka's subsequent lust for power to the fact that his little crinkled ears and the marked stumpiness of his sexual organs were ever the source of persistent ridicule.' At the age of eleven, Shaka attacked and almost killed two boys who had taunted him: 'Look at his penis; it's just like a little earthworm.' The insults and humiliations nurtured in Shaka a hatred of the E-Langeni people that he would later take out on them, and on much of Africa.

As Nandi and his aunts had assured him would happen, Shaka emerged from puberty as a man with huge bones, muscles and genitals, which he delighted in putting on public display. One of the stills for the colour brochure of *Shaka Zulu* shows how the girl Pampata 'rubs animal fat and ochre into Shaka's body during his coronation'. In adolescence, Shaka rebelled against the elders of both his mother's and father's clan, and went to serve as herdsman and warrior with another chieftain. It was during this time of exile that Shaka invented the style of warfare that made him the master of south-east Africa. Shaka abandoned the light, throwing assegai and ordered the blacksmiths to forge him a short, stabbing spear called iklwa, from the noise it made when pulled out of the flesh of its victim. He made his warriors throw their sandals away and dance barefoot on thorns. He drilled his impis to fight in a crescent formation, 'the horns', with two columns attacking the foe from the flank.

Like General Montgomery taking over the Eighth Army of Egypt, Shaka expected his officers to become as fit as the men. Those who could not keep up the pace of a sixty-mile route match were clubbed to death. This created a problem for William Faure, the director of *Shaka Zulu*. Few of the extras were tough enough to go barefoot, while some of the pot-bellied actors, cast as generals, looked as though they could not survive a route march longer than that from the taxi into a night-club in Soweto. But Henry Cele lopes at the head of an impi, as to the manner born. He is equally formidable in the scene where he orders the forging of iklwa. The smiths in Zululand, as in all southern Africa, were believed to possess sinister, magical power. They tempered the metal in the flesh of a skinned but living goat, or in human blood. Sorcerers watched over the forge in the forest, and only a brave man would go there at night.

When Shaka, in the film, hears of his father's death, he says: 'My conception was a moment of pleasure for him but the beginning of a life-long struggle for me. If I have tears to shed they are for myself.' He goes to the Zulu kraal where the elders have tried to install as the new King a cowardly half-wit. The wretch grovels and kneels to Shaka, who smiles, and puts him out of his misery with a casual jab of his spear.

When Shaka became their King, in 1816, the Zulus were one of dozens of Nguni clans. They co-existed, in spite of arguments over land, cattle and women. Before Shaka, the wars were really just stylised tournaments, in which the two sides hurled their spears, at a safe distance, and traded insults rather than blows. The women and elders cheered the young braves from the sideline. When Shaka went into battle, using his new short spears and his horn formation, he ordered the Zulus to slaughter the enemy to the last man, and often the women and children as well. 'Strike an enemy once and for all. Let him cease to exist as a tribe or he will live to fly at your throat again.' Within five years he was master of what is now Zululand, taking all those who surrendered into his Zulu army. From 1822 onward, Shaka dispatched his impis abroad. They moved south across Natal, driving before them a host of terrified peoples, the Sothos into their mountain fastness, the Xhosas into the British Cape Colony. His impis struck north and west into Swaziland and the present Transvaal. One of Shaka's commanders, Mzilikazi, failed in battle against the Swazis, and fearing execution if he returned home, took his army in flight to the north, not feeling safe from Shaka's revenge until he had reached the present Zimbabwe. He called his kraal after Shaka's, Bulawayo, which is how it remains today as capital of the Matabeles. Roy Campbell compared Mzilikazi's defection to Tito's quarrel with Stalin in 1948. Zulu people are strong in the present Mozambique and Tanzania.

In their panic dread of the Zulus, the other clans fought with each other for food and shelter. According to Donald R. Morris, the leading historian of the Zulus, two million people were killed in the few years that it took Shaka to build his empire. This was before either the British or Boers had come to the region except as solitary traders.

Those who remained under Shaka's sovereignty lived or died at his whim. One of his first acts as King was to conquer his mother's clan, the E-Langeni. He remembered and picked out all those men who, as boys, had tormented him, and had them impaled on stakes, to die in agony, pecked at by vultures. From this point in the film, impaling stakes are part of the set at KwaBulawayo. Shaka was always accompanied by his executioners, ready to club a man to death, or break his neck with a twist of the skull. He would kill a man for sneezing, or making him laugh when he was not in the mood. He killed whole regiments for the slightest failure in battle. Women who conceived, like Nandi, after the 'fun of the roads', were killed along with the man responsible.

One incident in the film reminded me of a more recent despot. It shows how traditional praise-singers who falter, grow faint, or are not putting their heart in their work, are slain by Shaka's attendants. Solzhenitsyn describes how, at a Communist Party meeting in Russia, nobody dared to be the first to stop applauding Stalin, and went on clapping till two of the old comrades died of heart attacks.

Some criticise the film for paying too much attention to Fynn and Farwell. It is true that from 1816, when Shaka became the Zulu King, till Fynn and Farwell arrived in 1824, the white man did not impinge on Zulu politics and society. But in the two years before Shaka's death, in September 1828, the impis had moved into Xhosa country, bordering on the Cape. The British mustered an army to face Shaka. He in turn wanted to send an embassy to King George IV. Shaka also wanted a bottle of Rowland's Macassar Oil to dye the hair of his ageing mother, and thereby prolong her life. Moreover, the whites had influence at the court of Shaka. Some took part in his military expeditions, though not apparently Farwell and Fynn as the film suggests. Fynn gave medical treatment to Shaka after a first botched attempt on his life, in 1824; and Shaka liked Fynn's company.

One striking episode in the film moves from the kraal, with its rotting corpses, into the Great House where Shaka and Fynn are talking at night. Shaka takes up the Bible and studies a plate of Christ on the Cross. 'Who was he?'

'A king.'

'Was Christ greater than George? His death, hanging from a tree, near weeping old women, is not worthy of a king. How did he come to die?'

'He was betrayed by those he loved the most.'

To which Shaka, thinking of the attempted murder, says, 'Yes, it is a mistake to love, especially for a king.'

He greets with a sardonic smile Fynn's protestation that 'with Christ in your heart, you are stronger than all the regiments on earth.'

Shaka rejects the love of Christ, and also the love of women. 'A man who builds a road to heaven must travel alone,' he says in the film, rejecting the girl who had rubbed ochre and animal fat on his body. The film includes one sexual encounter but Shaka appears to renounce and perhaps to murder the subsequent baby. Shaka kept a harem of more than a thousand girls, but according to Ritter: 'Although Shaka imparted full satisfaction to all his partners by means of Nguni "love-play" he was only able to deflower a reasonable number; according to Langazana they numbered "less than the fingers of two hands".' Donald R. Morris says bluntly: 'He was unquestionably a latent homosexual, and despite the fact that his genitals had more than made up for their previous dilatoriness . . . he was probably impotent.'

Shaka liked and trusted his father's sister Mkabayi, who had be-friended him as a child. But in the words of the actress Gugu Nxumalo, who plays the part in the film with sombre, heavy-lidded ferocity: 'Mkabayi is a wicked, rude, powerful and ambitious woman and the one who eventually plans Shaka's death.' The only human being that Shaka really loved was his mother, Nandi. Her death in 1827 drove Shaka into despair and madness. According to Fynn, who was one of the frightened witnesses, Shaka indulged in a day and a night of lamentation, and ordered several men to be killed on the spot:

> No further orders were needed; but as if bent on convincing their chief of their extreme grief, the multitude commenced a general massacre. Many of them received the blow of death while inflicting it on others, each taking the opportunity of revenging his injuries, real or imaginary. Those who could no more force tears from their eyes – those who were found near the river panting for water – were beaten to death by others who were mad with excitement. Towards the afternoon I calculated that not fewer than seven thousand people had fallen in this frightful, indiscriminate massacre.

After three days, Nandi was buried with ten of her handmaidens, their arms and legs broken then thrown still alive into the grave. Shaka gave orders that no crops were to be planted during the next year, and no milk drunk from the cows. All women found pregnant during the next year were to be killed, along with their husbands. He sent out regiments to the most distant kraals to enforce these orders and kill all those who had not sufficiently grieved for Nandi. He ordered the killing of milch-cows so that their calves should know the sorrow of losing a mother.

A year after Nandi's death, Shaka became obsessed with smelling out sorcerers and with diabolical science. He rounded up about three hundred women and asked each one if she kept a cat, which in Zululand as in Europe was thought to be a familiar of witches. Whatever the woman answered, Shaka killed her. He cut open a hundred pregnant women to study the growing foetus. These incidents do not come into the TV film, though there are others almost as blood-curdling.

The plot to destroy Shaka was hatched by his aunt, Mkabayi, who may have thought he had poisoned his mother Nandi. She enlisted the help of two of Shaka's half-brothers, and of the chamberlain at the Great House. The conspirators closed on him from behind and pierced him with spears. Zulu legend says that the vultures did not feed on the massive corpse. His aunt Mkabayi then ordered the burning of Shaka's kraal at KwaBulawayo, the Place of Killing. As the credits come on the screen at the end of the last instalment of *Shaka Zulu*, we see the smoke rise in a great pillar, blown sideways over the hillside, and hear only the rush of the wind in the grass. It is a fitting climax to this extraordinary film.

The story of Shaka brings to mind that of Siegfried, as it is told in the Wagner *Ring Cycle*. Both men are conceived in illicit unions and born under a curse. Both grow up in rebellion against authority. Both forge for themselves a weapon of magic power, the spear iklwa and Siegfried's sword. Both harbour incestuous passion, Shaka for Nandi and Siegfried for Brunhilde. Older women, Fricka and Mkabayi, sentence the heroes to die. Both are brought down by a spear in the back. Valhalla and KwaBulawayo burn after their deaths.

Shaka began his career in an Africa as remote from us as Siegfried's Germany. It was literally prehistoric because there was nobody to record events in writing. Yet by the time of his death, a few years later, Shaka was under the scrutiny of men such as Fynn, writing their diaries. Thanks to such records and to the film-work of William Faure, we have in *Shaka Zulu* a documentary drama set in prehistoric Africa. The implications are awesome. Arguments on the future of Africa always hark back to the past. The liberals talk of a simple, pastoral life before the slavers and racist exploiters. The right wing say that the blacks are 'straight down from the trees', that they never invented the wheel, lived in terror of sorcerers, and starved, when they were not eating each other. The film *Shaka Zulu* sets out to show what life was really like. Of course the Zulus were not typical Africans, any more than the English or the Albanians are typical Europeans. They lived by military conquest, and Shaka at least was exceptionally cruel. The Sotho King Mosheshwe, who led his people into their mountain fastness in order to get away from the Zulus, was peaceful and kindly. Shaka's atrocities frightened and shocked the Africans as much as they did the Europeans.

Although *Shaka Zulu* takes place one hundred and seventy years ago, before the Europeans came, it strikes me as all too topical. The Zulu politicians and generals may wear animal skins rather than Sam Brownes or safari suits, but nevertheless they remind me of men I have seen like Jomo Kenyatta, Omeka Ojukwu, Julius Nyerere and not least Idi Amin. Some episodes bring to mind the terror and anarchy of the Congo when I was there in 1964, or even when Conrad was there in the nineteenth century. KwaBulawayo merits the dying cry of Kurtz, in *Heart of Darkness*, the man who had gone to Africa to enlighten the natives. 'The horror! The horror!'

Obviously there was much to admire in Shaka's Zululand. He was, for what it is worth, a military genius. He inspired in the Zulus pride as well as terror. His drastic methods of birth control contained the population. The film-makers emphasise, as did the British who knew him, that Shaka was a man of enormous intelligence – quick, witty and capable, when he chose, of generosity and charm. Yet *Shaka Zulu* makes me uneasy. It also annoyed all sorts of South Africans.

Old-fashioned Afrikaners have never accepted television, and gave an unfriendly reception to *Shaka Zulu*. The Conservative MP for Soutpansberg, Tom Langley, said at a meeting in 1986: 'The Afrikaner never was what he is being shown as nowadays. I hope SABC is going to provide us with a parallel of *Shaka Zulu* for Afrikaners, so that Afrikaner children can also become proud of our history. The SABC is Americanising us.' He was applauded when he said that the late Albert Hertzog, who led the break from the National Party, was right to have warned against TV.

The white, English-speaking, middle class rejected *Shaka Zulu*, as they reject most things South African, especially its TV. Few of this type I met had seen even one instalment of *Shaka*. The *Weekly Mail*, the voice of north Johannesburg 'swimming-pool socialism', damned the series with Marxist sociology. The author says that Shaka's cruelties in the film are explained by sorcery and his evil genius: 'The effect of recourse to these "motors" of history is determined by the actions of leaders (spiritual or political) alone, and not by ordinary people. It is a perspective which denies the contribution of the Zulu people to the positive achievements of the Zulu kingdom. It obscures the oppression and exploitation of the people on which the power and wealth of the Zulu leaders was based.'

The same sort of attack appeared in newspapers written and read by black supporters of ANC. The Xhosas, Sothos and other former victims of Shaka hated the film. Some critics were Zulu, such as the group I met at Sobantu, one of the few townships around Pietermaritzburg that does not support Chief Buthelezi's Inkatha movement. 'No Inkatha member could stay here,' said one of the men in the front parlour, equipped with a TV set and a ghetto-blaster. A child slept in the corner, and a woman brought us in rum, beer and succulent pieces of beef. 'Do you have Women's Lib?' one of them asked me. 'We feel sorry for you white men who have to go straight home to your wives. We like to talk first with other men, hear the gossip, who's been interned, who's been let out.'

One of the things to which they objected in *Shaka Zulu* was how it showed a girl sitting beside him in company: 'That would never have been allowed in Zulu society. There'd have been the boys, the young men on one side and the old men on the other.' Objections started to pour forth: 'The architecture was pure American Indian . . . Shaka would not have been surprised at seeing himself in a mirror. We Zulus used to look into the water as a mirror . . . Shaka would not have been surprised by a horse.' They believed that no white men actually met Shaka, though Fynn was enjoying sex in Durban. One man defended 'the fun of the roads'.

In the history books we were taught we were savages that the missionaries enlightened. The missionaries stopped us using our old sex customs and did not give us any substitutes until the pill. Before that, men and women had sex without piercing, without defloration, which gave satisfaction to the woman as well as the man. They both had to use self-control. If a woman got out of line and got pregnant, she would be punished by sending her to live with the old men, who were past having sex. If she married, her partner would get only a small lobola (dowry), only one cow . . . Shaka was very particular when it came to sexual matters. He wouldn't allow the men any form of sex for two weeks before fighting.

The *Natal Witness* journalist, Khaba Mkhize saw the film *Shaka Zulu* as President Botha 'playing the Zulu card', as Lord Randolph Churchill played 'the Ulster card'. The Zulu leaders like King Goodwill and Chief Buthelezi gave the film their blessing before it appeared. Chief Buthelezi blamed the British for having portrayed Shaka as 'a bestial insane tyrant'. He said that men like Fynn had 'scattered sperm around KwaZulu as other men scattered footsteps'. The Afrikaners as well as the Zulus come down hard on the British in Natal. The South African *Sunday Times* published an essay by Louis du Buisson, author of *The White Man Cometh*, a critical appraisal of the early white pioneers in Natal. 'They lied, schemed and cheated their way into the confidence of the Zulu kings,' says du Buisson. They took Zulu girls and held powers of life and death over thousands. He blames the British like Fynn for having 'coerced King Shaka into a disastrous war against the Xhosa nation'.

The director of *Shaka Zulu*, William Faure, read and approved this attack on Fynn and the other British adventurers. Perhaps because I am English, I found something peculiar in this new-found friendship between the Zulus and Boers. Both, it is true, were beaten in war by the British; but they had slaughtered each other too. Certainly Faure does not support the present South African government. 'I suffered from the education system in the insanity of the fascist Verwoerd government,' he told me. 'This government has treated the Zulus like everyone else with arrogance and incompetence . . . My family are Treurnicht [right-wing] supporters. They hated the film.' He is hot-eyed, intense and passionate. But might not the film be seen, I suggested, as pointing the way to some kind of Zulu/Afrikaner alliance against the Xhosas and English-speaking whites? 'No,' said Faure, 'I don't think this government is bright enough to have sat down seven years ago and thought "How can we manipulate this film?" ' Perhaps not; but *Shaka Zulu* still makes me uneasy.

7
LADYSMITH

Black Week ... Thoughts on the Boer War ...
Churchill and Gandhi

F ROM PIETERMARITZBURG I went north to Ladysmith on one of the long-distance buses that now run in South Africa. Public transport used to be the monopoly of South African Railways, themselves a system of outdoor relief for the indigent Afrikaner. The Afrikaner/Socialist government of the 1920s nationalised most of the country's heavy industry and staffed it with hungry men who had drifted into the cities from the countryside. South African Railways offered a job for life to tens of thousands of slow, docile and loyal bureaucrats, including a team of two thousand gardeners, with a mobile seed bed, who planted and tended the flowers on even the smallest rail-halts. Buying a ticket and booking a seat on the train was almost as slow as the journey itself, which never exceeded 35 mph. South African Railways had its advantages. Some of the trains had an observation car at the back from which to survey the veld rolling backward into the distance. One sat down in the restaurant car at a table covered with neat blue cloth, at a place surrounded with silver for four or five courses. Over the last few years the railways have cut down the frequency and quality of the trains but have started instead a bus service, and, better still, permitted the competition of private owners. The driver is generally black and the hostess white, but when the coach stops at a café en route, the two of them share a table, and chatter genially. These details count in South Africa.

Like most small towns in South Africa, Ladysmith grew round the long main street, which also was wide enough to allow a team of oxen to turn. There is a late nineteenth-century church, a town hall built for a bigger town, and one hotel that flourished during the Zulu War. All three buildings survived the most famous siege in British military history. Like every visitor to Ladysmith, I force myself to reflect that on this dull and sleepy place there once depended the future and even the very

128

existence of Britain's Empire. Between October 1899 and April 1900, the Boers almost succeeded in crushing a British army and taking the whole of Natal. They were not at this stage of the war a band of guerillas. President Kruger had spent some of the wealth of the Transvaal gold to equip his troops with the latest field artillery, which they used with horrendous effect against the British in battles like Spion Kop. The British casualty lists were trifling compared with those of the First World War, but they included some of the greatest names in the kingdom. Fleet Street christened the early days of December 'Black Week'. A social historian, R. H. Gretton, wrote: 'The knowledge that the whole of our boasted arms were reduced to the pause of defeat, bit as with acid . . . It was one of the grim signs of that week that women then first began to buy newspapers, as men do, from the sellers in the streets.' While Britain waited in trepidation for the dreaded news of the fall of Ladysmith, most of the world exulted. The French and Germans gloated over the agony of the one people they both hated more than each other. The Russians prepared to march into India. The Catholic Irish, whether at home or in the United States, hurrahed for the Boers and sent out hundreds of volunteers to fight under John MacBride, a Fenian who, for his sins, was to marry the harridan, Maud Gonne.

The British survived 'Black Week', and managed to lift the sieges of Ladysmith, Mafeking and Kimberley. The sixty-eight-year-old Boer General, Piet Joubert, was too pious and kindly to carry on war à l'outrance. As a citizen and an advocate he had spoken against the war. After 'Black Week' he did not pursue his advantage, saying that 'if God offers you a finger, you do not take the whole hand.' His wife accompanied Joubert to battle; she loaded his guns, and on one occasion directed the Boer artillery. Perhaps it was she who persuaded Joubert on Christmas Day to fire shells loaded with plum puddings into the British garrison. Old Joubert was brave as the legendary Boers like Botha, Smuts, De la Rey and De Wet, but unlike them he knew that the cause was lost. 'Lucky the Afrikaner who does not survive the war,' he said, and died himself before it was over.

The battlefields of the Boer War depress me. I cannot grasp the intricacies of deployment of troops, of cover and fields of fire. Books like Thomas Pakenham's *Boer War* and Rayne Kruger's *Goodbye Dolly Gray* cease to grip me at just those battle scenes which ought to be most exciting. When I have been in countries at war, like Vietnam, Biafra, the Lebanon or El Salvador, I have never felt exhilaration to match the fear and depression. I would have hated the battle of Spion Kop, or the siege of Ladysmith. The Boer War depresses me most of all because I cannot sympathise with the British. I am a pro-Boer. The documents uncovered by Thomas Pakenham prove beyond question what I had always suspected, that Milner and the financiers like Alfred Beit provoked the war in order to get control of the wealth of Johannesburg. The Afrikaners fought for their homes, their families and their nation. Whatever we think of the Afrikaner's present attitude to the blacks, it was not their prime concern at the time. Moreover the same people who now are most anti-Afrikaner, the liberals, the *Guardian*, the trade unionists and the Irish, were at the time the most pro-Boer. The unjust war left a bitterness in the Afrikaners which found expression in 1948. To a large extent the apartheid system was aimed not at the blacks but the British. The simple piety of Joubert turned into the twisted ideology of Verwoerd.

It was therefore in sombre mood that I did the sights of Ladysmith. The town hall, which had a chunk knocked out of it by a shell, has now been repaired. So has St Paul's, the Anglican church, where plaques remember the three thousand who fell in action or died of disease 'during the successful effort to relieve the town besieged by the Boers of the Transvaal Republic and the Orange Free State. *Dulce et decorum est pro patria mori*'. The belief that 'sweet and proper it is to die for one's country', was dashed for ever by Wilfred Owen's sombre poem of the First World War, rebuking those who tell:

> with such high zest
> To children ardent for some desperate glory,
> The old lie: *Dulce et decorum est*
> *Pro Patria mori.*

At Sunday matins at Ladysmith, prayers were said for the troops on the frontier and in the townships, reminding us in this place of war that the battles continue. The Anglican nun who had preached the sermon afterwards handed out leaflets on Aids, 'the sin of homosexuality', Lot, and the other citizens of Sodom and Gomorrah.

Among those present during the siege of Ladysmith were two men who, four decades later, were prime antagonists in another, vaster tragedy for the British Empire. They were Winston Churchill and Mahatma Gandhi. The young Churchill had come to South Africa first as a newspaper correspondent, richly supplied with tins of pheasant and cases of claret and whisky. Outside Ladysmith he was taken prisoner by the Boers, escaped from Pretoria gaol and made his way to Mozambique, and then back to Ladysmith where he enrolled as a kind of honorary army officer. It was the only good news for the British during those dismal weeks. Mahatma Gandhi was at the time a lawyer in Durban, and leader of the campaign for Indian rights. When the Boer War broke out, he volunteered as a stretcher-bearer and stayed in Ladysmith during the siege. As far as is known, he did not meet Churchill, the man who later branded him as a 'naked fakir'.

Churchill and Gandhi are the respective hero and villain of Nirad Chaudhuri, the ninety-year-old Bengali, whose books have completely upset the received opinions on Indian independence and partition. Chaudhuri has set out to smash 'the myth that the decision to leave India was an act of wise and far-seeing statesmanship inspired by magnanimity; that it was executed in a masterly way by a brilliant military leader [Mountbatten]; that it brought into existence the largest democracy in the world; that it replaced an evil imperial system with a free association of nations; and that it opened an era of sincere and real Indo-British friendship.'

Chaudhuri's veneration of Churchill goes back to the First World War when, as a student in Calcutta, he applauded Churchill's opening of the Gallipoli Front. Later he hoped that Churchill would come to rule India. Churchill in turn was one of the first to applaud Chaudhuri's *Autobiography of an Unknown Indian* when it was published in 1951.

Chaudhuri's distrust of Gandhi goes back almost as far. He describes Gandhi's attitude to the British as blending servility with malice. He blames Gandhi's anti-British campaigns for stirring up hostility between Hindu and Muslim. He says that the 'Quit India' agitation during the Second World War was in effect inviting attack from Germany and Japan. In his latest book *Thy Hand, Great Anarch!* Nirad Chaudhuri writes: 'The worship of Gandhi is, in the British above all, unjustified imbecility and a sure proof of the degradation of the British character.'

Although Chaudhuri's attitude to the British Raj has won him few supporters in Britain, he does have a following among radical Indians, now disillusioned by government in all three secession states of the sub-continent. The Indian experience has considerable relevance to events in South Africa.

The Boer War made a big impact on India, as Chaudhuri recalls in his two-part autobiography. Some of the first names he remembers were those of such Boer War generals as Lord Roberts, Lord Kitchener,

Botha and Cronje. As a very small boy, he would ask his elder brother to climb on the trunks and read out the names of the regiments and the officers under the panoramic pictures of the Battle of Paardeberg and the Entry into Pretoria. Like all Bengalis, the young Chaudhuri had mixed feelings about the war: 'We thought of the Boers as a heroic people, and of their leaders, particularly of Cronje and Botha, as men of superhuman valour.' One half of him wanted the Boers to win; the other half identified with the British army.

Chaudhuri compares the whites in Africa, especially the Afrikaners, with Aryan Hindus, the conquering race from the north who came to rule the sub-continent. He regards the end of white rule in Rhodesia as one more example of abdication caused by failure of will. He writes with rare and refreshing candour of Indian attitudes towards skin colour. The Hindu caste system must be the oldest and most elaborate form of discrimination in the world. It involves the segregation of human beings according to marriage, jobs, place of worship and even physical contact, hence the name of 'untouchable' given to those of the *harijan* caste. The laws to free the *harijan* have still not proved effective; they are simply ignored. Gandhi himself, although he took up the grievances of the *harijan*, would not renounce the system of caste which accounted for their position. So strong is the caste feeling, even among those who are not Hindus, that Christian churches had to provide separate doors and of course separate communion cups for untouchables in the congregation.

I have mentioned how in the 1960s, the South African Parliament wanted to stop the integration of laundries, that is the contact in the wash, of clothes belonging to whites and clothes belonging to blacks. I gave this as an example of the absurdity of apartheid. It would not appear absurd to an Indian. The *dhobi* class of washermen earn good money because they are willing to do the 'unclean' work of handling other people's laundry, involving the risk of contact with menstrual stains. The dhobi wallahs are therefore considered as low as the 'sweepers' who take away night soil.

Some Indians reply that for all the faults of the caste system, it does not involve segregation by colour, like the apartheid laws. In theory the caste system is not related to colour; in practice it generally is. Few people on earth are quite as conscious of skin colour as are the Indians. The rulers of the sub-continent, the Indus-Ganges basin, have always been conquerors from the north, first the Aryan Hindus, then the Turkish and Persian Muslims and later the British. All these invaders were lighter skinned than the aboriginals.

According to Nirad Chaudhuri:

Varna or colour was the central principle round which Hindu society organised itself, and the orthodox Hindu scriptures know of no greater crime than miscegenation, or, as they call it, *Varna-sankara*, the mixing of colours ... This faith in the sanctity of *Varna*, colour, or caste endures and abides in Hindu society, and the fact – from the point of view of doctrine, the adventitious fact – that the inevitable intermixture with the indigenous element has made many Hindus dark-skinned, makes no difference to the hold and fascination of the ideal of colour. The Hindu regards himself as heir to the oldest conscious tradition of superior colour and as the carrier of the purest and most exclusive stream of blood which created that colour, by whose side the Nazi was a mere parvenu.

Colour continues to play a big part in the fixing of bride price. A light skin commands authority. The Prime Minister, Rajiv Gandhi with his mixture of Kashmiri and Parsi ancestry, is notably light-skinned. The North Indians look down on the darker South Indians, and all look down on black Africans. The colour consciousness of the Indians did not at first affect their British rulers, many of whom took Indian wives. The second Lord Liverpool, who was Prime Minister for almost fifteen years, in the early nineteenth century, was a quarter Indian. So, oddly enough, was Field Marshal Roberts, the British commander during the Boer War.

These thoughts about Churchill and Gandhi, the British in Africa and their Indian Raj, occurred to me in the Royal Hotel, which survived a direct hit from a shell during the siege. The Royal also survived some facetious jokes in the *Ladysmith Bombshell*, one of the siege journals that also appeared in Mafeking and Kimberley. Sample: 'There was a time at the Royal when you got eggs inside and shells outside. Now you don't.' There was no whisky available for the Scots on St Andrew's Night, November 30th, 1899. There is no shortage of whisky now in the Royal Hotel's Lady Chatterley Bar, kept by one of those Indians that you find in Natal, who is recognised as a character, as a teller of jokes, and a fount of gossip. I talked with some Afrikaner women, housewives spending an evening away from their husbands. Piped music tinkled through the Royal Hotel, the theme tune from the television *Shaka Zulu*. Some of the Zulu waiters were humming it.

8

PARYS

Paris in the Orange Free State . . . In Defence of the Afrikaners

ARYS, PRONOUNCED PAH-RACE, is the Afrikaans for Paris, which makes it exceptional in the Orange Free State, where places are named from the Bible, like Bethlehem, or from physical characteristics like Bloemfontein, the flowery spring. I stay in the Echoes Hotel in Boom Street, close to the Vaal River, which here is a placid stream, fringed by weeping willows, from which come the soporific buzzing of insects and cooing of doves. Somebody told me once that on Sundays the Transvaal bank of the river is lined with anglers, but fishing is not allowed in the more strongly Calvinist Orange Free State. On this Sunday, no one was fishing from either bank. 'We used to catch beautiful barbel,' said a Parysian, 'but now the water is overgrown with all those lilies you see. Somebody introduced those damn lilies from overseas.' The word 'overseas', with the accent heavily on the opening syllable, has come to be almost a term of abuse with Afrikaners. A pleasant torpor hangs over the riverside café where I am taking an evening beer. A fish rises noisily to an insect. A group of Afrikaner youths are exchanging jocular insults. One of them arm-wrestles the black waiter. Because the white is bigger and younger, he wins each bout, to his unfeigned joy.

Parys abounds in filling stations and junk food shops that cater for motorists passing through. Because it is outside the earth tremor belt of the southern Transvaal, Parys has factories using precision machinery. In most respects Parys is a slow and backwoods town. Except for the gold mines up in the north-west corner, the Orange Free State is not an industrial region. A few thousand Boers farm this immense plateau of rolling veld in much the same way as the first Voortrekkers. You can drive for miles without a sign of a farmhouse or African huts. Yet empty though it appears, the Orange Free State feeds part of Africa, and at harvest time you can see ripe maize stretching for miles. Now that Marxist schemes of collectivisation and soil erosion, have brought agricultural ruin to much of independent Africa, the more important it is that the Orange Free State produces a surplus of meat and grain. This can only be done by large-scale, private farming, in practice by whites, for there are few blacks in Africa with the know-how, or capital. Most countries in Africa have tried, for ideological reasons, to nationalise big farms, or split them up into hundreds of smallholdings. The result has been both agricultural and ecological disaster. Hence the famine in Ethiopia. The few African countries that still have a healthy agriculture are those like Zimbabwe, Malawi and Ivory Coast where whites as well as blacks are allowed to farm. These facts are unpalatable to the left-wing ideologue. It seems unjust that so few whites should farm so much of the land. It seems unfair because there are so many millions of Africans on subsistence farming. Nobody objects to the much greater corn farms of the American Middle West, or the sheep farms of Australia. Nobody would suggest that these should be turned into plots of subsistence farming for Indians or Aborigines.

White, townee South Africans look down their nose at the backveld farmers, rather like east coast Americans sneer at the Middle West. The Orange Free Staters have much in common with farmers in Minnesota or Iowa. They are cautious, conservative in opinion, God-fearing and dour. When I first came to South Africa, in 1964, I needed to have an interpreter to talk with the backveld Afrikaners. The farmers I met in the western Transvaal were courteous enough, but they could not conceal their suspicion of one who was not only an 'Engelsman' but an 'overseas journalist'. One lady showed me the charred remains of a doorpost burnt by the British during the Boer War. At another farm, our interpreter looked very embarrassed and urged me to leave. Later he said that the woman with whom we had talked had just been widowed under unusual circumstances. She had found her husband, a National Party politician, in bed with the African maid. He then committed suicide by setting fire to himself.

Nowadays it is rare to meet an Afrikaner who cannot or will not speak English. Television has popularised the language. Perhaps the Afrikaners have lost the fear they used to have of speaking English wrongly, or in a comical accent. They no longer resent the English-speaking South Africans. The old hatred of Britain has turned to scorn or pity. Because the Afrikaners now speak English, foreigners like myself have little chance to practise their Afrikaans. Even the blacks in Parys speak English as well as Afrikaans, and also two or three African languages.

Whereas, ten years ago, I wrote of some of the Afrikaners I met with a certain degree of mockery, now I feel it is they who are having a laugh at me. In Cape Town one evening, I fell into conversation with Manie, a Boer from the northern Transvaal, who had an assignment down in the south in his work as a draughtsman. It was late in the evening, shortly before the bar closed, and Manie had reached a state that was not so much aggressive as teasing. When he had finally gone, I wrote down what he had said to me, and wondered whether in fact he was drunk at all:

Listen, Rick . . . sorry, Dick, my memory's really terrible. I should really like to tell you what I think of overseas journalists, but I've been drinking since I came down from Jo'burg. I should really like to meet and talk to you when I'm sober, Nick . . . it is Nick? From Cape Town? Sorry, from London. Is that a big place, London? Now listen, Vic old chap [in a mock British accent], I hope you will not take offence when I give my honest opinion of the journalist. You won't take offence, will you, Rick? The overseas journalist is like a photographer who takes a naked woman as his model, a lovely woman, with perfect legs and boobs, red lips, beautiful eyes and hair, and he tells her to turn round and bend over and part the cheeks of her arse and then he photographs her arsehole . . . That's just my opinion, Nick, I hope you're not offended. Come on, have another drink . . .

Because the Afrikaners now speak English, one tends to forget how foreign they are to the English mentality. They are in the first place continentals, of Dutch, French and German ancestry, with a culture based on Calvinism and Roman law. They are also colonials, people whose ancestors went to settle another continent. They went to a land much further away from Europe than America, and severed from Europe for over two centuries. The ancestors of the Afrikaners, as of the first Americans, went from Europe during the seventeenth century, but while the Americans kept in touch with the ideas of Europe, the Afrikaners clung to their seventeenth-century way of life.

With all these differences, it is not surprising that Afrikaners appear odd to the outside world. A good example of this is South Africa's present Ambassador to the United States, Piet 'Promises' Koornhof, a long-time Cabinet Minister, and almost a caricature of the Afrikaner politician. He was one of the architects of apartheid and earned his nickname from his repeated promises, often postponed or broken, to do away with the system when it had proved a disaster. One South African newspaper hinted, politely enough, that Dr Koornhof might not come over well on American television. Like most Afrikaners, Dr Koornhof speaks an English not always easy for outsiders (when I telephone London, nobody at the other end can understand the local operators, who ask on behalf of 'Mr Waysht'), and sometimes he gets an idiom slightly wrong, like that Afrikaner judge who recently said of a crooked wheeler-dealer that, 'he had a finger in every tart in town.' With his huge nose and flapping ears, Dr Koornhof is a godsend to satirists like Pieter-Dirk Uys, who takes him off in stage performances. Not that Dr Koornhof minds; he is one of the regulars in the audience. His own speeches and television appearances are full of jokes, which range from the funny to the mysterious. A friend swears that he once heard Dr Koornhof conclude a debate with the words: 'And what is more, I agree with everything that I have just said.' In fact, Dr Koornhof may be going the way of the former New Zealand Premier, Robert 'Piggy' Muldoon, who started off as a dull political hack until he discovered that journalists printed his jokes. He achieved world fame when Nigeria warned New Zealand not to send a rugby team to South Africa, and Piggy advised the Lagos government to find a good taxidermist. So great became the compulsion to raise a laugh that Muldoon later went on the stage each night in the *Rocky Horror Show*.

We may howl with laughter at Dr Koornhof, just as we laughed at the Transvaal President Paul Kruger. Yet all the time, he may have been laughing at us. Taken to Britain and shown the marvels of Manchester industry, the Houses of Parliament, Stratford-on-Avon, the fleet at Portsmouth and the Tattoo at Aldershot, Kruger was asked what had most impressed him in Britain. 'The sheep are very big,' was all his reply. But Kruger's rude farmers took on and almost defeated the might of the British Empire. Perhaps the modern Afrikaners guess that although they make no appeal to the east coast America of black power, the women's movement, cocaine, abortion, gay pride – other Americans, further inland might warm to someone like Piet Koornhof – if they can understand him.

Over the last few years there has been a decline in jokes about 'Van der Merwe', the legendary Afrikaner bumpkin, stupid, sly, mechanically ignorant, greedy but indolent, hostile to blacks and Englishmen. The Orange Free State was the spiritual home of Van der Merwe. One story has Van on a radio quiz show, faced with the 64,000-rand question: 'Where was Jesus Christ born?'

After some minutes of agonised thought, he ventures the tentative answer: 'Bloemfontein.'

'No,' says the compère, 'I'm very sorry, Mr Van der Merwe, but the correct answer is Bethlehem.'

To which Van says ruefully, 'Ag' (pronounced like the German *ach*), 'Ag, I knew it was somewhere in the Orange Free State.'

Some of the Van der Merwe jokes were reworkings of stories told about Irishmen, Poles, even Scots and Jews. A few had the authentic Afrikaner ring, like Van der Merwe in London, watching some men repairing a road. 'Why do they need so many people to do that job?' he asks his friend. 'Just give me six boys, and I could do it myself.' There was a nice story of Van der Merwe, back from his farm in Zambia, meeting his school friend Nico Diedrichs. 'What do you do now?' Van asks, to which Diedrichs replies: 'Oh, I'm President of the Republic now.'

'Ag,' replies Van der Merwe, 'where I come from we have a black man doing that job.'

The Van der Merwe jokes do not offend the Afrikaners. I have seen an Afrikaner listening to a Van der Merwe joke told, not very capably, by an Indian. These days in South Africa, the English-speakers some-times strike me as odder than the Afrikaners. There was one example of this in Parys. Since there is no Anglican church in the town, I went to the Methodists, where an elderly visiting minister gave the sermon. He said that Methodism had once been strong in Johannesburg. Now the congregations were growing in some of the wealthy suburbs like Sandton, but three churches had closed in central Johannesburg: 'We are losing the support of the people who created Methodism, the Cornish miners, the working class of the great industrial centres like Birmingham.' As I was mulling over this piece of social history, the preacher suddenly changed to the topic of sin and temptation: 'You who come here,' he told an admittedly ageing congregation, 'are not going to be tempted by sins like murder or adultery.' Not even *tempted* by adultery? South African Methodists must be a race apart.

One of the harshest attacks I have read on the Afrikaners was published in 1930 under the title *Caliban in Africa*. The author, Leonard Barnes, had worked in London in the Colonial Office before becoming a journalist in Durban, where he contributed to *Voorslag*. Later, he went to work with Laurens van der Post at the *Cape Times*, in the period when that paper carried a series of leader page articles on the poet Virgil. Apparently Barnes succumbed to the lure of Communism, for during the Second World War he published a book called *Soviet Light on the Colonies*, claiming that Stalin's rule in Central Asia was altogether more wise and beneficial than Britain's rule in Africa. By 1969, Barnes had returned to reason, and wrote a defence of Biafra, with which I entirely agree. He never wrote anything quite as good as *Caliban in Africa*, and in particular, his attack on the Afrikaners. What he says of them is largely true; and yet I end up liking the Afrikaners for just the reasons that Barnes found them objectionable.

The book begins by making a clear distinction between the Boers, who started their Great Trek north from the Cape in the 1830s, and those of mainly British descent, who were opening up the American west. 'The Americans trekked *to* something; the Dutchmen trekked *away* from something.' To the young Leonard Barnes, this distinction reflected badly upon the Afrikaner: 'He moved not in search of liberty which he proposed to put to some positive use but merely because he resented being interfered with [*by the British in the Cape*] ... The routine work of the farm he leaves to managers and slaves, turning his own attention to the serious business of life – hunting game, visiting or entertaining his friends, and having rows with his enemies.'

There is some truth in this but it does not discredit the Afrikaner. The Americans trekked *to* something: the land that belonged to the Indians, and in the south and west to the Mexicans. The Afrikaners trekked into land that was virtually empty until they confronted the Zulus, and black people fleeing the Zulus. Many Americans trekked in pursuit of gold, especially after the finds in California. For the sake of gold they were ready to murder, swindle and rob. The Afrikaners not only did not search for gold but tried to prevent the exploration by others that ended in 1886 with the finds of Johannesburg, and the consequent inrush of foreigners. The Transvaal President Paul Kruger was right to predict that 'every ounce of gold taken from the bowels of our soil will yet have to be weighed against rivers of tears.'

Some of the Boers kept household slaves, in practice indentured labourers, but did not maintain the slave plantations that brought such wealth to Americans in the South. They hunted game but did not wantonly slaughter animals in the way that Americans wiped out the buffalo herds. They fought the Zulus, Sothos and Matabeles but did not try to exterminate them, as did Americans to some Red Indian tribes (or Australians did to the Aborigines). The Afrikaners have never regarded the blacks with hatred. Even Barnes concedes this: 'The Dutch do not suffer from that involuntary reserve which keeps the Englishman a little aloof from natives, however he may respect and like them. On the contrary they will sometimes deal with natives more open-heartedly and in a certain way more sympathetically, even when consciously despising them.' The Afrikaner, Barnes declares, was capable of spontaneous benevolence, as an act of grace, but he could not grasp the idea of permanent obligations. He believed in freedom for himself but not as a common possession. 'Rousseau's theory of the social contract is equally beyond him,' Barnes says with a patronising sneer.

Why should the Afrikaners have shared their freedom? The blacks they encountered were either savage and hostile nations, such as the Zulus, or servants who came to work on the wagons and farms. The Boers had no authority over the Zulus and therefore no obligation to them. Towards their servants or slaves, the Afrikaners felt a personal obligation, but this did not extend to political obligation, let alone to acceptance of Rousseau's notions. If the Boers had heard of the theory of 'social contract', they would have called it absurd. They regarded themselves as settlers not colonists. In this they resembled the British settlers in Kenya around the turn of the century. The settlers in Kenya were always at odds with the Governor and the colonial service, who took it upon themselves to guard the rights of the natives. It was accepted wisdom, in liberal circles, that Britain's colonial service gave good government to the blacks, in contrast with countries like Kenya, Southern Rhodesia and South Africa, where there were white settlers. Uganda and the Gold Coast (Ghana) were models of justice, prosperity and contentment; but look at them now, in the grip of famine, disease, corruption, tyranny and despair. The only countries in Britain's former African Empire, still enjoying a measure of decent government, are those like Kenya, Zimbabwe and South Africa, where there were once or are still white settlers.

Nor is it true that the Afrikaners were only trekking *away* from something. They had their grievances against British rule in the Cape: the abolition of slavery, the interference of missionaries, the pressure on land from the Xhosas, Coloureds and British. However the trekgees, or trek fever, did not diminish once they had left the Cape. The Voortrekkers were not content to remain in the great, empty plateau between the Orange and Vaal Rivers, the present Orange Free State. They went east over the Drakensberg Mountains, into Natal, where they met and fought with the Zulus. They pushed north into the Transvaal and founded a series of tiny republics, now forgotten. But still, trek fever burned. As late as 1875, a number of Boers from the Transvaal and Orange Free State set forth on an expedition north and west, across the Kalahari Desert, and into Angola. Some of these Thirst Trekkers, as they were called, had some kind of grievance against their government; others were just victims of trek fever. Such a man was Johannes van der Merwe, one of the Voortrekkers from forty years earlier. Now, at the age of eighty-two, a rich man, comfortable on his fine estate, Van der Merwe resolved to join with the Thirst Trekkers. It is true that he rode in a comfortably furnished wagon, accompanied by his excellent native chef, but Van der Merwe was nonetheless crossing one of the grimmest deserts on earth. He arrived in Angola in perfect health and went on to live to be ninety-two.

What were the Thirst Trekkers trekking from? Kipling would have us believe that they could not abide 'the smoke of a neighbour's fire'. Perhaps such feelings contributed to the trek fever, although the Boers were not unsociable. The actual trekking forced them upon each other's company. Most of them took a delight in freedom, out in the wilderness, under the great sky of Africa. The trekkers compared themselves with the Children of Israel, moving towards the Promised Land. Whenever they found a rivulet, heading north, they called the place Nelspruit, or source of the Nile. When the Thirst Trekkers came to Angola, they gloried in finding wild cattle and beehives, the land flowing with milk and honey.

After this long attack on the trek mentality, Barnes came to what he clearly believed was final proof of the worthlessness and unfitness for power of the Afrikaner: 'The truth is that the French Revolution, the Industrial Revolution and the conquests of the scientific spirit have all passed him by. His outlook is virtually unaffected by the profound modifications which these movements have made on the psyche of the civilised world . . .' Reading and re-reading those words, I find that my old and furtive liking for Afrikaners is now in danger of turning to hero worship. Could any people, even as long ago as 1930, have been so brave and magnificent as to ignore the three most loathsome phenomena of the last two centuries, the French Revolution, the Industrial Revolution and 'the conquests of the scientific spirit'? The sad truth is that even the Afrikaners have not wholly escaped the influence of these modern abominations.

The Afrikaners, as Christians, reject the basic French revolutionary concept of human perfectibility. Nobody can believe in Original Sin and

Rousseau's Noble Savage. The French Revolution and all its consequent 'isms' sprang from the hope of building a heaven on earth. In particular the Revolution produced the twin evils of socialism and nationalism which blossomed as Jacobinism and Buonapartism, to reappear this century in the still more virulent form of Communism and Fascism. The two 'isms' invariably go together; two sides of the same dud coin. The Afrikaners have toyed with both these ideas. During the twenties, they joined with the British socialists to form a National Labour government. During the thirties, Boer patriotic pride became infected with Hitlerism. But even then, at its worst, Afrikaner nationalism was not aggressive. It did not seek conquest or lebensraum. Its motive force was resentment against the British. In this it resembled Irish Republicanism. The Afrikaner Nationalists, like the Irish Republicans, took the side of Germany in the two world wars, regarding England's difficulty as their own opportunity.

Apartheid could be described as an 'ism'. Its leading exponent, Dr Verwoerd, was nothing if not an ideologue. But whereas the ideologies of the French Revolution claim universal validity, apartheid only applies to South Africa. No other country has such a mixture of races, nations, religions, languages, cultures and different levels of civilisation. Even in the United States, where English is the official language, and everyone thinks of himself as American, there still are ethnic divisions, and separate suburbs for Anglo-Saxons, Hispanics, Asians and blacks. In South Africa, only the ANC aspires to a multi-racial society, or what Americans used to call the 'melting pot'. The South African government favours what is now called 'multi-nationalism'; if they had used that word in the first place, instead of apartheid, they might not now be in such a mess.

The Afrikaners are an intensely democratic people when it comes to class; but they do not believe in democracy as a philosophical concept. They do not want to share their democracy with others who live in the same country, like Coloureds and blacks. Their refusal to give the vote to the foreign whites of Johannesburg caused the Boer War. Democracy to the Afrikaner means thinking himself as good as the next man. The humblest Afrikaner peasant or miner feels as important as President Botha. The noisy and incomprehensible squabbles within the National Party, as well as the right-wing groups, have a precedent in the angry debates of the Boer War on how to conduct the military and diplomatic struggle. Far from forming a laager in time of peril, the Afrikaners are always ready to quarrel, to inspan their oxen, to trek off in different directions. Bickering lost them the Boer War. It is the characteristic vice of an overly democratic people who fear a domestic tyrant more than a foreign conqueror. In this respect, the Afrikaners resemble the ancient Athenians; it makes them vulnerable to attack from a more authoritarian people, the Spartans or Soviet Russians. The Afrikaners will no more share democracy with the Africans than did the Athenians with the barbarians. (From *barbaros*, foreign, literally stammering, from the unfamiliar sound of foreign tongues.)

Democracy suits the Afrikaners, a small homogeneous nation, with little distinction of class, wealth or lineage. Afrikaner democracy much resembles that of Americans two hundred years ago, a society based on black slavery. But few people now talk of democracy in this, its original meaning of popular sharing in government. Elections, in all the Communist world and most of Africa, are fraudulent. The people, the *demos*, have no share in government. Most of us now, when we talk of democracy, mean not the franchise but freedom. A 'democratic' country is one with the rule of law, freedom of speech and civil rights. Democracy, in this sense of freedom, does not depend on democracy in the sense of franchise. The English enjoyed their essential freedoms for hundreds of years before the introduction of universal suffrage. Tsarist Russia was far more 'democratic', in this sense, than Communist Russia. South Africa is democratic in this sense even for those who have no vote. Black South Africans have more freedom of speech, more justice at law and more rights to enjoy the fruits of their labour than whites in the Soviet empire.

If the French Revolution has passed the Afrikaner by, the same cannot be said for the other two horrors mentioned by Leonard Barnes. They now accept the Industrial Revolution. At the time of the Boer War, ninety per cent of the Afrikaners lived in the country. Now, ninety per cent live in the towns. The Anglo-American Corporation, the giant of manufacture and mines, may still be run by English and Jews, but its profits support a government run by the Afrikaners. The Afrikaners themselves control a part of the mining, the steel industry, oil manufactured from coal, and the railways and airlines. The Afrikaners delight in the most detestable product of the Industrial Revolution, the motor car. The machine indulges the ancient trekgees, or trek fever. The Afrikaner thinks nothing of driving throughout the night from Pretoria down to Durban, or all day and night to the Cape.

No longer can it be said, alas, that Afrikaners ignore 'the conquests of the scientific spirit'. They now accept the grossest perversion of science. It cannot be too often repeated that Dr Verwoerd was both a psychologist and a sociologist. An Afrikaner, Christiaan Barnard, invented what is in some ways the final atrocity of the scientific spirit, the transplantation of hearts from dead to living people. South Africa bears the shame of pioneering another abuse of medical science: a 'surrogate grandma' gave birth to her daughter's triplets.

But probably no other people on earth are still as free as the Afrikaners from most of the strange ideology of the twentieth century. This helps to explain their isolation. Afrikanerdom is under attack from the Soviet Union, the Commonwealth, the United States, the United Nations, the World Council of Churches; from Freudians, abortionists, feminists and all those who desire to reshape human nature. The Afrikaners are now in that state described by Evelyn Waugh in the *Sword of Honour* trilogy, of being at war with the twentieth century.

9
KIMBERLEY

A Corporation Town . . . 'A Diamond is for Ever' . . .
Kimberley in the Days of 'Paddy' Cohen

THE NEAREST THING to pornography in this puritanical country is found in the *Financial Mail*, South Africa's answer to the *Economist*. In a publication supposedly aimed at men in the business community, it is startling to see a full-page colour advertisement showing a girl dressed in what the caption describes as, 'a saucy mix 'n' match camisole, bra, tanga, G-string and suspender belt, in white, black and pearl'. A few pages later, one finds some still more startling advertisements for gold as an ornament, one showing a man and a woman's hand (the wrists encircled with gold) placed on the woman's neck, the other showing a woman's gold-laden hand gripping her crotch, over a caption: 'Gold, I feel great when I put on a few ounces.'

By contrast, the diamond advertisements are demure, showing only the head, shoulders and one hand of a girl, whose ear and finger sparkle with gems. The stone on her finger, according to André, the advertiser, is 'an extraordinary diamond' of 1.02 carat. 'Every diamond is rare,' André continues, 'but a diamond of a carat or more is only one in a million. And, like love, becomes more precious with time. A miracle among miracles. Born from the earth. Reborn on a woman. The extraordinary Diamond Solitaire. When a woman's achievement becomes a woman's good fortune. A diamond is for ever.'

Kimberley, where the diamonds first came from, is now one of the dullest places on earth. It is a corporation town for De Beers, who run a secretive and suspicious bureaucracy. De Beers is part of the Anglo-American Corporation, which owns almost everything in South Africa, starting with diamonds, then gold and other mining, agricultural land, brewing, much of the English press, including *Financial Mail*, and manufacture almost every conceivable product – perhaps even the saucy mix 'n' match camisole, bra, tanga, G-string and suspender belt, in white, black and pearl.

The Anglo-American Corporation had its origin with the finding of diamonds at Du Toit's farm, near Kimberley, in 1869. Prospectors arrived from all over South Africa, England and Europe. The camp site turned into Kimberley; the first diggings became the 'big hole' from which three and a half tons of diamonds were mined by 1914. The profligate or unlucky prospectors fell away, leaving the diamond fields to men like Cecil Rhodes, Barney Barnato, Alfred Beit and eventually the Oppenheimers, who still run De Beers and most of Anglo-American. Monopoly put an end to individual prospectors, the diggers, fossickers or 'kopje wallopers' as they were known in South Africa. Like every visitor, I saw the 'big hole', surrounded by barbed wire and empty beer cans. Nobody digs there now, or anywhere in the Kimberley region. The Corporation gets its stones from Lesotho, Botswana and the immense 'forbidden zone' in the deserts of Namibia.

The discovery and the mining of stones is now unimportant compared with keeping control of the distribution. In Cecil Rhodes's time, the Kimberley miners would readily flog or hang anyone guilty of IDB, 'illicit diamond buying', which put at risk the market value of stones. Today, the role of the lynch mob has been assumed by the Central Selling Organisation (CSO) based in London, which over the years has managed to keep a monopoly on the distribution and sale of gem and industrial stones. The world's second largest producer of diamonds, the Soviet Union, has always remained within the CSO, and its state diamond corporation has close, though secretive, links with De Beers. When one De Beers executive was spotted not long ago in a box at the Bolshoi Ballet, a company spokesman blandly said he was just changing planes in Moscow.

The De Beers promotion team enables the Soviet Union to unload diamonds on to the US market. After the Second World War, when tens of thousands of US soldiers were coming home to marry their sweethearts, De Beers employed a New York advertising agency to promote the sale of diamond engagement rings: the greater the diamond, the greater the love for the girl. In his book, *The Diamond Invention*, Edward Jay Epstein showed how N. W. Ayer, the advertising agency, coined and promoted the slogan, 'A Diamond is Forever'. All went well until, in the mid-sixties, the Soviet Union put on the market many thousands of small, less than half-a-carat diamonds which De Beers were obliged to sell through the CSO. Accordingly N. W. Ayer started a new campaign to promote small diamonds, stressing 'the importance of quality, colour and cut' over size. Women were encouraged to think that a small diamond could be as perfect as a large diamond. De Beers then dreamed up the 'eternity ring', made of hundreds of tiny Soviet diamonds, and sold to a new market of married women. The Soviet Union returned the favour. A Soviet general leads a Cuban and African army against the South Africans in Angola; but on the commercial level, the Soviet Union has told Angola, a major diamond producer, to stay within the De Beers CSO.

If South West Africa falls to a Marxist regime, it does not mean that De Beers would lose control of the diamonds. The threat to De Beers comes not so much from the Soviet Union as certain countries within the Western camp. More worrying still, Australia has found an enormous diamond field. Even this probably does not worry De Beers so much as the fear that diamonds may lose their glamour. Many nations, for instance the French and Spanish, have never much cared for the stones. The Princess of Wales is typical of a generation of women who now prefer other jewels, or pearls. Even here in South Africa, women wear artificial diamonds, quite indistinguishable from the real thing, but costing only a tenth of the price.

A diamond has little value at all except when sold through De Beers. A diamond under a carat is literally unsellable, as are stolen diamonds of any kind. South Africans have special reason to know this. Those who have tried to get their money out of the country by smuggling diamonds have found they fetch only a fraction of what they cost. It seems that diamonds have no intrinsic value, while gold is a fixed and reliable asset. Someone worked out that an ounce of gold would have bought a top quality man's suit in 1776, in 1918, in 1945 and in this decade. The advertisements in the *Financial Mail* reverse the truth. It is gold that, like love, becomes more precious with time. A diamond is not for ever.

After seeing the 'big hole' and plodding round Kimberley in stupendous heat, I pushed open the swing doors of an old-fashioned saloon. The bar was deserted. Only the creak of the ceiling fan disturbed the silence. At last an elderly Coloured barman brought me a bottle of beer, and railed for a time against the government and the Afrikaners in general. An English-speaking South African stopped for one drink, and told me that Kimberley was a dying town. He left, and an Afrikaner took his place. He drank large brandies and told me that he had come out of prison just that morning, and gone to the barber to have two of his teeth pulled. Not to the dentist? No, man, to the barber.

It was all rather a change from the bar described in one of my favourite books, Louis Cohen's *Reminiscences of Kimberley*:

> Standing near, as the story goes, is a royal rogue from Russia, with deep scars received in Siberia, marked upon his cheeks, who regards with an unloving, half-enviable glance, a frowsy-looking Pole in jack boots, who is standing 'fizz', and whispering Yiddish to his guests, while the champagne corks go off like file firing. He has evidently had a good time, for he flashes a huge bundle of notes, and openly exchanges some of them over the bar for a hundred pounds in gold, for which favour he allows the proprietor one per cent . . . Around that bar, too, you could see detectives mingling and drinking with the fish they hoped to catch (except when overnight there had been sensational IDB arrests), broken-down grandiose captains, jewelled gamblers, stinking of scent, liquor-loving lawyers, cocking drunken eyes from under their hats, Irish 'pathriots' of most combative and fiery inclinations, a few flabby actors, unwashed and unabashed, with last night's triumphs plastered on their puckered faces and lingering on their tongues, newspaper reporters, down at heel and hungry for a 'wet', ready and willing to read their tremendous paras on the last IDB case.

Louis Cohen was a relative of those remarkable East End Jews, the Joels and the Barnatos, who made a fortune out of the Kimberley diamonds and, later, the gold of the Witwatersrand. Louis was different because his father had married an Irishwoman, and though he made several financial killings during his thirty years in Kimberley and Johannesburg, he ended up as a scribbler for the scandal sheets, and a jail-bird. 'Paddy' Cohen had come up to Kimberley in 1871, at the age of seventeen, and went into diamond buying with Barney Barnato, who later became a millionaire in the class of Rhodes, Alfred Beit and Sir Ernest Oppenheimer. Barney Barnato had come out from London with nothing but a supply of cigars, which sold at a premium in the diamond fields. With their meagre capital, he and Cohen started to trade in diamonds.

In those early days in the diamond fields, the future magnates were still only maggots, as Cohen later remarked. Most of the pioneers did well. Later, the fame of Kimberley's wealth attracted a new sort of prospector:

> Rabbis, rebels, rogues and *roués* from Russia and the Riviera, transports from Tasmania, convicts from Caledonia, ex-prisoners from Portland, brigands from Bulgaria, and the choicest pickings of the dirtiest street corners in all

Europe, many of whom were very devout, but nearly all decidedly improper. Dalgettys and Jack Sheppards, and Cagliostros, and Artful Dodgers, all came here to escape the grinding poverty which had driven them from their native heaths; or, in many cases, the punishment of their crimes. Unfrocked clergy-men, with the air of saints and the souls of sinners, who had never known the stain of work; broken, stalwart soldiers, with fair moustaches and freckled faces, caring for nothing but billiards and brandy; lawyers who knew Horace well, but Holloway better; and *divorcées*, with a variegated past printed on their features, who had plucked the periwinkle blossom not wisely but too well . . .

Soon 'Paddy' Cohen and Barney Barnato were prospering:

> We had acquired a pony, and in the morning, perhaps from six to eight, I would go out kopje walloping, and many a time make twenty or thirty pounds before breakfast . . . It was no uncommon occurrence for a diamond buyer to make seven or eight hundred pounds on one stone. Indeed I have known of a single piece of cleavage sold five times in a day, and each man that bought and sold it became richer by nearly a hundred pounds or so.

As they prospered, the young diamond merchants developed a taste for good living. 'Well, on this auspicious evening, we strolled into Halibur-ton's bar to make eyes at Mrs Hart (that gorgeous pea-hen over whom Lowenthal and Abrahams shed blood), and moisten our lips with a glass or two of wine.' By dawn the next day, Cohen had won twelve hundred pounds at hazards, from Lynch, the gentleman gambler. Barnato and Cohen spent most of their free time in bars and billiard-rooms:

> I learnt that Barney was a very fair cueist, and sometimes would go halves with him when the stakes were not too high. He invariably won; if he lost he would promise to settle the next evening (he never carried any money for fear anybody would hear it rattle), and when that time came, handicap his opponent for the return match, and come home triumphant and blessed. I found he could box, too, and many a time have seen him have a bout in the back saloon of Grussendorf's canteen in Stockdale Street. To be sure he had nothing to beat, only strong yokels, but he always proved victorious, and then had a drink with them. And he was a splendid domino player – hardly ever beaten. When I came to London in 1882 he took me to Petticoat Lane, and showed me with some pride the eating-place where he had graduated as a domino professor. He beamed on that old coffee-house as Rhodes would have beamed on Magdalen College.

This last was a reference to the way Rhodes had used some of his fortune from Kimberley to take a degree at Oxford and later endow the

scholarships which still bear his name. Cohen was much in awe of
Rhodes:

> I have many times seen him in the Main Street, dressed in white flannels,
> leaning moodily with hands in his pockets against a street wall. He hardly
> ever had a companion, seemingly took no interest in anything but his own
> thoughts, and I do not believe if a flock of the most adorable women passed
> through the street he would go across the road to see them. Rhodes was a
> great and good personality, but he would have been a greater and better had
> he married . . . It is such stupidity to compare, as some parasites have done,
> Barney Barnato with the great Rhodes. One was a mighty patriotic Empire
> builder, the other merely a money getter, who lived only for 'monish', when
> he got it trembled for its safety, and died overbalanced by the fear of losing
> it.

Barney Barnato committed suicide by jumping off the side of a liner
bound for Cape Town. Cohen, who had been with him on the voyage,
was always ambivalent in his attitude to his far more successful cousin.
Yet for all Cohen's disparagement, the reader ends up feeling a great
affection for Barney Barnato. His cheek and Cockney gaiety have a ring
of the music hall and its faded, modern descendant, the 'Carry On'
series of films. There were dozens of stories about his ignorance of the
world of art; of how, when a dealer announced that the Constable had
arrived, Barney said, 'What's the copper here for I wonder?' One London
hostess wanted to show off a valuable French work of art:

> As they were parting the goddess bent in an irresistible and charming manner
> towards him and said invitingly, cordially beaming the while with the sunniest
> and most fragrant diffusing of smiles: 'Good night, Mr Barnato. I am glad
> to have met you. I like you.' Then leaning forward whispered, 'Come and
> see my Watteau.' Barney looked as if someone had pinched him, took off his
> glasses, wiped them, and, glancing keenly at his fair inviter, ejaculated, 'Eh?'
> 'Yes,' repeated the lady with emphasis, 'you must come and see my Watteau.'
> 'Do you mean it?' queried the millionaire, as if striving to discover if the lady
> was in earnest. 'Well of course I do' responded the merry dame showing her
> white teeth. Barney's face gave birth to a broad, enraptured grin, and he
> winked in a peculiar manner to himself as he replied in a subdued tone, 'All
> right. When's the old man out?'

It might be Sid James in 'Carry on Kimberley'.
The kopje wallopers, who went out buying diamonds from the local
Afrikaner farmers, were also described as Boer verneukers, or swindlers.

The kopje wallopers, such as Cohen and Barnato, gave some of the stones to brokers to sell on commission: 'So we gave them a chance, and some of the dear souls took it, for many of them diddled us more than the kopje wallopers did the Dutchmen. You see it was a game of catch-as-catch-can, and the first catch, of course, was the Dutchman.' The Boers, as the Dutch farmers were called already, were swindled over their diamonds, their property, and the goods, like coffee and sugar, they had to buy at inflated prices. Ike Sonnenberg cheated the Dutchmen at 'Nap', and 'Tommy Wilkie', also known as the 'Brighton Baker' introduced the three-card trick, 'to the ecstasy of the elect, and the great wonderment of the unsophisticated Dutchmen who took to the pastime fully assured of its fortune-making elements'. When the Brighton Baker died a few years later, they put this epitaph on his gravestone:

> Here lies a man who pitched the broads,
> Who ofttimes got as drunk as fifty lords.
> From Dutchmen he got many a score,
> Die carte gewinn, und die twee ye verloor.
> ['This card wins, and those two lose.']

Like Barney Barnato, Cohen had rather a soft spot for the Afrikaners, even when he verneuked them:

> Quiet, simple folk they were . . . Not one of the men was uncivil, they were more than kind and honest and sympathetic, especially the Boers, and these last would have remained so to this day had it not been that in times to come, the scum of Germany and Whitechapel – they have crystallised into 'magnates' since then – taught them to be otherwise . . . I could a tale or two unfold, if I liked, but there is a blue pencil suspended over my head, like the sword of Damocles, fear of which stays my hand, to the great relief of certain South African financiers.

Unfortunately for Cohen, he later forgot this sword of Damocles, i.e. the British libel laws. He began writing his reminiscences in 1907, after a bankruptcy. They were published first as a serial in *The Winning Post*, a magazine devoted in equal parts to racing tips, society scandal and City news. One of the men whom Cohen had known as a youth was J. B. Robinson, now Sir Joseph, and one of the richest capitalists in the world. He had started life in the Orange Free State, keeping a country winkle, or shop, and buying wool from the Afrikaners. At Kimberley, he went into land and diamonds; then he moved to Johannesburg, where he bought the whole suburb around his house, calling it Mayfair. When Cohen's reminiscences began to appear in *The Winning Post*, readers were understandably eager for gossip about the early life of one of the most famous men in the City. They were not disappointed.

Early on in the reminiscences, Cohen remarks that 'Robinson had a diamond office in the main street, where, dour and sour, he sat waiting for customers.' After these testing jabs, Cohen unleashed his big punches:

> Sour visaged and unsympathetic, he looked as yellow as a bad apple, and green with spleen like a leek . . . Before the financier came to Kimberley he was an honest Free State trader in the Boer winkle and wool-buying vocation, which two professions combined are sometimes called Boer verneuking. (If you don't believe me, ask Leopold Albu, who swears when he is knighted he will call himself Lord Verneuker – with Robinson's permission.

Cohen dwells at length on Robinson's military aspirations:

> I call to mind when he was Colonel of the Diamond Field Horse, and I a trooper in the same regiment, how fond he was of parading us, and getting salutes, and giving them for all the world as if he had a winkle again, and we all cheap wool to sell. There is no doubt he is a great soldier, as mercenary as Marlborough, as cold as Wellington, as ambitious as Napoleon, as greedy as Blucher, and as patriotic as Keir Hardie. He conquered the world of wool, and now he can't look a sheep in the face.

He remarks on the fact that Robinson had not served in the Boer War: 'You, Sir J. B. R., not only failed to show us your fighting powers, but never put hands in pocket except to buy a halfpenny paper to read something about your precious self.'

Perhaps emboldened by Robinson's lack of response to these early articles in *The Winning Post*, Cohen went on to call him 'a soldier who disdains to fight, a politician with no politics, an orator without speech, a financier *sans* spirit or tact, a music-lover bereft of hearing, a philanthropist lacking charity, a man without friends and a patriot without country'. He then went on to make the specific accusation that Robinson had on one occasion sold a Boer a sack of coffee weighted with pebbles.

Sir Joseph ignored these articles until, in 1911, they came out in book form as *Reminiscences of Kimberley*, whereupon he sued for damages, hiring as counsel Sir Edward Carson, the prosecutor of Oscar Wilde and, later, the Ulster Unionist leader. In an unwise defence, Cohen called various witnesses who claimed to have been at Kimberley at the time, including one Emile Berger who said he was told by Robinson of the trick with the coffee. However, the judge in his summing-up described Cohen as 'steeped to the eyes in malice' against the plaintiff, and the jury awarded Sir Joseph £1,000 damages.

This was not the end of Cohen's troubles. His income of £175 a year was insufficient to meet Robinson's claim for damages and costs. He had to go bankrupt again. Then in 1913, Sir Joseph took the unusual step of bringing a private prosecution for perjury, charging that Cohen had entered into conspiracy with Berger, now an admitted liar. In 1914, at the age of sixty, Cohen was sentenced to three years' penal servitude.

The story has a happy ending. In 1922, Sir Joseph was cheated out of his promised peerage when the Lords discovered how he had just milked £200,000 out of his own South African company, in one of those property swindles at which he was adept. When he died in 1929, *The Times*'s obituary said of Sir Joseph roughly what Cohen had said in his lifetime: 'His despotic egotism tolerated no partner or equal. His many boards of directors were content to be his clerks. Always litigious, he generally had a case going on in the courts. His intense egotism, and a sort of rasping intolerance offered no invitation to friendship or sympathy.'

In 1922, the year Sir Joseph was turned down for the peerage, Cohen was back in South Africa, meeting old friends and publishing his *Reminiscences of Johannesburg and London*. These are as racy and outrageous as his Kimberley book. When Sir Joseph Robinson died, Cohen was back in England, still writing books and articles. He died at the age of ninety-one leaving behind those reminiscences which are worth more than all Sir Joseph Robinson's diamonds and gold.

10

PRETORIA

Property Boom . . . Kruger and the Jews . . . Afrikaner
Nazis . . . the Jews Today . . . and the Irish

I N ONE OF the shopping arcades in Pretoria, there is a young black paper
boy, selling the English-language *Pretoria News* and the Afrikaans *Die
Transvaler*. Each time that a white man or woman approaches, the boy
holds out one of the two papers. He can tell by the shape of the head,
the clothes, or perhaps the expression, whether his customer is an
Afrikaans or English speaker. So much for the whites who say that 'we
all look alike to them'.

A foreigner like myself cannot always see the difference; but everyone
in Pretoria has a prosperous look compared with elsewhere in South
Africa. Whereas, a hundred years ago, the centres of wealth and population were down on the coast, now almost three-quarters of all the
whites live in the Transvaal. The shift began in 1886, with the first finds
of gold on the Witwatersrand, since when Johannesburg and its black
twin city, Soweto, have grown into the present metropolis.

Gold is still mined in parts of the Transvaal, but coal is now more
important than either gold or diamonds. The Transvaal has huge deposits
of iron as well as coal, and therefore the capability of producing steel,
and therefore a major share of the steel-consuming industries such as
automobiles. Port Elizabeth, once the 'Coventry of South Africa', had
already lost much of its automobile production even before the strike at
General Motors which I described in an earlier chapter. The coal of the
eastern Transvaal helps South Africa to defy international boycotts. It
generates much of the electricity. Oil produced from the coal of the
Transvaal helps South Africa to resist the possible threat of a ban on
petroleum.

The southern Transvaal is now the industrial heart of South Africa;
according to Marxist theory, it should be ripe for revolution. An engineer,
called Andrew Kenny, who works in one of the power stations, thinks

that there may be unrest but not of the kind that Marx predicted. In an extraordinary article in the London *Spectator*, Mr Kenny explained how the white working class was turning increasingly to the radical right, to parties such as the AWB which are racist, fascist and socialist. This does not mean that the whites dislike the blacks; but they no longer get a differential in pay, commensurate with their skills and education. They fear that the state-run electricity, steel and coal-oil corporations are using the blacks to depress white wages. Andrew Kenny discussed the possibility of a white, radical protest movement, similar to the strike and civil war of 1922. He also re-drew the political map of South Africa; where there are coal seams, there will be votes for the radical right; where there are swimming pools, there will be votes for the Progressive Federal Party.

The Transvaal suffered less than the Cape during the last four years of black unrest; and in the Transvaal, Pretoria suffered less than Johannesburg. The Cape and Natal have a high proportion of English-speaking whites and therefore of would-be emigrants to Australia, Britain and the United States. The Afrikaners in the Transvaal belong to Africa. The Portuguese, who are now about 40 per cent as numerous as the whites of British origin, are also committed to stay here. 'Pretoria is the place for the come-what-may hard-liners' says one who speaks with authority, John Swanepoel, executive director of the Institute of Estate Agents. House prices have tumbled in the Cape, Natal and the posh northern suburbs of Johannesburg; in Pretoria there is a property boom. The Transvaal has become the redoubt, or laager, of the remaining whites in Africa.

Pretoria used to be thought of as just a dull, administrative centre, and poor relation of the exciting Johannesburg. Now it is richer in business and social graces, without having lost its small town air. There are still some of the nineteenth-century brick country houses, surrounded by gardens and orchards and sometimes fragrant with roses. The Boulevard Hotel is more comfortable, friendlier and serves better food than any establishment I have found in Johannesburg, even at three times the price. The well-to-do in the government and the quasi-governmental bodies, the Army, the SABC, the steel and electricity corporations, all the bureaucrats of this swollen state, live well in Pretoria. According to a statistic I read, the Greater Pretoria area has five per cent of the population of Greater New York but seventy-five per cent of the acreage. This means that most of the whites can live in spacious homes, surrounded by gardens, jacaranda groves, jacuzzis and swimming pools.

In spite of their Calvinism, the Afrikaners have always enjoyed the lekker lewe, the sweet life here on earth, which used to consist of hunting, gossip, tobacco, coffee and Cape brandy. Now, the lekker lewe extends to expensive motor cars, holidays in the Cape or in Greece, golf, adultery and a set of credit cards. Ever since the 'Information scandal' of ten years ago, when Ministers and civil servants were found to be spending secret funds on holidays in the Seychelles and tickets for Wimbledon, there have been many tales of corruption within the National Party. This helps to explain why the humbler class of Afrikaner, the kind who work in the steel works and electricity stations, are moving away in disgust to the right-wing factions. The demagogues of the AWB, and even the primmer Conservative Party, wail at the decadence of the Afrikaners, harking back to the days of the Great Trek and the Boer War and 'Oom Paul' Kruger.

President Kruger's old house is now a museum and the most attractive tourist sight in Pretoria. When you have bought your entrance ticket, postcards and maybe a scroll of the Last Message from exile in Switzerland, you walk through the living rooms and bedrooms, whose furniture is as heavy and dark as the clothes of Kruger's family in the photographs. Out in the garden stand the two railway carriages from which Kruger conducted the war and the policies of his ever shrinking Republic, as he was shunted east to the border with Mozambique, and at last to exile. The most endearing feature of Kruger's house is the stoep, or verandah, looking on to the street. It was here that Kruger, slouched in an easy chair, puffing his pipe, and sometimes hawking into a brass spittoon, conducted affairs of state. Anyone could approach him with a request, a complaint, or merely to have a chat. This was Boer democracy at work.

To the uitlanders of Johannesburg, this ugly old man on his stoep was an ignorant peasant obstructing the march of science, progress and industry. The pro-Boers contrasted the homely and God-fearing Kruger with the cosmopolitan, greedy, lecherous citizens of Johannesburg, which Randolph Churchill described as 'Monte Carlo superimposed on Sodom and Gomorrah'. Certainly Kruger despised the social arts. He believed that dancing was bending the knee to Baal. When invited to take into dinner the beautiful wife of Ralph Williams, the British agent in Pretoria, this surly old man inquired: 'What do I want with this woman?'

Kruger deplored the first discovery of gold, but later determined to get his share of the proceeds. By 1890, the Transvaal government was collecting £300,000 a year in revenue from the mines, a sum that rose greatly after the sinking of deep-level shafts. President Kruger got more money from the leasing of land, from freight charges on Transvaal railways, from public utilities such as water, above all, from sale of concessions.

Kruger disliked the uitlanders in Johannesburg, most of whom were British or Anglo-Saxon and therefore potential servants of the British Empire. He welcomed and gave advancement to other kinds of uitlander. Some were German and Irish, two races hostile to Britain, but most were Hollanders, as the Afrikaners call the Dutch. They took most of the top jobs in government. The Hollanders also constructed the railway line from Pretoria down to the Mozambique coast, a route which Kruger rightly believed was a guarantee of his independence.

The Liberal press represented Kruger as a victim of the Jews. The *Manchester Guardian* argued that Beit and other mining financiers wanted to bring down Kruger in order to make the Transvaal safe for British investment. They had a good case, as Thomas Pakenham proves in his book on the Boer War. But if there were Jews on the side of Johannesburg and the British Empire, so there were Jews on the side of Kruger, and many more who admired him. Kruger's liking for Jews was a cause of fury and scandal up to and during the Boer War, involving him in a feud with one of South Africa's greatest writers, Eugène Marais. This feud helps us to understand the odd love-hatred between the Afrikaners and Jews, which is one of the themes of South African history.

Visitors to the Kruger house invariably give a glance and perhaps a smile at the two stone lions adorning the stoep. They look Chinese rather than African, anxious rather than fierce, indeed more like a pair of chow dogs than the monarchs of the veld. It comes as no surprise to learn that the statues were given to Kruger by Barney Barnato, the Cockney Jewish financier who made a packet out of Kimberley before moving on to the Transvaal. Barney Barnato ran the Johannesburg Waterworks Company, and it was in this capacity that he first visited Kruger. He often went to Pretoria to confer with the bureaucrats over permits required by his engineers, architects and contractors. Unlike the stuck-up Rhodes, Barney enjoyed the circumlocution and small-talk required in doing business in Pretoria. The Boers enjoyed his wit and his fund of stories. Kruger, especially, found Barney a genial companion. 'They would sit for hours on the stoep of the white house,' says Barney's biographer Stanley Jackson, 'drinking cups of coffee, while Barney puffed his cigarettes and Kruger constantly refilled his pipe bowl from his moleskin pouch and blew his huge nose with a bandanna handkerchief. They coughed in unison and periodically interrupted their friendly dialogue with a fairly accurate use of the spittoon between them.' Old Kruger was getting deaf, but when Barnato's jokes had been translated from Yiddish to Afrikaans and yelled into his better ear, he laughed out loud and sometimes called to his wife to hear the story repeated. Unlike most of the uitlanders, Barney did not demand the vote for the citizens of Johannesburg. He did not believe in it. Only once, when Barney suggested a local council, with mayor and alderman and councillors, did Kruger become indignant: 'Have I not given them their railways? Instead of going on their knees in gratitude, they invite me to a ball in honour of Queen Victoria.'

Although he got on well with Kruger, Barney Barnato represented Johannesburg, and himself. Some of the uitlanders who had gone first to Kimberley, and then to Johannesburg, ended up in Pretoria, working for Kruger. The foremost of these was Sammy Marks, a gentle and amiable man who nevertheless became an object of hatred to some Afrikaners. President Kruger sold him several concessions, including those for the manufacture of jam and bricks, but Marks made most of his wealth from liquor. He paid Kruger £1,000 a year for distilling rights, and did so well that after four years he sold the concession for £120,000. Marks also had a share in the still more controversial concession for dynamite, a basic essential of mining. Kruger had sold the concession first to Edward Lippert, a cousin of Beit, who had fallen foul of the uitlanders in Johannesburg, and bore them a grudge. When Rhodes went up to Bulawayo to treat with the King of the Matabeles, Lobengula, Lippert followed him, apparently with a rival offer from Kruger. The British sent Lippert back to Pretoria, where his resentment rankled. He took great delight in selling dynamite to Johannesburg at £5 a case, when less than half that price would still have earned him a handsome profit. 'Oh Lippert, E. Oh Lippert, E., what crimes are committed in thy name,' the uitlanders jested. But anger against him was one of the strongest motives in the Jameson Raid, and indeed the Boer War.

Perhaps Kruger enjoyed the sight of Lippert cheating the uitlanders. He certainly got on better with Jews than with cold and haughty Englishmen like Rhodes, and the hated Milner. The Transvaal Afrikaners, because of their isolation, had not been exposed to the anti-semitic virus which swept through Russia, Central Europe and Germany during the nineteenth century, creating an exodus to Britain and the United States. Calvin, unlike Luther, had not condemned the Jews. Afrikaners like Kruger regarded the Jews as the People of the Book; but of only half the book. In the early days of Johannesburg, Kruger had granted four stands, or plots of land, to each of the different Christian communities for the building of churches and chapels; but to the Jews he allotted only two stands. When the Rabbi protested, Kruger sucked at his pipe, lay back in his chair and delivered his judgment: 'You people believe in only half the Bible, the others believe in the whole of it; when you do the same, I will give you the other two stands.' It is apparently true that Kruger opened the first Johannesburg synagogue, 'in the name of the Father, the Son and the Holy Ghost'. Yet many Jews revered him. In his *Reminiscences of Johannesburg and London*, Louis Cohen writes of Kruger:

> No clot of blood clings to his shabby frockcoat and frayed trousers, no brutalities tarnish the sheen of his quaint top hat, no memories of torture bleached his grizzled locks, no blasphemy pastured on his kindly mouth. No laurelled crown, purple or ermine, it is true, adorned his massive head or ungainly body, and lent a gorgeous dignity to his exalted rank, yet in that sallow-skinned, swollen-faced man of ugly presence, austere aspect, and ambling figure, there dwelt the soul, like glowing iron, of a great patriot and of a herculean hero of many valorous deeds.

This view of Kruger as hero was shared by few of Cohen's contemporaries. Most supported Rhodes in his attempted coup d'état, the Jameson Raid, intended to free Johannesburg from the oppressive role of Pretoria. Three years later the uitlanders took the British side in the Boer War. Nor was Kruger a hero to all the Boers. He held a narrow majority in a series of general elections which, so his enemies said, were rigged. The opposition accused Kruger of taking bribes, nepotism, cheating on his official expenses, and stifling economic growth. Some Afrikaners joined in mining for gold and took the side of the uitlanders in politics. The opposition to Kruger was sometimes anti-semitic. One of his angriest critics, the journalist Eugène Marais, is now remembered because he later became a poet and author of three extraordinary books on animal life: *My Friends the Apes*, *The Soul of the Baboon* and *The Soul of the White Ant*. These books are not well known outside South Africa. Like his contemporary, Olive Schreiner, Marais was not an easy or sympathetic writer. His vision of life was harsh and joyless, perhaps because of his drug addiction. Yet more than any South African writer, Marais expressed an empathy with the natural world of the veld. Perhaps only an Afrikaner, an African for centuries back, would have dared to call a book by the rash, almost absurd title, *The Soul of the White Ant*.

Marais early acquired his fascination with animal life. In the year of his birth, 1871, Pretoria was still just an assemblage of farms, most of which were infested with mambas and puff adders. The child Eugène kept scorpions and a tarantula for pets. His parents had come from the Cape and boasted a higher level of culture than most of the Transvaal Boers, so Eugène acquired a good education. Although he later became a pioneer of the Afrikaans language, and one of its major poets, Marais never wrote it as easily as the English he learned as a child.

Eugène's elder brother Henry had started life as a journalist and was one of the first Pretoria men to join in the gold rush. There were three coaches a day from Pretoria to Johannesburg, and if you caught the 7.15 you could be at the stock exchange before lunch, mixing with people like Barney Barnato and Louis Cohen. The Pretoria newspapers, like those in Johannesburg, were filled with news and rumour about the gold fields. When he was eighteen, Eugène Marais joined the *Pretoria Advertiser*, whose standards of accuracy and fairness fell short of those on the *Eatonswill Gazette*. The young Eugène Marais was soon attacking the superstition and graft of the Kruger government, which refused to exterminate locusts because they came from God; which refused to employ the latest method of bringing rain, by shooting into the atmosphere, in case one of the bullets killed an angel; which authorised President Kruger to take a personal loan at half the prevailing rate of interest. When he was still eighteen, Eugène Marais was barred from the Volksraad, the Transvaal's miniature parliament. The next year he was editor of an opposition newspaper, and made the acquaintance of leading uitlanders, such as Percy Fitzpatrick, later Sir Percy, the author of *Jock of the Bushveld*, who even then was plotting to get the Transvaal into the British Empire. When he was twenty-one Marais became the editor of the first Afrikaans-language newspaper, *Land en Volk*, which needless to say was opposed to President Kruger. One of its first stories suggested that Kruger, in spite of his presidential salary of £7,000, had put in two different expense accounts for a visit to Colesberg, although he had been a guest of the Cape Colony government. President Kruger sued him for criminal libel.

The political tone of *Land en Volk* appealed to some of the uitlanders in Johannesburg. They resolved to take over and pump new money into the paper, while keeping its reputation as an independent voice. A group of rand millionaires, headed by Charles Leonard, invited Marais to dinner in Johannesburg, where they made him this handsome offer: to buy *Land en Volk* for £2,500, retaining Marais as editor at £50 a month. Marais needed the money to marry his sweetheart, Lottie Beyers; he doubtless told himself that the change of ownership would not affect his politics, which were anyway hostile to Kruger; nevertheless, one is taken aback by Marais's eagerness to accept a bribe.

Although Marais later became a distinguished writer, his newspaper *Land en Volk* was not what we call 'quality journalism'. It was an arrant scandal sheet. After the general election in 1893, which Kruger is said to have won by the rigging of votes, his electoral officer, Jan Kock, was given the well-paid job of Secretary of the Executive Council. Gunning in vain for Jan Kock, Marais discovered a good dollop of dirt on his brother Frans, the landdrost, or magistrate for the Christiana district. The story was given to *Land en Volk* by Constable Willem Oberholzer, a mounted policeman working for Frans Kock. Over the last few months, Constable Oberholzer had grown aware that Landdrost Kock was sending him out on long and frequently pointless missions into the bush. One day Kock ordered the mounted policeman to ride to the border to do a count of the native huts, a trip that involved an absence of several days. Constable Oberholzer left next morning but during the afternoon encountered a native, illegally holding a gun. He arrested the man and returned with him to Christiana, arriving at nine that night. Here *Land en Volk* took up the story of Constable Oberholzer's homecoming:

> Reaching his house, he knocked on the door, but no one came to open it. He knocked once more, and again nothing happened. The house was in darkness. When he knocked once again, his wife came to the door. He could see that she was trembling. Constable Oberholzer greeted her impatiently, pushing past her to the children's room. He was hungry, and he was after the bread he had hidden beneath their bed. Under the bed he found Landdrost Kock, dressed only in a pair of trousers and a vest.

Angry scenes followed, during the course of which Constable Oberholzer said he was offered £150 by Kock's brother Jan to forget the matter. However the Constable heard that his wife had been seen several times in a state of déshabillé with Landdrost Kock, and he would not stay silent. He took the story to *Land en Volk*, who printed it all with glee. Landdrost Kock sued Marais for libel. When the case appeared in court in 1894, Marais pleaded 'truth and justification'. The counsel for Landdrost Kock was Charles Leonard, the very same man who had managed the purchase of *Land en Volk* as a weapon against the Kruger government. The judge threw out the libel action, saying that adultery had been committed, or at least intended. Johannesburg crowed over this victory. The *Star*, which then as now championed the mining financiers, reported the case at length, under a memorable headline:

The wife whom Marais had wed from the proceeds of *Land en Volk* died of puerperal fever after the birth of their first child. Even before his marriage, Marais had taken morphine; now he became an addict. Grief and the drug deranged him and lent an hysterical edge to his journalism. The doctor who had attended his wife was an alcoholic. This may have had nothing to do with her death, but in Marais's tortured mind, the loss of his wife was tied up with the liquor licence given by Kruger to Sammy Marks. He learned that Marks had contributed £10,000 to the statue of Kruger that stands to this day in Church Square. He raged in *Land en Volk*:

> Let our children be taught that the statue is not being erected by a grateful people to honour a great leader, but by a Jew who obtained the money for it by selling liquor to our own people, for which he had a monopoly. Let our children know that the price paid for the statue consists of the tears of widows, the lamentations of orphans and the poverty and misery of entire families ... Let it stand as an image of all that the Transvaal child should hate and let our children be taught to pass the statue with abomination in their hearts.

When the Boers were in flight in 1900, and Kruger was in his train in the eastern Transvaal, frantic for money to keep his army supplied, he took loans at enormous interest rates, putting the country in hock. This revived the accusations of 'selling out to the Jews', and started the legend of 'Kruger's millions', allegedly stashed in the veld. Yet after his death in exile, Kruger's enemies in the Transvaal and England found no proof of graft or embezzlement. His family never grew rich. The lekker lewe meant no more to Kruger than cups of coffee, snuff and a full pipe, at ease in his rocking chair on the stoep.

It is well known to the outside world that most of the National Party leaders who came to power in 1948 had sympathised with the Germans during the Second World War and some, like Vorster, had been interned. It is less well known that a group of South Africans, backed by Hitler, nearly succeeded in mounting a coup d'état in 1941. The murder of the Prime Minister, Jan Christian Smuts, was to have been the signal for an uprising led by three thousand well-armed conspirators, banking on the support of most of the Afrikaners. The plot was foiled, thanks largely to the determination and courage of one Afrikaner detective, Jan Taillard. The ringleader, Robey Leibbrandt was captured and put on trial, in the course of which part of the story came to light. Yet until a few years ago, most South Africans were unwilling to learn what happened during the war on the home front, and how near they came to taking Germany's side. The National Party themselves were sensitive on the issue. Although proud of having refused to fight for the British Crown and Empire, they had belatedly come to see the evil nature of Hitler and Naziism. Whatever the faults of men like Vorster, Malan and Verwoerd, they would not have countenanced crimes such as Auschwitz. They therefore tried to forget their one-time admiration for Hitler.

The English-speaking South Africans were just as eager to bury the past. The disloyalty of a large proportion of Afrikaners had shocked them, and proved the fragility of the Union. The reconciliation after the Boer War was proved to have been a sham. The English-speakers, even more than the Afrikaners, are shy of discussing their differences in public. The mutual hostility of the two white races, which used to be known as the 'racial problem', was until recently far more of a threat to South Africa than the discontent of the blacks.

The taboo on discussing what happened during the Second World War appears to have first been broken by SABC which put out a TV drama series on tension between the English-speakers and Afrikaners in some small town in the Orange Free State. From all accounts it was excellent drama and caused no offence to either side. Then, in 1984, Hans Strydom, a journalist on the Johannesburg *Sunday Times*, published a book on the failed coup d'état: *For Volk and Führer: Robey Leibbrandt & Operation Weissdorn*. Although the story is told with imaginary dialogue – 'Hitler raised his hand limply in acknowledgment. "Bring me the file, Schaub" ' – Strydom has based his book on recorded facts, on Leibbrandt's unpublished memoirs, and interviews with some of the leading characters, including Taillard, the detective. This book on Leibbrandt interested but did not shock the South African public. The attempted coup d'état has so far entered the realm of popular knowledge that it was made the central incident of a novel, *The Power of the Sword*, by Wilbur Smith, whose books of adventure, generally with a South African setting, are best-sellers all over the world.

The man who aspired to be South Africa's führer was Sydney Robey Leibbrandt, born in 1913 to a father of German ancestry and a mother whose maiden name was Joyce, a cousin of William Joyce, 'Lord Haw-Haw', the Irish Nazi hanged by the British after the war. Young Robey Leibbrandt was brought up to believe in a mixture of German, Irish and Afrikaner nationalisms, whose common feature was hatred of England. On leaving school, Leibbrandt served six years in the Army, the police and the railway police, but his chief claim to fame was boxing. At nineteen he became the light heavyweight champion of South Africa, knocking out 'Wildcat' Mandy; however he broke his thumb, and could not take part in the 1932 Olympics at Los Angeles. At the Empire Games in London in 1934, he knocked out the British champion during the opening seconds, only to be disqualified for a low blow, a judgment he put down to British prejudice. His hour of fame as a boxer, and also his call to political destiny, arrived with the Olympic Games in 1936, in Berlin.

With experience of more than a hundred wins, nine-tenths of them by a knock-out, Leibbrandt went to Berlin as a favourite. He also went in the hope of meeting 'that legendary figure Adolf Hitler', as he expressed it. In character and physique, he was a model Nazi: blond, blue-eyed, muscular, brave, fierce, loyal, arrogant, humourless and determined. Like Hitler, he was a vegetarian; he slept on wooden boards; he trained himself to withstand pain. The Berlin press and public gave an ecstatic welcome to Leibbrandt, especially when they discovered that he spoke good German. When Leibbrandt knocked out a sparring partner, a German professional boxer, in less than a minute, one of the journalists wrote in awe: 'He is mauling his sparring partners like a sadistic tiger.'

Leibbrandt was thrilled by the splendour and pomp of Nazi Berlin, and the flattery it accorded him. He quarrelled with other Olympic athletes who criticised the Nazis, and even complained that the anti-semitic posters had been removed. The inspiration of Hitler fired Leibbrandt during the crisis after his third successful bout, when he found he had broken his right hand. The Olympic doctors and the South African team insisted that he drop out of the contest, but he himself wanted to fight in the quarter-final against the French champion, Mich-elot. His new German friends offered to serve in his corner. His political minder, Freiherr von Vlietinghof, sent Leibbrandt a copy of *Mein Kampf*, marked at the passage on boxing:

No other sport is its equal in building up aggressiveness, in demanding lightning-like decision, and toughening the body in steely agility. Naturally in the eyes of our intellectuals this is regarded as wild. But it is not the duty of a race-Nationalist State to breed colonies of peaceful aesthetes and physical degenerates.

Inspired by the Führer's precepts, Leibbrandt entered the ring with one hand useless and deadened by pain-killer. He lost on points. The Johannesburg *Star* correspondent, Frank Rostron wrote:

> He fractured his right hand last night and fought a remarkable one-handed contest against the moderately good Frenchman tonight. He was the victim of a doubtful decision. He was unable to bear the pain of using his right which he sent over a dozen times during the contest. However, I again consider that the Springboks should have received a verdict of a close fight. This view was supported by all the British judges.

The Olympic Games were then as now a triumph for the totalitarian spirit. Germany won the greatest tally of medals, outstripping the United States; Italy did better than France; Japan did better than Britain. After the Games were finished, Hitler held a reception for the German team, to which were invited thirty foreign athletes who had shown themselves favourable to the Nazis. They included Robey Leibbrandt. When Hitler asked him how he had come to speak German, Leibbrandt replied: 'I have German blood in my family. We also learn it at school, and I have made a special effort to improve it since I became an admirer of yours. *Mein Kampf* has become my Bible. I know it almost by heart.' Leibbrandt's infatuation with Hitler grew more intense when he was asked to attend the Nuremberg Rally that autumn. After a brief return to South Africa, where he won the heavyweight as well as the light heavyweight title, Leibbrandt went to study athletics in Sweden, Finland, Czechoslovakia and Hungary. In the autumn of 1938 he accepted an invitation to attend the Reichsakademie for Physical Culture in Berlin. He was there on September 4th, 1939, when the South African parliament voted by eighty votes to seventy-six to enter the war against Germany on the side of Britain and France.

This was hardly a vote of confidence in the new Prime Minister, Jan Christian Smuts, who no longer carried his own Afrikaner people. The economic depression of the 1930s had devastated the farming community and driven still more Afrikaners into the towns where they lived in poverty. The radical discontent against the capitalists expressed itself in a mixture of socialism, nationalism and anti-semitism, the same ingredients that had brought Hitler to power. The intellectuals of Stellenbosch and the kaffiehuise in Cape Town worked out the ideology of the Afrikaner; the masses joined in 1938 in the Ossewatrek (the ox-wagon trek), commemorating the Great Trek of a hundred years earlier. The leader of the procession was Johannes van der Walt, the world champion heavyweight wrestler, a big-hearted but stupid man, unfailingly known to the press as the 'gentle giant'.

Unlike Smuts, the mass of the Afrikaners had not been reconciled to the British. This anti-British feeling was what inspired, during the 1930s, the growth in secret or semi-secret societies, dedicated to Afrikaner nationalism. The most respectable of these was the Broederbond which, in spite of its sinister reputation, is comparable to the Freemasons, the Catholic Knights of Columbus, or even the Rotary Club. Whereas the Broederbond was exclusive and was a club, the Ossewabrandwag (the ox-wagon firewatch) was a mass organisation, holding great rallies, sometimes by torchlight, resembling the Nazis or Ku Klux Klan. By the end of the 1930s the OB numbered some four hundred thousand. The OB had a military wing, the Stormjaers, or Stormchasers, closely modelled on Hitler's Stormtroopers.

The hundreds of thousands of Afrikaners who, if not pro-German, were certainly anti-British, represented a threat to Smuts's government. Most of the Afrikaners loyal to Smuts had volunteered for the forces and now were serving up in North Africa or Ethiopia, leaving South Africa to be guarded by the police, many of whom sided with Robey Leibbrandt, their former colleague. There was a large, and pro-Nazi, German community in South West Africa, which had belonged to Germany before 1914. In short, South Africa was one of the few countries that Hitler might have won to his side by means other than military conquest. Its minerals and the control of the shipping routes might have altered the course of the war.

With so much to gain, and such good chance of success, the Nazis bungled their coup d'état in South Africa. Although they had many potential supporters, including the four hundred thousand members of the Ossewabrandwag, the Germans were lacking in agents answerable to Berlin. The National Party politicians like Malan, Verwoerd and Vorster, were ready to go to gaol in opposition to Britain, but they were not potential Quislings. The leader of OB, Hans van Rensburg, had met and admired Hitler, but he too refused to order acts of sabotage; some said he had done a deal with Smuts. The German intelligence service did not even possess a radio contact with South Africa. Therefore the Germans decided to send out Robey Leibbrandt to start a revolt. They trained him in sabotage, in marksmanship and radio. His task as leader of Operation Weissdorn (white thorn) was to raise and arm a group of three thousand rebels and then to assassinate Smuts. This would create a state of chaos in which to seize control of the government.

The Germans had first intended to send Leibbrandt by submarine, but could not spare a ship for the operation, perhaps a sign that they did not take the plan seriously. They therefore decided to send Leibbrandt by yacht with an expert sailor, Christian Nissen, who had been dropping agents in Wales. At Paimpol, in occupied Brittany, Nissen spotted and commandeered a beautiful, twenty-two-metre yacht, the *Kyloe*, which he had seen and admired on the Fastnet Race in 1938. Leibbrandt travelled to Paimpol on April 1st, 1941, to rendezvous with Nissen, his crew and the radio specialist chosen to land with him in South Africa.

Even before the sailing, Leibbrandt had started to show his arrogance and pig-headedness. He did not trust the radio operator. He would not join with the crew in making the yacht ready, but got drunk instead and went to bed with a French girl. During the journey into the South Atlantic, Leibbrandt quarrelled with all the crew. He decided to leave behind the radio operator. He also refused to put ashore at Lamberts Bay, and resolved not to meet the German agent at Cape Town. He refused to hand over to Nissen his $14,000 expenses money, and when Nissen persisted, pulled a gun on him. Three miles from the shore at Mitchell's Bay, some two hundred miles north of Cape Town, Leibbrandt ordered the crew to lower him into a dinghy with his gear. He was swept ashore on a desert, in the Forbidden Zone, so called because of its state-protected diamond wealth. For three days Leibbrandt trudged inland, bearing a suitcase, a kitbag and a radio transmitter, weighing together one hundred and eighty pounds. He accomplished this on a few morsels of sausage, eaten against his vegetarian principles, and sips from a bottle of soda pop. When he reached a village, no one believed his story of why he was there; but they did not report him to the authorities, and eventually he was given a lift to Cape Town.

At Cape Town, Leibbrandt made no attempt to meet the German vertrauensmann (trusty) but looked up a former girlfriend who shared his political views. She passed him on to her brother, who was a Stormjaer. He passed Leibbrandt on to the OB staff in Bloemfontein. Leibbrandt offended everyone with his arrogant behaviour but at last got an interview with the OB Commandant-General, Hans van Rensburg, in a Pretoria suburb. In his memoirs, published in 1956, van Rensburg had this to say about Robey Leibbrandt:

> I found him curt, brimful of self-confidence, impressive and not inclined to accept any view but his own. To me, he hardly seemed able to form a picture of the South African scene at that time; possibly because he had spent all his time in a sort of 'closed shop' with the OB and the SJs. Presumably he thought that the whole of South Africa was peopled by such men which – unfortunately – was very wide of the mark.

At their first interview, van Rensburg offered Leibbrandt the job of training the Stormjaers, but flatly refused to accept his authority or to lead a campaign of sabotage. At their second meeting, van Rensburg's bodyguard kept their guns on Leibbrandt and his lieutenants. Van Rensburg called Leibbrandt 'only a German agent', at which Leibbrandt grabbed the Commandant-General's collar, yelled at him 'Smuts's lackey', then pushed him into the open fire. The bodyguard seized hold of the prize-fighter and hurled him physically out of the house.

By his arrogance and stupidity, Leibbrandt had dished the Nazi cause in South Africa. However he still had the support of some extremists inside the OB and most of the Stormjaers, who numbered eight thousand in the Transvaal alone. Most of their members were in the police, the prison service, the railway police, the municipal fire brigades and the ambulance service. Among the men that Leibbrandt recruited was the illustrious Johannes van der Walt, the world heavyweight champion wrestler, who had led the wagon train in 1938. The conspiracy by a boxer and wrestler was more distinguished by courage than brain-power. They carried out some daring raids to obtain explosives, rifles and ammunition; but their security was weak. Having antagonised the Ossewabrandwag, the only nationwide organisation, their operations were limited to certain parts of the Transvaal. The police were soon on Leibbrandt's trail and would have captured him and his colleagues, but for the fact that most of the individual constables were reluctant to make an arrest. When van der Walt was captured, friendly policemen let him out of his cell in Johannesburg. For six months Leibbrandt was able to wander about the Transvaal; he came near to shooting Smuts, who would not give up his walks in the countryside.

The policeman, Jan Taillard, who captured Leibbrandt on Christmas Eve, 1941, had first to resign his job and pretend to become a Nazi supporter. He won Leibbrandt's confidence, and steered him into an ambush outside Pretoria. Taillard himself was knocked unconscious by those who arrested Leibbrandt. The Nazi brute was ferocious up to the end. As he was taken into Pretoria Central Police Station, Leibbrandt spotted a sergeant who had been on a previous raid. Breaking loose from two policemen, he raised his hand-cuffed arms and felled the sergeant, shouting, 'You bastard, you shot one of my best men!' Then he remembered the wrestler, van der Walt, and shouted defiantly: 'But my Hannes is still free!' But not for long. The police raided van der Walt's hiding place and shot him in the spine. He was crippled and died in agony only a few months later.

During the four-month trial, which ended in March 1943, Leibbrandt began by giving the Nazi salute but then kept silent. Before hearing his sentence, Leibbrandt delivered one of those speeches from the dock which are de rigueur in South Africa; witness Nelson Mandela. After a eulogy of Adolf Hitler, Leibbrandt declared: 'Whatever the sentence will be is of minor importance. The idea of freedom has been planted again in South Africa. You can be assured that nothing is capable of breaking this Afrikaner heart. In that spirit I exclaim "To hell with mercy!" I demand that justice be done. Long live the Afrikaner volk! Long live National Socialist South Africa! God be with my comrades! *Die Vierkleur hoog*! [The four-colour (flag) high!]'

The judge sentenced Leibbrandt to hang but Smuts commuted the sentence to life imprisonment. The old man said that he could not send to the gallows the son of a valiant Boer War comrade. Perhaps he did not want to make Leibbrandt a martyr. When the National Party came to power in 1948, one of its most controversial acts was releasing Leibbrandt. This was soon after the war, when the world was learning with horror the full extent of the Nazi crimes. There were furious demonstrations, especially from Jews and ex-servicemen. But Robey Leibbrandt was no longer an Afrikaner hero. He was just an embarrassment. He lived in obscurity in remote small towns; he failed in business and found no publisher for his memoirs. He died almost forgotten in 1966.

The Wilbur Smith novel, *The Power of the Sword*, is loosely based on the story of Robey Leibbrandt, as was a play by Cas van Rensburg. One of the two leading characters is a light heavyweight boxer who goes to Berlin, becomes an admirer of Hitler and later returns to South Africa as a German agent. Naturally, Mr Smith has used his author's licence to change many details in the career of Leibbrandt. Fair enough. But whereas Mr Strydom's historical book was published only in South

Africa, Mr Smith's fictional work has sold millions of copies around the world. Because *The Power of the Sword* is based on fact and introduces historical personalities like Hitler, Smuts, Verwoerd and Mandela, readers may come to regard it as true. Comparing these books by Mr Strydom and Mr Smith, one sees at work the process by which historical fact is turned into legend. One also begins to understand why Mr Smith's South African stories of love and war and adventure outsell the anguished and sensitive novels about apartheid by writers like André Brink and Nadine Gordimer.

The ending of *The Power of the Sword* suggests that the Nazis had taken over the South African National Party. This was the fear of many in 1949, especially of course the large Jewish community. The Jews who had survived Hitler's 'final solution', were at this time in a state of agitation over the founding of Israel. The international left, which accused the British in Palestine of fascist brutality, regarded the rise of the National Party as one more threat from the neo-Nazis.

Since 1948, the National Party's main white opposition has come from the Jews. The British South Africans sneered at the 'Nats' as dim Afrikaners, sour republicans, prating Calvinists, 'hairies' and 'yaapies' – an expression derived from the word ja or yes – but they had no reason to fear them. The Jews regarded with outrage and horror a government that had released Leibbrandt from prison. Jews such as Helen Suzman and Harry Oppenheimer have always been prominent in the party that now goes under the name of Progressive Federal. A small but influential number of Jews, including Joe Slovo and Ruth First, have always been powerful in the South African Communist Party. Because of South Africa's isolation from Europe, these Jewish Communists did not join in the disenchantment with Stalin and all things Russian that followed the end of the war. They did not hear, or did not want to hear, of the Gulag Archipelago, the purges and treason trials, and the persecution of Jews.

Many, if not most, South African Jews are still opposed to the National Party government; but few, I suspect, would still regard it as anti-semitic. Israel is now one of the few states friendly towards South Africa. Presidents Vorster and Botha have made official visits to Israel. Several thousand Israeli citizens have second homes and businesses in South Africa. Both countries face hostility from their neighbours and from the world at large, at any rate from the left and the United Nations. The white South Africans approve of the tough Israeli reaction to terror attacks from over the border. When South Africa, in 1982, sent in a group of commandos to shoot up the ANC in neighbouring Lesotho, some of the Afrikaner press uttered words of caution. The liberal, English-language papers, most of which are part of the Oppenheimer group, were more favourable to this ruthless action.

The international left, which supported the Jews in 1948, has now swung round to the cause of the Arabs. The Palestine Liberation Organisation (PLO) and Colonel Gaddafi support the ANC, which is anti-semitic, or as it prefers to say 'anti-Zionist'. Some of the ANC blamed Zionists for the death of Samora Machel, the Mozambique President, in a plane crash. As I recounted earlier, I heard a white clergyman telling an anti-semitic 'joke' in Cape Town's Anglican Cathedral.

The new right-wing populist movement, the AWB, employs as its emblem a kind of swastika with broken arms, and its leader, Terre Blanche, is a demagogue in the fascist mould. Yet South African Jews have not taken alarm as they would have done thirty or even twenty years ago. Perhaps anti-semitism was never very important to Afrikaner Nationalists. They admired Hitler not because he hated the Jews but because he hated the English. That was what was meant by the 'racial' question. Now the word 'racism' is misused in order to bracket together two quite different phenomena: the old anti-semitism of Europeans, and how the whites regard the blacks in Africa. Anti-semitism has its roots in suspicion and envy of Jewish knowledge and enterprise. The blacks in Africa pose a threat to the whites, not by their knowledge and enterprise, but by their lack of these and other requirements of modern civilisation. The 'racist' may dislike both Barney Barnato and Idi Amin, but not for the same reasons. In so far as the word 'racist' has any meaning at all, it now has a dozen meanings. The word, when applied to South Africa, causes only confusion.

It is odd to reflect that Robey Leibbrandt, racial theorist and Afrikaner Nationalist, was half German and half Irish by blood. Three virulent strains of bigotry coursed through his system. The relationship between German, Irish and Afrikaner nationalisms is worth a brief inspection.

Most Catholic Irish Nationalists came out for the Afrikaners during the Boer War. The British Consul in Mozambique attempted to check the flow of the Irishmen who arrived at Lourenço Marques to take the train to the Transvaal to fight for Kruger. Oddly enough, this Consul was Roger Casement, who later was hanged for his part in the Easter Rising. The volunteers for the war against Britain were formed into an Irish Brigade under John MacBride (who also, in 1916, was executed by Britain). While MacBride fought, his future wife Maud Gonne was stomping the platforms of Europe and the United States to denounce the war, the British Empire, and Jewish financiers. Many Catholic Irish but still more Protestant Irish fought in the British Army. The mound at the end of the Belfast football ground is known to this day as Spionkop, after the fatal hill near Ladysmith.

At the outbreak of the First World War, a few of the Irish and rather more of the Afrikaners saw England's difficulty as their opportunity, to use an old Irish expression. A few Boer War officers mounted a coup d'état which was soon put down by the greatest of Boer generals, Louis Botha. The Germans tried to bring off in Ireland the same kind of revolt that Leibbrandt later failed to achieve in the Second World War. Sir Roger Casement, knighted for his humanitarian work in the Congo and in Brazil, had left the British Foreign Service and dedicated his life to the Fenian cause. He opposed Britain's entry into the war and offered his services to the Kaiser. He addressed British prisoners of war and tried to recruit the Irish among them to join a Republican army. He had no success, for until the end of the war, most Catholic Irish were loyal to King and country. In 1916, the Germans sent Casement by U-boat to Ireland, to join in the insurrection planned for Easter Monday. It is hard to imagine two conspirators resembling each other less than Casement and Leibbrandt, the first intellectual, sensitive, shy and homosexual, the other a bullying, muscular oaf. But whereas Leibbrandt stayed at freedom for half a year, Casement was apprehended as soon as he put ashore. The Post Office conspirators got no support in Dublin or anywhere else in Ireland. Whereas in South Africa, during the Second World War, there was wide popular sympathy for a man like Leibbrandt, Ireland in 1916 did not want a rebellion. The Fenians and the IRA had little support until the British hanged MacBride, Casement and other conspirators, turning them into martyrs. The Fenians then mounted a highly successful terror against the British and the Protestants. The Republic of Ireland was born from bombs, shooting, the burning of homes and mutilation of cattle.

Between the two world wars, the Irish Republicans and the Afrikaners turned to the fascists for inspiration. The Irish Prime Minister Eamon De Valera modelled his country's constitution on Mussolini's Corporate

State. Many Catholic Irishmen fought on the side of Franco in Spain. The malevolent harridan Maud Gonne became an admirer of both Stalin and Hitler, perceiving correctly that both hated England. Her son, Sean MacBride, the Chief of Staff to the IRA, made several visits to Nazi Berlin to ask Hitler for weapons. From June 1940, while Britain battled alone against Hitler's Germany and Mussolini's Italy, the Irish Free State maintained a demure neutrality. In May 1945, when news reached Dublin of Hitler's death, De Valera called at the German Legation to offer condolences.

After the Second World War, the Irish Republicans lost their admiration for Hitler. Instead they supported the Jewish search for a homeland, especially applauding such anti-British terrorist groups as the Stern Gang and Irgun Zvai Leumi. Just as the Fenians of the nineteenth century looked for arms and support to the United States, the modern IRA looks to the Soviet Union. The arms come from Czechoslovakia; the ideology comes from Marx. The new techniques of terror are learned from experts such as the PLO and Colonel Gaddafi's Libya.

Although Southern Ireland has now cut its last ties with Britain, assuming the title of a republic, intellectual fashions come from London. Modish opinions like easy divorce, abortion and gay liberation have now been followed by anti-apartheid hysteria. The ancient Sean MacBride, former IRA Chief-of-Staff and client of Hitler, re-emerged as United Nations man in charge of the liberation of South West Africa. For his services to the African freedom fighters, MacBride received the Lenin Peace Prize. His mother would have been proud of him.

By the 1980s, the Irish Republic had grown obsessed by South Africa. Shop girls in Dublin went on strike rather than sell South African oranges. The sponsors of a sea-angling contest off County Wexford solemnly banned South African fishermen. Nelson Mandela was made a freeman of Dublin.

11

JOHANNESBURG

Old Johannesburg . . . Apartheid crumbles . . . Gold . . .
Black Affluence . . . Murder . . . Introducing H. C.
Bosman. . . in Marico . . . Bosman's Johannesburg

ON MY FIRST day back in Johannesburg after an absence of almost
four years, I went with a friend to a bar off Commissioner Street,
close to the spot where the miners camped in 1886. Among the customers
was a stout, bad-tempered Californian, who told us he was a businessman, selling napalm to the South African Air Force. 'I deal with General
Earp,' he announced, naming the Air Force commander, 'and I'm telling
you that man is a lineal descendant of Wyatt Earp, the sheriff . . .' At
about this point, he started to get annoyed with his mild-mannered, South
African business partner. The Californian took umbrage at something his
colleague had said on the recent death in a plane crash of the Mozambique President, Samora Machel. The Californian started to raise his
voice, and yelled at the other: 'You pusillanimous piece of pinko pig
shit!' Then he took an enormous swig at his whisky, lost his balance,
and executed a perfect back somersault off his bar-stool, fetching up in
the angle between the wall and the floor, still holding his whisky and
still yelling abuse at the man who did not share his robust views on
Communism.

A few blocks west on Commissioner Street, I went down the steps to
the Jameson's Bar, under the management of two Yorkshire girls. One
of the black drinkers, an immigrant from Zimbabwe, started to tell me
about the drug trade. Most of the dealers, he said, were Indians, but
most of the pedlars were white or black, and the most notorious place
was Bok Street, off Twist Street, in the Hillbrow district, half a mile
north of here. He told me that one of the Hillbrow hotels, where I had
stayed ten years ago, was now a brothel for girls of all colours, working

174

around the clock. On the other side of me there were two middle-aged white women, one Afrikaner and one Rhodesian, who had been trying to get off with two Afrikaner young men. The atmosphere turned all of a sudden nasty. One of the young men said to the Rhodie woman: 'Look, lady, I just don't want to go to bed with you.' The other woman gripped my arm and made some tearful remarks in Afrikaans on the lines of how sad it was when all you wanted to be was friendly, and other people took offence. 'I will bet you anything that they are married,' the young Afrikaner said to me when the women had left – to try their luck at the small Portuguese hotel down the road. This was where I was staying.

Close to Jameson's and my hotel is the best resort of Johannesburg, the upstairs bar of the Guildhall Tavern, on Market and Harrison Street. The balcony looks on to the City Hall and Market Square, whose stalls covered with veld flowers offer a splash of vivid colour among the prevailing sandstone and cement. This was the site of the outdoor stock exchange, 'between the chains', where Barney Barnato and 'Paddy' Cohen won and lost fortunes. Around the walls of the Guildhall bar are prints of the old Johannesburg, and even a portrait of Cecil Rhodes.

The Guildhall is also a haunt of the press which once reported from all over Africa. I have met here people I knew in the Congo in 1964. One of the regulars is Christopher Munnion, witness of many a coup d'état, massacre, famine and folly. I remember him from Uganda, in the days when Idi Amin was calling himself the King of Scotland and keeping his wives in the fridge. Chris was clapped in Makindi prison, hearing the screams of people battered to death with sledge-hammers. Not long ago, Chris was told by his office to get a visa to go back to Uganda. 'I went to the Uganda High Commission in Nairobi,' he was recounting, 'and told the lady there that the last time I had been in Uganda, I was imprisoned. I told her I was a prohibited immigrant. I told her I was a resident of apartheid, racist South Africa. She opened my passport, banged in a visa stamp, smiled and said "Enjoy your trip".'

The 'wind of change' blew south through Africa, bringing anarchy, war, famine, corruption and hopelessness to Nigeria, Congo, Sudan, Ethiopia, Uganda, Angola and Mozambique. A few countries like Kenya, Tanzania and Zambia retain the trappings at least of civilian rule, and even the vote. But all of them fear and distrust outside observers, such as the press. Even Zimbabwe, the latest hope of the liberal 'friends of Africa' will not accept foreign journalists based in South Africa. They know Zimbabwe too well. The journalists who have seen what has happened, north of the Limpopo River, tend not to share the faith of the rest of the world in a black-ruled South Africa, under the rule of Nelson Mandela, Chief Buthelezi, or any other aspirant politician.

The death of Samora Machel was not an occasion for grief at the Guildhall. His freedom fighters had come to power by sowing land-mines over the country, causing much loss of life and limb to the Portuguese conscript Army. The Soviets, who had supplied Machel with the land-mines, set him upon the disastrous course of collectivisation of agriculture. This brought famine, as it had done in the Soviet Union during the 1930s. As Stalin had blamed all opposition on 'Trotskyists' and 'German agents', so Samora Machel blamed South African agents. Machel was a spendthrift, even by African standards. He wasted much of his country's few foreign reserves on a sumptuous Washington Embassy. After a visit to Sandhurst, he bought himself a collection of British dress uniforms.

The outside world was quick to blame the death of Samora Machel on South Africa. Even today, there are some who believe that the pilot was lured to his death by a false beacon. At the Guildhall, attention was focused upon the fact that one of the few undamaged relics of the disaster was a half empty bottle of Scotch; this probably came from the cockpit, which was the least damaged part of the plane. One of the regulars at the Guildhall, Ray Kennedy, had been to the scene of the crash near Komatipoort, on the Mozambique border. The little town lives off the railway, built by Kruger's Republic a hundred years ago. The train spends most of its time now moving to and fro over the border. On the South African side, it is filled with the meat and vegetables needed in starving Mozambique, then shunted into the Mozambique border town, where it stops in front of the state cement works. Here the train is loaded up with cement, and also with video sets and electronic equipment, bought on the black market down at Maputo, the former Lourenço Marques. These and the cement are then shunted into South Africa. The outside world had never heard of Komatipoort, but it has its place in history. It was there, in 1900, that Winston Churchill finished his great escape from Pretoria Central Prison to Mozambique. He was hidden under a pile of goods in a railway freight van. Later the same year, President Kruger bade farewell to his country at Komatipoort.

The huge, hideous city of Johannesburg rose from the highveld here, where we are looking from the balcony of the Guildhall. It is one of the only cities in the world to have sprung from nothing. There was no village, no grove of trees, no river, not even a well. It was a gold mine, pure and simple. The City Hall began as a kind of diggers' parliament, rebellious against Pretoria. It was typical of Johannesburg that when the city fathers planned to hold centenary celebrations in 1986, they would not invite President P. W. Botha. This old part of Johannesburg grew from the mines and is still devoted to business with high-rise banks, insurance companies, department stores and hotels. It is dead on Sunday; so is everywhere in South Africa. Late at night and on Saturday after-noons, the streets are deserted and menacing. Going on foot, you keep one eye open for robbers, the other for public places like bars, where you can dart for shelter, as rabbits like to remain in reach of a burrow.

Old Johannesburg extends beyond the commercial centre to take in everywhere there are flats or rows of houses, rather than individual villas. These are the poorer districts like Mayfair, founded by the abhorred Sir Joseph Robinson; Brixton and Turffontein, where the Afrikaners used to clash with the Lebanese and the Portuguese; the pleasant-sounding but not very pleasant La Rochelle and Rosettenville, where the Madeirans live; and Orange Grove for the less prosperous Germans and Italians. Coming from the airport, you pass by Kensington, built by the Norwich Union Insurance Company, on the condition it never included a bar.

Just north of the old city centre are Hillbrow, Joubert Park and Berea, with bed-sitters and flats for the young and the old. Hillbrow is even more tatty than I remember: I watched three white girls, soliciting car-drivers, their legs stretched out in the road and their skirts hoiked up to show thighs and more. We went to the bar of a big hotel where a blonde transvestite was dancing with one of the 'troopies', South African Army soldiers. When I stayed once in Hillbrow, my tenth-floor hotel bedroom looked straight down into the Fort, the old gaol. By day I could watch the prisoners marching at the double; at night, I could watch the armed sentry patrolling the parapet.

The richer whites of Johannesburg live in the green, northern suburbs which stretch for miles over the veld to where they will one day join with the green southern suburbs of Pretoria. There is so much space that every house has a garden and maybe a swimming pool, a garage for two or three cars, and quarters for the servants. Most houses have a security fence and often a guard dog and some kind of 'neighbourhood watch'. Nevertheless, the atmosphere is uneasy. Many North Johannesburg people fear their servants. They remember the stories from Kenya in Mau Mau times, of aged butlers and faithful nannies who cut the throats of the household. And Archbishop Tutu still further alarmed the whites when he said in an interview with the *Washington Post* (quoted in the *Daily Telegraph*, January 11th, 1986): 'Virtually all school buses in South

Africa carry only white children. They are the softest of soft targets . . .
Most white households still have their morning coffee brought to them
by black servants. Suppose the ANC, or whoever is behind all this, were
able to contact even just a quarter of those servants and say: "Look, here
is something that we want you to slip into their early morning coffee." '

The security of the population hangs on their motor cars. If they
have petrol and a sufficient warning, they can escape attack – as the
Voortrekkers could do in their cumbersome wagons. But if the petrol
runs out? Or when the blacks all have cars, as many already do?

Life in the northern suburbs of Johannesburg is otherwise indistinguishable from that of north Sydney, or Dallas or Los Angeles, where
there are barbecues, swimming pools, the latest in cars and interior
decoration, and much obsession with sunshine, health and plastic sur-
gery. Hell is the country 'where it is always afternoon'. I would rather
live in the centre of London, Paris, Vienna, Rome or New York than
even the greenest suburb. Those who make their money out of the city
should live in the city. So it should be in Johannesburg. Although I am
grateful to friends with whom I have stayed in various northern suburbs,
I feel more at ease in that garish, cosmopolitan but in some way attractive
dump.

Whereas in the northern suburbs, the only blacks one meets are servants,
some of the old part of the city is now partly multi-racial. The blacks
have always gone into town to shop because of the poor facilities in
Soweto. The cheap food and clothing stores for the blacks were once to
be found near the railway station. Now the blacks are as plentiful as the
whites in the shops along Market and President Street. The main depot
for buses and taxis going to Soweto is just behind the Carlton Hotel, the
grandest establishment in Johannesburg. The rich or merely pretentious
blacks drink in one of the Carlton bars. But blacks are found in every
kind of place of entertainment. More often than not, they outnumber
the whites.

The blacks look to Johannesburg for escape from some of the many
restraints of Soweto. Their family and their neighbours cannot spy on
them in the anonymity of the white metropolis. The men can conduct
affairs or squander the housekeeping money without their wives knowing.
The protection racketeers of Soweto have no control on the white-owned
premises of Johannesburg. The political militants of the ANC, the
'comrades', cannot ask nosey questions.

In central Johannesburg there is an easy relationship between the races, such as you cannot find in the northern suburbs or in the townships. Back in the 1960s, when the apartheid laws were strict, I went to multi-racial parties in Hillbrow and in the northern suburbs where most of the whites were anti-apartheid activists (or BOSS informers) and any blacks were sure to be ANC. Everyone struck political attitudes. It was like a charade or one of those deeply sensitive TV plays on apartheid: the Theatre of Embarrassment. So it is when a visiting English bishop, or liberal politician on the make, is taken to see a 'typical' township family. No black who disagreed with the ANC would dare to express an opinion in public for fear of a beating or even the necklace. The white who visits a township shebeen will meet with courtesy but he cannot talk in private or confidence. Johannesburg, on the other hand, is neutral territory. Anyone can talk there without fear of the 'comrades' or the Security Police.

Whereas twenty or even ten years ago, the whites in South Africa had little idea what the blacks were thinking, now you can hear as much as you want about how they live, what they earn, how they were educated, how they want to bring up their children, their views on sex or religion, and how they esteem Mandela, Tutu, Biko, Buthelezi and P. W. Botha. You are not likely to meet the sort of people you see on the foreign TV: the ANC spokesman, trade union leaders and radical clergymen. One thing you quickly learn is the great diversity of the blacks in Johannesburg. They are quite as cosmopolitan as the whites; quite as much immigrants. I once met a man who was born in Sophiatown, the black suburb flattened during the early days of apartheid, but it is rare to meet a middle-aged black who is actually from the Johannesburg area. One hundred years ago, blacks were as few as whites in this part of the Transvaal. Few go back more than a couple of generations. Most are Sothos or Tswanas from other parts of the Transvaal or the Orange Free State. There are Zulus from Natal and Xhosas from the eastern Cape. There are many blacks from foreign, independent states such as Swaziland, Botswana, Lesotho, Zimbabwe and Mozambique. I have talked to blacks from all those countries within a week. The blacks as much as the whites have come here only to make money. Its white public relations people call Johannesburg the 'Golden City', or even 'the City with the Heart of Gold'. The blacks call it 'gold' in their languages. Just as the whites in Johannesburg think of themselves as English, Afrikaans, Portuguese, Germans, Italians, Irish or Scots, the blacks who have come here keep their separate identities. As far as they can, they stick with their own people. 'It is not easy to live with the Xhosa people,' a North Sotho told me.

The ANC and its foreign supporters claim that the blacks have risen above their tribal differences in common dislike of apartheid. A radical black politician, the kind of person you see on TV, will tell you he has no tribe nor even a mother tongue. He will not even admit where he comes from. Visiting whites are told, and believe, that all the Soweto people now speak a common language. There is indeed a patois based on the primitive lingua franca used in the gold mines. Much of Soweto's turbulent youth are now detribalised in the sense of losing respect for their parents, their elders and their traditions. But this does not give them a nationhood; still less a common ideal. Skin colour confers no real unity.

The whites of Johannesburg stick with their own kind: English with English, Afrikaner with Afrikaner, Portuguese with Portuguese. There is still less mingling over the colour line outside work. You see a mixing of races at office parties; also in theatre, show business, above all music. Young people, black and white, seem to enjoy the same kind of Afro-American music, played, so I am told, with a special South African tone. There are many bars offering country and western, modern and Dixieland jazz. In these sorts of places, the races mix cheerfully. There is some sexual encounter over the colour line, though mostly, I think, between white women and black men.

An African in the Jameson Bar asked me if race relations were better in London than here in Johannesburg. The answer is in some ways no. The battles one sees on the TV screens between stone-throwing blacks and helmeted white policemen are not reflected in everyday life. The blacks I have met in Johannesburg shops, offices, newspapers, churches, hotels and bars have been invariably courteous. Even those whites who resent the end of the colour bar would not betray this in public. They are correct but reserved. When the apartheid restrictions first started to crumble, five or ten years ago, many people of both races were eager to find what the others were thinking. Soon the novelty wore off. Few of the whites in Johannesburg speak an African language, as some do in Natal, the east Cape or the northern Transvaal. Most people prefer to relax with their own kind.

Racial tension is found where the non-whites move physically into districts designated as white under the Group Areas Act. A survey, by two researchers from the Rand Afrikaans University, showed that twenty-five per cent of the population of Hillbrow, Berea and Joubert

Park were what they called 'black', and less than half the resident population of Mayfair was white. Of the 20,000 non-whites living in Hillbrow, Berea and Joubert Park, 9,000 are Coloured, 6,000 are Indian and 5,000 African. The report said there were 5,600 Indians living in Mayfair, and 1,000 Coloureds and Africans. Indians have bought much property in the expensive north Johannesburg suburbs of Sandton and Houghton, generally using Europeans as front men. This predominance of the Indians and Coloureds over the Africans reflects their relative wealth, more than their need for property. According to the same report, published in late 1986, there is a shortage among Africans of 500,000 housing units; 52,000 among the Coloureds, and 44,000 among the Indians. In areas allocated for whites, there is a surplus of 37,000 units. This reflects demographic trends. Over the last five years there has been a net emigration of whites. The non-white population grows at four per cent a year.

The Asians and Coloureds are moving back into the same central Johannesburg districts from which they were barred by the apartheid laws. The blacks are making their first incursion. A newspaper editor told me that fourteen out of his seventeen black reporters now were living in 'white' Johannesburg. A wealthy black businessman is a near neighbour of Helen Suzman in Houghton. Some of these blacks want to get away from the threat of the 'comrades'; some want to make a point against the apartheid system; some merely want to enjoy Johannesburg's glamour.

The rich do not have to worry that a few blacks in Houghton will affect the property value. The influx is more disturbing for poor whites facing a threat to their safety and standard of living. The whites of Mayfair took to the streets last year in protest. The voters of Hillbrow turned out their Progressive Party MP and elected instead a National Party man, an Afrikaner. We face the same problem in Brent, Birmingham, Bradford and Bristol. The whites in Brixton, south London, are no more 'racist' than those in Brixton, Johannesburg. The same goes for the whites of New York and Miami, who have erected a de facto segregation by suburbs quite as strict as the Group Areas Act.

Some ten years ago, the Progressive Reform Party (as it was then called) was holding a local election rally, attended by Helen Suzman and Harry Oppenheimer, the chairman of Anglo-American. Before the meeting began in the City Hall, a series of lantern slides was shown depicting

Johannesburg – skyscrapers, black women, white babies and slag-heaps
– to the accompaniment of an adman's voice: 'We call it the Golden
City. The majority of its people call it Igomi, gold . . . Each of us has
an opportunity worth more than its weight in gold.' This was followed
by a campaign song:

> Let's have a new deal for the golden city,
> Putting a smile on the city's face,
> A new deal for the golden city,
> Let's make the city a better place.

After a speech by Mr Oppenheimer, whose millions of dollars of wealth
come largely from gold, the meeting ended with exhortations to make
the vote 'the beginning of a new gold rush; to vote PRP and stake your
claim for a golden future.'

One day in the same year, 1977, I happened to witness the closing
down of the last pit in the last Johannesburg gold mine. This was the
Crown Mine, one of the oldest and most profitable, the one that was
always shown to distinguished visitors such as the British royal family.
The top of the pit had already been sealed and boarded over, and all
that remained to be done was cutting away some of the metal, a duty
performed with a blow-lamp by Les Donald, a Scotsman who had
worked at the Crown for thirty-two years. He took me to the engine
room to show off his pride and joy, the giant hoists that raised the ore
from the ground and carried the miners to and from work, noble
machines from Metro-Vickers, installed before the First World War.
'They used to take two hundred and fifty skips a shift with never a
breakdown,' Donald told me. 'They're as good now as they were when
they were first installed. If you do hear a bit of a rattle, it's only the
clutch and they can easily be replaced . . . It's rather pathetic, closing a
mine. The Crown had its fair share of accidents but nothing really bad.
It was always a lucky mine.'

Ten years after the closure of Crown Mine, its site has become an
amusement park, done up to resemble a mining camp, with noisy saloons
and barmaids dressed from the 'Naughty Nineties'. The promoters have
tried in vain to evoke the atmosphere of the city described by the great
'Paddy' Cohen: 'Johannesburg men smoked like Sheffield and drank
like Glasgow, and the odour of the barmaids, whose pretty faces were
each worth a pocketful of guineas, perfumed the glittering canteens of
a city where the sun is made of flaming gold and the moon is made of

silver.' Lust for gold and a sense of high adventure brought tens of thousands of men and a few wild women to the Witwatersrand, as it had brought them to California, Australia, the Yukon and Alaska. Waltzing Matilda and Dangerous Dan McGrew had stepped into modern folklore. The romance of gold still lingered after the mines themselves had fallen under the ownership of the great corporations, like Harry Oppenheimer's Anglo-American. The potency of the legend made a best-seller of Wilbur Smith's *Gold Mine*, a tale of skulduggery with a gigantic pit disaster. In spite of its South African setting, *Gold* was also a highly successful film with Roger Moore as the hard-living, hard-punching mine engineer.

Now the campaign against all things South African has turned its attention to gold mining and, in particular, accidents. This was shown in 1986 after the accident at a Transvaal mine in which 177 workers, most of them black, were killed. The Granada company's *World in Action* team prepared a report showing convincingly that the owners, Gencor, had used polyurethane foam although it was known to be dangerous. However Granada were also trying to make political points. They suggested that Gencor's mining was part of a 'drive to win the maximum output of gold which pays for members of the Army, the police and the vast bureaucracy needed to maintain apartheid'. A relative of a dead black miner was heard to complain that she had not received Gencor's condolences, though she did expect compensation money. The fact that the black corpses were given only a cursory post-mortem showed that 'even in death the apartheid system wants to exact the final indignity.' A black trade union leader spoke at length, and we saw black miners interrupting the funeral service held by a white Christian minister. The commentary described South African mining as 'an industry that kills six hundred a year, one for every ton of gold.' (When you think that gold costs $400 an ounce, these lives are not cheap.) It is odd, to say the least, to hear the Afrikaners accused by the British of lust for gold. The Boers did their utmost to halt the invasion of Anglo-Saxon and Jewish uitlanders; and during the subsequent Boer War, Afrikaners died in thousands against the armies of British financial imperialism.

Before Granada and the press condemn the South African gold mining industry, they might try to discover how gold is exploited elsewhere in Africa and the world. This is not always easy, as I discovered when writing a book on an international mining company. South Africa is one of the few countries where you can freely examine mining conditions. It is hard these days to get a visa to visit Ghana, the former Gold Coast, and still one of the major producers of gold in Africa.

The Granada television company and the press have not so far given us much information about the conditions of work in the world's second greatest gold-mining country, the Soviet Union, whose tonnage could equal South Africa's by the end of the century. A recent Channel 4 television programme 'The Nuclear Gulag' gave us a distant glimpse of one or two of the 2,000 labour camps in the Soviet Union today. The amateur cameramen risked their lives to take this film; in contrast to Johannesburg, where you could film from your hotel window into the Fort prison.

It can no longer be said that South Africa's gold industry runs on cheap black labour. For some years now, the mines have enforced a system of equal pay for equal work. The last obstacle to the advance of the blacks, the law which refused them a blasting certificate, has now been abolished. In the last two decades, black miners' wages have risen four times as fast as the cost of living. The present gap between average earnings of whites and blacks is due to a difference of skills. The great majority of the blacks have received only three years' formal education. Here again, it has to be pointed out that blacks who were educated in South Africa have much higher skills than those who grew up in foreign states like Lesotho, Swaziland, Mozambique and Malawi.

The prosperity of the miners has brought dissension, as well, to the black community, increasing the gap between the employed and the unemployed, as well as between rival tribes and political groups. The present leadership of the black National Union of Mine Workers (NUM) is using industrial power to achieve political ends, as Arthur Scargill did with his miners' strike in Britain a few years ago. Like Scargill, the South African NUM was unable to win sufficient support for a strike in 1986. Thousands of miners stayed at work, in spite of threats which proved real when thirty-five non-strikers were murdered. Most Zulu miners support their own Inkatha unions against the NUM and others which follow the banned ANC. There are frequent clashes, with dozens killed, between miners at pits in the Orange Free State. The government, through its censorship, tries to play down these fights, which appear to have tribal origins. They are said to involve Xhosa miners, loyal to ANC, and migrants from Lesotho. We should not look down on the blacks for what we call tribal differences. During the British miners' strike, the fiercest battles occurred between the strikers of Yorkshire and those who remained at work in adjoining Nottinghamshire. Although the Notts and

Yorkshire men are indistinguishable to the rest of the world in their accent, rough appearance, tattoo marks, and fondness for lager and football hooliganism, these two tribes nourish a mutual hatred that goes back to the days when Nottinghamshire was in Mercia, and Yorkshire was part of Northumbria.

The new-found prosperity of the blacks is not restricted to miners. The change in the standard of living of blacks over the last twenty-five years is far and away the most important development in South Africa. Yet it has gone almost unnoticed. When I first came to Johannesburg, I was shocked and depressed by the woebegone look of the blacks, their poor physique and cowed behaviour. Now it is rare to see a black who is not smartly or even nattily dressed. The black executive in a three-piece suit and bakelite briefcase no longer attracts attention. Whereas once the black man driving a car was either a white man's chauffeur, or a comic tyro, with all his family packed in an old jalopy, now he sits casually at the wheel of his BMW or Mercedes. One of the elderly regulars at the balcony of the Guildhall Tavern watches for hours the cars proceeding down Market Street, noting with horrified relish how many are driven by 'them'.

With the breakdown of the apartheid laws, it is simple to find out what the blacks earn. You merely ask them. Those who have no 'matric' and are working in unskilled or semi-skilled work, like drivers, earn about £50 a week, which is worth much more here because of the low cost of living and income tax. Here are some of the notes I took after talking to Norman Raborife, aged thirty-one, employed as a maintenance man for Lipton's, a subsidiary of the Unilever company. The Soweto riots of 1976 had prevented him from taking matric, so he had gone to work in a gold mine before moving to Lipton. His pay of R800 a month (roughly £60 a week) was sufficient: 'I can live on that.' He said that foreign-owned companies such as the British Lipton's paid better than local South African firms, and offered better promotion. The manager of his department was Irish, and highly respected, but there were good opportunities for blacks. He had with him the Lipton's house magazine and showed me the photograph of a senior black executive.

In the kind of pub I like, most of the Africans come from the medium economic range. The wealthy or upwardly mobile blacks go to the smart hotels, night-clubs and country resorts. The existence of a class of blacks who own sports cars, dress in the Paris fashion, and holiday in Europe or the United States, was shown by the publication of *Tribute*, a hundred-and-seventy-page, bi-monthly, glossy magazine, aimed at the black conspicuous consumer. 'Join the club, buy a racehorse,' invites the two-page advertisement for the Thoroughbred Breeders Association of South Africa. And just to prove that the club is not for whites only, the ad shows Richard Maponya leading his horse, With Haste, and its white jockey, into the winners' enclosure. Although Mr Maponya is one of the few who is rich enough to enjoy all the things one sees in *Tribute*, many thousands are near enough to aspire to this kind of affluence.

Like glossy magazines all over the world, *Tribute* is geared to the needs of its advertisers for luxuries such as foreign air travel, resort hotels, fashion, cosmetics, jewellery, wine and liqueurs. Some of the eight-page advertising features show off a combination of products, by posing a group of models of both races and sexes, wearing expensive clothes, sipping brandy, while lounging against an expensive car in front of a country hotel. The first issue of *Tribute*, on holidays in the Cape, showed a number of elegant blacks on board the Blue Train, a change indeed since the days when South African Railways were a stronghold of the apartheid system.

Many advertisements show cheaper products like hair spray, cosmetics and ordinary shoes. The advertisers of drink and cigarettes do not have to include any warnings on health, or drunken driving. One full-page picture shows a convivial group of whites and blacks, surrounding a table of half-drunk bottles and glasses of wine, under the heading: 'Long lunches and great friends and old jokes and Benson and Hedges.'

Some *Tribute* advertisements smack of Madison Avenue. For example, the blurb for a 3-Series BMW: 'I drive this car because it is the quintessential Sports Sedan. I drive it because in a world filled with automotive trivia, it alone represents an enduring philosophy.' 'Play it again Swissair,' says an advertisement over a picture of Louis Armstrong, the trumpeter. However, it is no longer unusual for rich Sowetans to fly on holidays. In one of the many stories on cocktail parties, receptions and fêtes which adorn the pages of *Tribute*, one finds, for example, photographs of a wedding attended by five hundred guests: 'Soweto pharmacist Kwanele and his bride, who is soon to qualify as a pharmacist, will be spending their honeymoon in Greece in May.'

Although the advertisements in *Tribute* show a belief in consumer capitalism, the editorial line is mildly radical. There is an article on the writer Bloke Modisane who died in exile, and other South African blacks who have gone abroad like Nat Nakasa, Letta Mbula and her husband Caiphus Semanya. There is an article on the Mandela children, and an interview with Hugh Masekela, son of a Scottish mining engineer: 'If all

Christians were like Father Huddleston or Archbishop Tutu I would be in church every Sunday. But the irony of it is that a guy like Botha or Hitler can claim to be as Christian as them . . .'

Besides the radical chic, *Tribute* carries articles on a black Johannesburg copy writer, and Peter Motale 'who turned a pirate taxi service into a transport empire'. There is a feature on how to fight the feeling of disappointment that sometimes follows success. In its emphasis on achievement, *Tribute* is very American, and its editor Maud Motanyane has worked as a journalist in the United States. She told me she modelled *Tribute* on *Ebony* magazine. It is aimed at men as much as women. I asked Miss Motanyane if she agreed with the view I had heard from white South Africans, that black South African men were very clothes-conscious, more so than black women, and much more than white men. 'There may be some truth in that,' she said, then added tartly: 'They have better taste.' Unlike such glossy magazines as *Playboy* and *Cosmopolitan*, *Tribute* does not go in for sexual titillation, with articles on how to improve your love life. 'We believe in the family,' said Miss Motanyane.

Of course most of the blacks who live round Johannesburg are not part of the glossy world of *Tribute* magazine. There are many poor; or in modern parlance 'people living below the poverty line'. (Who draws this line?) The relative wealth or poverty of the black South Africans is best measured, not by some abstract principle, but by comparison with other African countries. Perhaps the most prosperous of these is Kenya, and also one of the few with a partially free press. An article in the Nairobi *Sunday Nation* last year had the courage to make the comparison between Soweto, Johannesburg, and Soweto, Nairobi, a shanty town which was named after the famous South African suburb. According to the *Sunday Nation*: 'Nairobi Sowetans have little to compare themselves with. Their South African counterparts are better, by far, educated, have a minimum wage of 1,200 shillings (about £46) and have access to better medical facilities . . . but the lives of the Nairobi Sowetans are a nightmare.' Kenya is one of the most prosperous countries in independent Africa. Much of the continent, especially those countries that suffer Marxist regimes, like Ethiopia, Mozambique and Angola, have been reduced to mass starvation. Black South Africans now have a higher standard of living than most Europeans under the Soviet system.

The advance of the black South African owes nothing to agitation either at home or abroad. Quite the contrary. The ANC has deliberately tried to wreck the educational system which is the cause of black advance. They have used the threat of the necklace to try and stop youngsters taking the vital matric exam. Supporters of ANC abroad have asked for sanctions to bring South African industry to a standstill. The ANC, quite logically in its own terms, fears the increasing prosperity of the blacks.

A Gallup poll conducted in Britain in 1986, showed that 'across all political persuasions and age groups, respondents believed apartheid to be more restrictive and oppressive than it really was and that lives of whites were in danger every day.' (Johannesburg *Star*, October 30th, 1986.) These were the judgments given on certain statements about South Africa:

> 'Blacks are not allowed into white hotels and restaurants': true 75 per cent, false 9 per cent.
> 'Blacks and whites are not allowed to marry each other': true 46 per cent, false 14 per cent.
> 'Whites are served first in a shop even if they come in after blacks': true 46 per cent, false 14 per cent.

These answers reflect the view of South Africa given by Britain's press and TV, especially TV, which by its nature can show what life is like. The BBC could, for instance, interview black and white customers in a pub; it prefers to show Archbishop Tutu and Winnie Mandela. Television must be partly to blame for another answer given to Gallup. To the proposition, 'the lives of the whites are in danger every day', the response came: true 58 per cent, false 31 per cent. From what they read in the papers, or see on TV, the British believe that white South Africans spend every day in danger of death, presumably at the hands of the black South Africans.

In fact the swart gevaar, black danger, is less of a bogey now than it was a hundred years ago, when Johannesburg was appalled by a series of sexual attacks on white women. As Louis Cohen recalls in *Reminiscences of Johannesburg and London*:

> The Black Peril curse also wore an ugly aspect, and day after day one heard of the growing audacity of the natives. A lady, Mrs Norman, taking her courage in both hands, had pluckily, in self defence, shot a villainous nigger dead, but that meritorious act did not check the evil. Sir Drummond Dunbar formed a ladies revolver club so as to teach the young how to shoot, but at

the first muster of members, the obliging Sir Drummond got his little finger accidentally shot off.

'Oh,' whispered a female of fashion to a Boer official's wife, retailing the incident and trying to put on side, 'have you heard the news? Sir Drummond has had his digit shot off.'

'Alamagtig!' sighed the Boeress, to whom the strange word signified something more serious than a finger, 'I do feel so sorry for his poor wife.'

There is much more concern about swart gevaar in New York, Paris and London than there is in Johannesburg. Sexual assaults by black men against white women are rare. Although there are muggings by blacks against whites, the motive is robbery rather than racial hatred. In the overwhelming majority of the crimes committed by blacks, the victims are also blacks. Here is a typical Monday news item:

Nine people were murdered in Soweto at the weekend, among them former student leader Miss Masabatha Loate (29) who was hacked to death in Orlando West, police in Soweto said. The body of a 22-year-old man was found in the backyard of an Orlando West home at 6 a.m. on Saturday. He had a bullet wound in the back of his head. On Saturday, at about 8.30 a.m. the body of a 19-year-old youth was picked up by police in front of house 1093 in Zone 1, Meadowland. He had a bullet wound in the back.

The terrorists of the ANC direct their attacks almost exclusively against their fellow-blacks. The introduction of a state of emergency and internment of many young 'comrades' broke the terrorist organisation; but there were isolated acts of violence. In November 1986, young thugs smashed up sessions of the matric exam and threatened reprisals against those students who took part; they gave one boy a necklace. The censorship is intended to play down terrorist acts; but even the stark reports are poignant, such as the one of January 3rd, 1987: 'A black man and a black woman were set alight by about 20 black radicals at Endemi in Soweto on New Year's Eve, while a black woman was set alight by about 90 radicals in White City, the Bureau of Information reports.'

Not all the necklace attacks have been committed by ANC, or even by blacks. Four coloureds in Port Elizabeth were sentenced to death for killing another and then setting fire to the body to make it look like a necklace. In the Transvaal, Anton Werner Stoop was sentenced to death for the murder of David Mthutang, whom he attacked and then set alight. The victim was a mineworker at Dube Deep, and a member of

Zion Christian Church. After the sentence was read in court, the widow said she would like to have Stoop 'sent straight to the gallows'.

It takes an unusual crime to arouse the jaded interest of Johannesburg; and such was the murder of Roger Smith in 1982. Nothing since has so far challenged the title given it by the press at the time of 'South Africa's Crime of the Decade'. A local crime reporter, Paul Langa, published an instant book on the case, giving a résumé of the evidence in court, enabling one to sort out what happened. Those sentenced to death were only three of at least eleven people who knew of the plan to murder Smith and had at least some intention of taking part in the crime. Only four were Africans and the rest were British citizens, some resident in the United Kingdom. The case provided a startling glimpse of social life and race relations in modern Johannesburg.

Roger and Maureen Smith, who each had a child or two by a previous marriage, came out from England to South Africa in the mid 1970s. He was a quantity surveyor, perhaps something more. She was the daughter of Harry Mullocks, known also as Arthur Mullocks, who ran a firm of insurance assessors in East Ham, London. At the time of the trial, Mr Mullocks denied the allegations made in court that he and associates were involved in illegality.

The murdered man, Roger Smith, was by almost all accounts a rough sort of person, given to drink and bad language, who may or may not have made a pass at his teenage stepdaughter, Karen Wood. He refused to give a divorce to Maureen Smith, because, so it was said in court, he was blackmailing her with the alleged illegal activities of her family and friends. She therefore decided to have him murdered and first called in the assistance of certain British people. These plans came to nothing so, in June 1982, Maureen Smith did what prosperous women in northern Johannesburg normally do when they have a problem: she went for advice to her African maid, a shrewd and not very scrupulous woman called Asnath Dekobe. 'I worked for the first two weeks,' said Mrs Dekobe in court, 'and in the third week the madam said that the life she was leading was not a good one. I asked her why. She said the cause of the "whole thing" was in bed.' This was the first and last mention of sexual motivation in murdering Smith.

A few days later, Mrs Dekobe continued, Mrs Smith rang her up to say that her husband was planning to kill her, and she wanted to kill him first. Then: 'On a Wednesday, Mrs Smith said I must leave my work and come and have a chat with her. "Assie," she said. "Madam," I said. "I want you to go and get me people who can kill him [Mr Smith]," she said. I said I had no experience of tsotsis [young black criminals]. She said I must go and try.' Then Mrs Smith put her hand in her bra and took out R400 (a rand was then worth slightly less than a US dollar) and said to her maid: 'Go and look at these people and tell them this is only a deposit.' Now Assie Dekobe was too smart to get involved in hiring murderers, so she took the money and more that Mrs Smith was to give her, and kept it for herself. She did, however, give R200 to the chauffeur Jack Ramogale and told him Mrs Smith was wanting to find a killer. Thus began the downfall of much the most likable and most pitiable of the people, black and white, involved in the murder of Roger Smith.

It is rather unusual, even for wealthy South Africans, to employ a chauffeur, but Roger and Maureen Smith lived in Kelvin, one of the newest suburbs out on the high veld, where no buses have started to run to Johannesburg. Kelvin is almost side by side with the Alexandria township, a smaller and, then, more peaceful place than Soweto, so African labour is very handy. The Smiths thought they would save money by running only one car and hiring Jack Ramogale as chauffeur at R220 a month, with free lodging and board, and permission to watch the family television set. The Smiths, whatever their other faults, were friendly and generous to their servants. And Jack Ramogale, one of three people sentenced to hang, was the only person involved who expressed any liking for the deceased, or any remorse for the murder. He said at the trial, 'I like Mr Smith very much.'

'Why kill him then?' asked Mr Justice van Dyk.

'It is because of the job. If it was not because of the job, I would not have been involved in this thing.' (Jack, a Sotho, spoke little English, but Justice van Dyk spoke Sotho, having been raised, like Jack, in the northern Transvaal.)

Later, the court was to hear what Jack Ramogale meant by saying the murder of Smith was 'because of the job'. Like many young Africans, he had come to the big city hoping to find a well-paid job to support his family, including an elderly mother, as well as to raise a family of his own. He was extremely dutiful, almost passive to those in authority over him, particularly towards Mrs Smith and the maid Assie Dekobe, a middle-aged woman. Also, of course, he craved the enormous sum of R5,000 which Mrs Smith had promised him if he managed to hire a killer.

It was characteristic of Jack Ramogale that he went to find an assassin at the local Zion Christian Church. The 'ZCCs' as they are sometimes called, have millions of followers in South Africa for what is a blend of

Pentecostal Christianity and traditional beliefs. It is a puritanical Church. Women have to abstain from using scent or make-up or wearing trousers. The men like Jack Ramogale may not smoke or drink. Throughout the suburbs of Johannesburg on a Sunday afternoon, one sees the Africans, devout and well-dressed, taking part in such outdoor services.

'I took Mr Smith's motor car,' Jack Ramogale told the police, 'and went to 19th Avenue, Alexandria, where my church is and searched for Sam Sekwela. Sam and I know each other.' Samuel Sekwela took up the story. 'I was at church on that Sunday (July 18th). Jack told me there is a white lady who is trying to kill her husband, in which then I said to him let us proceed to 17th Avenue where Vukani lives.' This was one of the nicknames of David Mnguni, the man who actually did the murder. The three of them, Jack, Sam and Mnguni, went to the Smith home at Kelvin where Mrs Smith asked (according to Sam's testimony), who was going to do the work. Jack pointed to Mnguni. Then, according to Jack, Mnguni raised the question of payment. 'Before Mrs Smith replied, Vukani [Mnguni] asked for R12,000. Mrs Smith said she only had 10,000 . . . they then agreed on this amount.'

It was a generous fee by South African standards. A black South African taxi-driver with whom I was talking about the case asked how much Mnguni was offered to do the killing. When I said R10,000, the driver practically crashed his taxi with astonishment. I asked him how much it would cost to get a man murdered in Soweto (the township he lived in), to which he replied R100, or even as little as R50. According to Jack Ramogale, he, Mrs Smith, the maid Asnath and Mnguni, agreed that the money be paid out on the Saturday after the murder, at the Pan-African Shopping Centre. 'Thereafter we went to church,' Jack told the court.

On the night arranged for the murder, July 20th, 1982, Jack drove Roger Smith from his office back to his home, where Mnguni was waiting. 'After I brought back Mr Smith,' Jack told the police, 'I parked the car and together with Mr Smith, went into his house, where Mr Smith, his daughter Karen Wood [actually stepdaughter] and I watched television.' Also in the house that evening were Karen's boyfriend and Mrs Smith's aunt, who was on a visit from England.

'I later left the lounge,' Jack Ramogale continued, 'and went to the kitchen where I found Mrs Smith and Asnath. Mrs Smith then asked me if the people – meaning Sam and his friend – were outside and I answered affirmatively. I then went to my room.' Between eight and nine that evening Mrs Smith told Jack what was to be his part in the plot: to get Mr Smith outside by turning off the mains switch for the current supply which was in the garden. There Mnguni would be waiting. At this point Jack suffered torments of fear and conscience:

> I then went back to the kitchen where I told Mrs Smith I was scared and did not know what to do. Mrs Smith then said to me that I must remember the R5,000 that was promised to me. Asnath also told me I must go and switch off the mains switch and that Mrs Smith had promised me R5,000 . . . I then turned off the mains switch. I was scared and ran to my room where I crept under the blankets. I heard someone scream outside and then I heard Mr Smith calling me to come and help. I then felt sorry for Mr Smith and thought that I should die with him.

Jack did run outside, but the deed was already done. The hired killer, Mnguni, later told the police: 'The woman's husband came out and went to the mains switch. I followed him. When he lifted the door, I stabbed him in the back. We fought there. There were stones . . . The man tried to run away. I chased him and prevented him from getting away. I stabbed him twice in the front. I then went out through the gate and left.'

So many people knew of the plot that it was easy to find the culprits. The police chose to prefer charges against only three of those involved: Maureen Smith, Jack Ramogale and of course David Mnguni, the man who had actually wielded the knife. The defending counsel for Mrs Smith, the impressive Lionel Weinstock, based his argument on the unhappiness of her marriage, and on the influence of those around her who, so he implied, had egged her on to the crime. The argument that Smith had provoked his own murder because of his bad behaviour, did not impress Mr Justice van Dyk.

The largely black audience which, by the end of the trial was packing the courthouse, showed little sympathy for Maureen Smith and indeed made loud and hostile comments. She did not take the witness stand but she caused a sensation by fainting and later having an epileptic fit. The public gallery gave its support to Jack Ramogale. He was so clearly well-intentioned.

'On Sundays I go to church. Also on Saturdays – but that is just for choir practice. I do not smoke and I do not drink. I am born of a Christian family and they taught me to obey them.' He repeated in court what he had told the police about the night of the murder: 'The manner in which he [Mr Smith] screamed made me run outside to see if I could help him. The screams he made were heartbreaking to me. I would have tried to fight with Vukani [Mnguni] because my heart was sore.'

At this point, Mr Justice van Dyk interjected: 'It would have been easier if you had told your employer about the plans – and less dangerous.'

To which Jack answered: 'I was instructed not to tell him and I was afraid to tell him that Mrs Smith wanted to kill him. I once thought of telling him but I was frightened. I was afraid that he would approach Mrs Smith and ask her [if it was true]. And if he did that she was going to deny it and I would be in trouble.'

Jack's advocate, Andrew Booysens, called as a witness Gordon Isaacs, a full-time lecturer in social work at the University of Cape Town, studying for his doctorate on the subject of 'crisis psychotherapy and minority groups'. The South African government had sent him abroad ten years before to study 'crisis intervention'. The court was told by Mr Isaacs that Jack's childhood history 'revealed no apparent chronic or acute problems except excessive poverty and cultural deprivation and an injury to the leg which his mother describes as a process of witchcraft – in that a thorn which was embedded in his foot created a septic sore with the result that healing was long in duration'. Previous employers said that Jack was reliable, trustworthy and a hard worker. However: 'When authority is presented to him in the form of (1) mother/father figures, (2) authoritarianism and command figures, (3) kindness, he has little sociological resource to self-protection.' Since he believed that death is in the hands of the Deity and that killing is punishable by the wrath of the ancestors, Jack was persuaded to take part in the crime, 'to please and fulfil the role of obedience towards authority with a lucrative reward at the end, i.e. monetary gain'.

In his evidence on behalf of Jack Ramogale, the sociologist Mr Isaacs raised what he called the 'black/white authority' issue. The same point was raised, albeit in an obscure fashion, in an exchange between the judge and Riaan Strydom, the advocate for the actual killer David Mnguni:

STRYDOM: It has been conceded that Mnguni came from a low socio-economic background and that he lived for the moment . . . The influence exerted on Mnguni by the offer of R10,000 was most important. He was a materialistic person. He was a person who was easily influenced by friends, as we heard when he left the woman he loved because his friends said she was weak.
MR JUSTICE VAN DYK: In our land, whether you accept it or not, a white has a certain influence over a black. We could decide that, as an adult who

worked for himself, Mnguni might have grabbed the chance of a quick R10,000.

It seemed for a moment as though the judge was about to accept the sociological argument that being black and poor somehow excuses crime; even that 'we are all guilty.' Then older wisdom reasserted itself and Mr Justice van Dyk concluded: 'All of South Africa knows that it is wrong to kill a man, except in very specific circumstances. Even the Bible says it – for those who still read it. No other sentence than the ultimate one would suit their dark and evil crimes. All three accused are therefore sentenced to death.'

David Mnguni was hanged, but the sentences on Maureen Smith and Jack Ramogale were later commuted to life imprisonment.

While most well-read people have at least heard of Olive Schreiner, Laurens van der Post, Nadine Gordimer and Roy Campbell, not one in a hundred knows even the name of the man whom Campbell called 'the only literary genius that South Africa has produced'. This was a reference to Herman Charles Bosman, whose catastrophic and violent life ended in 1951, when he was forty-six, and still at the height of his comic and sinister genius. Although Bosman is now well known to the South African public thanks to the dramatisations and readings given by actors, as well as the publication of some of his work in paperbacks, he is still disliked by the English-speaking literati, so that you cannot find a copy of Bosman at some of the best bookshops in Cape Town or Johannesburg. For although he wrote in English, and he was steeped in English, French and American literature, Bosman took his inspiration almost exclusively from his fellow Afrikaners, out in the Transvaal countryside or in Johannesburg, the garish but vital metropolis, sprung from the high veld. As far as he had any politics, Bosman shared the prejudices of those Afrikaners who came to power in 1948, and have ruled South Africa ever since.

In Bosman's life-time, the South African 'racial problem' was taken to mean the hatred against the English-speaking ascendancy felt by the Afrikaners, the Boers who had lost a bitter war, and lived in poverty on their farms, or were driven to look for work in alien cities like Johannesburg. Bosman wrote as well about the relationship of the Afrikaners and the blacks, what we would today call the 'racial problem'; but it was not in his nature to look at the blacks or anyone else as a 'problem', still less as an object of pity, guilty conscience or indignation. The characters in his stories, especially the Afrikaners of the Marico, the poor western Transvaal, appear with a clarity and a truthfulness that can make one gasp. These are the opening words of a story written in 1930, in which the narrator 'Oom' (Uncle) Schalk Lourens describes a raiding party against some Africans in the 1890s:

> Kaffirs? [said 'Oom' Schalk Lourens] Yes, I know them. And they're all the same. I fear the Almighty, and I respect His works, but I could never understand why He made the kaffir and the rinderpest. The Hottentot is a little better. The Hottentot will only steal the biltong hanging out on the line to dry. He won't steal the line as well. That is where the kaffir is different.
>
> Still, sometimes you come across a good kaffir, who is faithful and upright and a true Christian and doesn't let the wild-dogs catch the sheep. I always think that it isn't right to kill that kind of kaffir.

Those two paragraphs, when I read them first, gave me a double shock. In modern South Africa, more than in Britain or the United States, there is now a prudery about race relations comparable to the prudery over sexual matters in the Victorian age. Yet Schalk Lourens's reflections were true of the way that a simple Afrikaner thought of the blacks in the 1930s, and may well be true of his thinking today. But in modern South Africa, few people of any race are honest enough to say what they think of the others. The whites are especially guilty of humbug. Many prominent black and Coloured authors defend Bosman's use of derogatory words like kaffir, as being appropriate to his characters.

The second shock I received when I read those two opening paragraphs of *Makapan's Caves* was linguistic. It was the first English prose I had read that was clearly and unmistakably South African, quite apart from the use of such words as 'biltong', 'kaffir' and 'rinderpest', although these and others more obscure are common in Bosman's tales of the Marico. His writing is South African in its syntax, construction and almost its voice. You hear the words spoken with a South African accent. For, as somebody once observed, Bosman wrote Afrikaans in English. The undertones of Afrikaans both flavoured and enriched his English, just as the Irish adds charm and elegance to the writing of Yeats, O'Casey or Kavanagh. But just as the best Irish writers have shunned whimsy or blarney, so Bosman never indulged in Afrikaner folksiness. 'Oom' Schalk Lourens and the other Marico Boers are shown without sentimentality. Bosman is harsh and sardonic. For instance, in *Makapan's Caves*, Schalk Lourens's father gives this parting advice to the men going to battle:

'Don't forget to read your Bible, my sons,' he called out as we rode away. 'Pray the Lord to help you, and when you shoot always aim for the stomach.' These remarks were typical of my father's deeply religious nature, and he also knew that it was easier to hit a man in the stomach than in the head: and it is just as good, because no man can live long after his intestines have been shot away.

After the massacre of the Africans in Makapan's Caves, 'Oom' Schalk accidentally shoots dead a 'good kaffir' who had attached himself to the white man's party.

Even Bosman's funniest stories are touched by sadness, often with horror as well. Some are literally gallows humour, for Bosman himself spent four months in a condemned cell. One apparently trifling story describes a young woman during a church service trying to catch the eye of her boy friend, the schoolteacher. We think she is merely lovesick until, after church, she sadly reflects that she will now have to swallow sheep-dip for an abortion. This was another subject on which Bosman wrote with expert knowledge.

Bosman's writing was pitiless and amoral. He viewed the racial and other prejudices of the Afrikaners with neither approval nor condemnation; simply with laughter. When a third-rate troupe of actors arrive with *Uncle Tom's Cabin*, the director gets a black eye and decides to make some changes:

> He made Uncle Tom into a much less kind-hearted negro. And he also made him steal chickens . . .
>
> After a few more misunderstandings with the public, André Maritz so far adapted the play to South African conditions as to make Uncle Tom threaten to hit Topsy with a brandy bottle . . .
>
> True, there were still one or two little things, Elder van Zyl declared, that did not perhaps altogether accord with what was best in our outlook. For instance, it was not right that we should be made to feel so sentimental about the slave girl as played by Hannekie Roodt . . . They said that when Hannekie Roodt walked off the stage for the last time, sold down the river, and carrying the bundle of her poor possessions tied up in a red-spotted rag, a few of her mistresses's knives and forks could have been made to drop out of the bundle.

The narrator of Bosman's early stories, 'Oom' Schalk Lourens, grew up in the nineteenth century and fought in what we British call the Boer War. His children had died in a concentration camp, so that 'taken all in all, we who had trekked into the part of the Marico that lay nearest the Bechuanaland [Botswana] border were very bitter against the British.'

The Marico people feel uncouth compared with the English, who carry handkerchieves, wear socks and bathe each morning. In spite of their sneering, they are impressed by the Englishman, Webber, who studies agricultural science: 'When his cattle had the heart-water, or his sheep had the blue-tongue, or there were cut-worms or stalk-borers in his mealies, Webber would look it all up in his books. I suppose that when the kaffirs stole his sheep he would look that up, too.'

At the outbreak of the 'Second Boer War' the burghers, or citizen soldiers of the Marico, go to join a commando outside Mafeking. 'We had to go and shoot there a man called Baden Powell ... We made a fine show with our horses and wide hats, and our bandoliers, and with the sun shining on the barrels of our Mausers.' Their officer, the veld-kornet, gets them to Mafeking, after frequently stopping to ask the way from Africans, and there they are routed. 'And the stars shone down on the road that was full of guns and frightened horses and desperate men. The veld throbbed with the hoof-beats of baffled commandos.' As a burger of the Republic, 'Oom' Schalk knew what his duty was – 'and that was to get as far away as I could from the place, where, in the sunset, I had last seen English artillery'. These Boer War stories are told with such exquisite delicacy that even we the readers are never quite sure whether Schalk Lourens is conscious of his own timidity as well as the cowardice of his fellows. These stories also reflect the bitterness of the Afrikaners against those, like Paul Kruger, who led them into defeat and captivity. At the end of *Mafeking Road*, Schalk Lourens recalls: 'Our veld-kornet was the first to be taken prisoner. And I often felt that he must feel very lonely on St Helena. Because there were no kaffirs from whom he could ask the way out of the barbed-wire camp.'

The Bosman stories are partly responsible for the many South African jokes about Van der Merwe, the archetypal Boer hick, who is ignorant, stupid, lazy, sly and dishonest. 'Oom' Schalk Lourens always complains of the hardship of farming: 'There is the ploughing, for instance. I used to get aches in my back and shoulders from sitting on a stone all day long on the edge of the lands, watching the kaffirs and the oxen and the plough going up and down, making furrows. Hans Koetzee, who was a Boer War prisoner at St Helena, told me how he got sick at sea from watching the ship going up and down, up and down, all the time.'

The Marico Boers are not very good with machinery. When a car breaks down, it is inspanned to a team of long-horn oxen. The post office keeper, Jurie Becker, is proud of his rain gauge which shows there has been no rain for three years:

'Look, you can see for yourself. Nil.' Jurie Becker also tried to explain the rain instrument to the kaffirs on his farm. But he gave it up. 'A kaffir with a blanket on hasn't got the brain to understand a white man's inventions,' Jurie Becker said about it, afterwards. 'When I showed my kaffirs what this rain gauge was all about, they just stood in a long row and laughed.'

Although the Marico Boers accuse the blacks of stealing cattle and sheep, they themselves rustle across the border: 'I mean, the Bechuanas as far as Malopolole know how broad-minded Oom Koos Gerber is to this day about what brand-marks there are on the cattle that he brings back to the Transvaal. That is why the Bechuanas have given him the name of Ra-Sakeng. It means "He-Who-Walks-Too-Near-The-Cattle-Kraal".' Although the Marico Boers are Calvinists who despise African superstition, they sneak off to the witch-doctors to hear their fortunes. 'Oom' Schalk Lourens is furious to be told that his sister had asked after his safety during the war:

> Especially as the witch-doctor said to her, 'Yes, missus, I can see Baas Schalk Lourens. He will come back safe. He is very clever, Baas Schalk. He lies behind a big stone, with a dirty brown blanket pulled over his head. And he stays behind that stone until the fighting is finished – quite finished.' ... I think I have said enough to show you what sort of scoundrel that old kaffir was. He not only took advantage of the credulity of a simple girl, but he also tried to be funny at the expense of a young man who was fighting for his country's freedom.

Although Herman Bosman is now best-known for his stories about the Marico, in western Transvaal, he actually spent only six months there, as a schoolteacher in 1925. Whereas his early Marico stories, related by 'Oom' Schalk Lourens, hark back to the nineteenth century and the Boer War, his later stories, set in the front parlour of Jurie Steyn's post office, are vehicles for satirical comment on matters of interest at the time, 1950, the year before Bosman's death. The Marico farmers chew over such ponderous subjects as psycho-analysis, grand opera, cattle shows or cremation, and make them absurd. For example, Gysbert van Tonder relates how he went with two back-slapping Americans making an anthropological study of native customs on the Limpopo:

> He said he could still remember how one of the Americans slapped Chief Umfutusu on the back and how Chief Umfutusu, in his turn, slapped the

American on the ear with a clay-pot full of greenish drink that the chief was holding in his hand at the time ... Later on, when Gysbert van Tonder and the Americans came to a Mshangaan village that was having some trouble with hut tax, the American who kept the diary was able to write a lot more about what he called an obscure African ritual that that tribe observed in welcoming a superior order of stranger. For that whole Mshangaan village, men, women and children, had rushed out and pelted Gysbert and the two Americans with wet cow-dung.

Stories like that, which Bosman wrote for a weekly paper, were really part of his journalism; but then, with Bosman fact and fiction tended to merge. His novels, two of them unfinished, were toned down accounts of his own career, which included murder, blackmail, abortion, three unhappy marriages, with chronic debt and drunkenness. His journalistic reports were often as wild and hilarious as his fiction. Apart from the Marico stories, almost everything Bosman wrote was about Johannesburg. Nobody else has managed to catch so well the verve and charm of that overgrown mining camp, which sprang from nothing in 1886, and even in Bosman's time had almost completely replaced its original buildings with others, even more hideous. Although Bosman spent seven years in Europe, mostly in London, he never, as far as I know, wrote about anywhere outside the Veld and his beloved Johannesburg. Whereas most South African writers have aimed for audiences in Europe and the United States, Bosman wrote only for and about South Africans.

Since Bosman's writing about Johannesburg is autobiographical, it is time to examine his life-story. There are now published memoirs by Bernard Sachs, who was at school with him and by Aegidius Blignaut, a journalistic colleague, as well as a life by Valerie Rosenberg, who has found much valuable information. We still have not got the full story, because there is much about Bosman that modern South Africans fear to contemplate. His life story is not for the squeamish any more than his writings, and they can be embarrassing for South Africans as Dorothy Driver admits: 'For who has not squirmed at that slandering in post office and voorkamer (*front room*), at his riding roughshod over some sensitivity or other, at that canny tongue, that sharp ear, those circles he runs round our white, English-speaking consciences?'

Herman Charles Bosman was born on February 5th, 1905 to Jacobus Bosman, a mine labourer, and Elisa, née Malan, at Kuil's River near Cape Town. They moved to Johannesburg, where Jacobus Bosman got a job as a waste packer, down a gold mine. Although poor and Afrikaners, the Bosmans managed to get Herman a place at Jeppe High School, which had been founded on English public school lines. His schoolfriend Sachs says that the young Bosman was studious, undisciplined and contemptuous of authority, and that he wrote an essay defending Goliath 'an easy-going, well-meaning giant who minded his own business but was being pushed around till he met his sad end at the hands of the cunning David'.

From Jeppe Bosman entered the new University of the Witwatersrand. Under the influence of Sachs, he briefly joined the Young Communist League 'but when he discovered that it was only trying to replace the present social order by a more rigorous one, he soon opted out.' By this time Bosman was a devotee of Edgar Allen Poe, Baudelaire and Verlaine, but he must have known where his genius lay, for he wrote an article in the College magazine on Chaucer's *Canterbury Tales*, noting the framework of a pilgrimage for presenting diverse stories, like his Marico.

In the year Bosman qualified as a teacher, 1925, his father was killed in a mining accident, and his mother married an Englishman with a grown-up son. At the beginning of 1926 Bosman married Vera Sawyer, a bank clerk. Apparently the marriage was not consummated and later was annulled by Vera's family, against the wishes of Bosman, who stayed on good terms with Vera till the end of his life. Two days after the marriage Bosman took up a teaching post near Zwingli in the Zeerust-Groot Marico district of western Transvaal. He lodged with an Afrikaner of Irish descent called Flattery, who greeted him every morning with the unusual expression '*Die beste van die more*', which Bosman eventually realised was 'the top of the morning to you'. Bosman was often in trouble during his six months in the Marico. When he was teased by Flattery's daughter, a girl of his own age, Bosman hurled a knife which lodged in her back, narrowly missing the kidneys. Soon afterwards he bought a hunting rifle and took it down to Johannesburg on his winter holiday. On July 18th, 1926, Bosman returned home late to find his younger brother fighting his twenty-three-year-old stepbrother David Russell. He went for his rifle and shot Russell dead.

After four months in custody at the Fort, almost the only Johannesburg building left from the nineteenth century, Bosman stood trial for murder. He showed no sign of remorse. When a woman spectator stared at him in the witness box with fascinated horror, Bosman winked, causing her to collapse in hysterics. His friend Sachs believes that Bosman wanted to know what killing felt like. He was sentenced to hang and placed with one other prisoner in the condemned cells of Pretoria Central, whose many distinguished former inmates include Winston Churchill. Bosman's experience is recalled in *Cold Stone Jug*, a novel all the more grim because he could not stop clowning:

> 'You condemned men mustn't laugh so loud' he [the night head warder] complained. 'The hard labour convicts got to sleep. They got to work all day. You two don't do nothing but smoke cigarettes all day long and crack jokes. You'll get in serious trouble if the Governor finds you keep the prisoners awake at night, romping about, and laughing in the condemned cell.'

In reality, Bosman recalls: 'We were afraid to trust our heads to the hard pallet, in case when we woke up in the morning it would be to find the sheriff standing at the door, with the death warrant.' Bosman's companion was hanged but he was reprieved.

On leaving prison in 1930, Bosman published the first and almost the best of his Marico stories, *Makapan's Caves*. He also contributed, under the name Herman Malan, to scandal and blackmail sheets. According to Sachs, Bosman would 'feature some leading luminary of the city in *The Sjambok* posters and then go along to the victim and promise to desist if he coughed up'. One of his targets was Sachs's brother, Solly, a prominent left-winger and head of the Garment Workers Union, then engaged in a strike: 'Herman approached the clothing bosses about using *The Sjambok* against Solly. For a consideration of course. One morning Joh'burg awoke to find about one hundred *Sjambok* posters placed at strategic points with the wording "Solly Sachs Dances With Kaffir Girl".' Sachs sued for criminal libel and won.

At about that time, Bernard Sachs spoke at a meeting outside Johannesburg City Hall, supporting his brother: 'To my great surprise and consternation I found Herman leading the hecklers in their assault on the platform with eggs and tomatoes. And then I suddenly saw one of our harridan female comrades plaster him across the forehead with a mineral water bottle.' Bosman was knocked out. The next edition of *New LSD*, for February 5th, 1932, carried the headline: 'Blignaut and Malan fight 300 red scum'; but Bosman took it all as a joke. He told Bernard Sachs next day: 'You know, Ben, when I looked in the mirror this morning, I could read on my forehead "Australian Mineral Water Works".'

Bosman tried all kinds of journalism. He approached a rich Jewish radical for £100 to start an anti-Nazi newspaper.

'And if I don't give you £100?'

'Then we'll start a pro-Nazi paper.'

He was sentenced for blasphemy after printing a pornographic story *A Nun's Christmas*. He was had up on thirteen indecency charges after a poster appeared saying 'Joh'burg girls stuffed . . . more than one way'. Witnesses for the Crown included the President of the Johannesburg Branch of the National Council of Women, and also the Bishop of Johannesburg, who said he did not know what 'stuffed' meant, but thought that the posters were foul and lowering to the prestige of white women, because they were carried by blacks.

A photograph of Bosman at this time is well described by the poet David Wright: '. . . striking, light-coloured eyes – personable – an Afrikaner face; elegant trilby hat – a smile part sardonic, part rueful – a precipitation of gaiety and intelligence'. He wore two-toned shoes, to look like a Portuguese gangster. Women were hypnotised by his brilliant blue stare. He took up with and married a neurotic pianist, Ella, who Sachs believes was a lesbian. Ella was crazed with hatred of Bosman's mother, Sachs recalls: 'It is quite stunning to listen to her describe with all the necessary mime, how when Herman's mother visited him she had hit her about the ankles with an umbrella and made her hop – "like this and like that". All this in front of Herman. And when my wife told Herman that his mother had died of cancer, he sent up a hurrah, kissed my wife and then kissed me.'

The Bosmans left in 1934 for England, where they remained for over six years, including stays in Brussels and Paris. Throughout this exile Bosman wrote for South African magazines, on South African themes. He earned his bread by writing for seedy publications such as *The Sunday Critic*, subsidised by the Empire Movement. It was padded with fake advertisements, and Bosman wrote under pseudonyms like the 'Dowager Lady Raglan'. He and Ella lived at the top of Shaftesbury Avenue, near the British Museum, where they founded a publishing house under the names of Arnold and Eleanor Roosevelt Godbold. The records of the Crown Estate Commission show that 'Mr Godbold had been using residential premises for business purposes, was in arrear with rent and had made unauthorised decorations to the landing' – apparently pictures of Adolf Hitler. He spent September 3rd, 1939, the outbreak of the Second World War, in a pub in Lamb's Conduit Street, doubtless the Lamb, which has always been a haunt of Bohemia. The Bosmans were sent back to South Africa in 1940.

After two years in Johannesburg, Bosman in 1943 obtained the editorship of the *Zoutspansberg Review and Mining Journal*, a bi-weekly newspaper at Pietersburg in the Northern Transvaal, a centre of Afrikaner Nationalism. The *Journal* supported the pro-British Union Party. Here Bosman met Helena Stegman, a schoolmistress, and made her pregnant. He found a syringe and the right ingredients for an abortion, from which she almost died. The National Party newspaper published hints of the scandal, and Bosman was taken in handcuffs from his editorial office. He sat in court with the African prisoners, wearing sandals to show off his carefully crimsoned toe-nails. The prosecution failed because the syringe was not found, but Bosman was sacked. He married Helena. Meanwhile his divorced wife Ella got pregnant by Bosman's successor as editor of the *Zoutspansberg Review and Mining Journal*. There is a picture from this time of Bosman, with stetson hat at a rakish angle, strolling along through Johannesburg with second and third wife on either arm. Shortly after the picture was taken, Ella died from an abortion. This time Bosman was threatened with trial for manslaughter; but once again, the police lacked evidence.

From the end of the Second World War to his death in 1951, Bosman wrote well and furiously. He was happy to be in Johannesburg after the years in gaol, in London and Pietersburg. He loved the drab streets of Johannesburg, where all of a sudden: 'Blazes of colour reflect from the silvery grey scales of the fishes, from the dusty windows and the dirty wet pavements. Down the street a Hindu in a red fez comes striding along after his cart which is laden with fresh veld flowers.' He loved street processions. In London he had marched with Communists, Mosleyites, Scotsmen on their way to the Cup-Tie, unemployed Welsh miners and the Peace Pledge Union. Nothing compared with joining a line of marchers going down Jeppe Street, to boo at the *Rand Daily Mail*, the symbol of British capitalism. The marchers swigged Jerepigo wine, to the fury of their leader: 'Drinking wine like that out of a bottle, and in the street. And in front of the *Rand Daily Mail*, too. What if they had taken your photographs, drinking wine, when all the boys were booing.'

When the National Party swept into power, in 1948, Bosman jumped three times on his hat for joy. These were his people. Although he undoubtedly disliked the English-speaking ascendancy, as symbolised by the *Rand Daily Mail*, Bosman was not against blacks. But neither was he a sentimentalist. There is a passage in one of his unfinished books that no one would dare publish today. It described a third-rate Johannesburg bakery which boasts that its products are untouched by hand. But when the electricity fails, the dough for the slab cake and cream cake is pounded under the bare black feet of Big Jim Fish as the sweat pours off him as though from a shower-bath.

Although Bosman never won fame, or critical recognition, or even a good living, he did at last make enough money to rent a home of his own. He and Helena his wife threw a house-warming party on October 13th, 1951. The next day, Bosman woke with a hangover, and died the same evening.

The life and writings of Herman Bosman help to explain to outsiders the two peculiar and baffling features of modern South Africa: the character of the Afrikaners, and what one can only call the Johannesburg phenomenon. These two things largely comprise the problem of South Africa, a problem with no solution. They are both undefinable in the terms of the rest of the world because there is nothing like them anywhere else in the world. They are best comprehended through works of imagination, like Bosman's stories.

Bosman expresses the thoughts not just of the Afrikaners but of the backveld Boers who would not themselves write down their ideas and feelings. Although he wrote in English, lived a few years in London, and came under the spell of the French decadent poets, Bosman was almost immune to the ideas of modern Europe. Because of his own experience, he was opposed to capital punishment; yet did not believe it was wrong to take life. He felt none of the guilt so typical of the English middle classes: guilt over the poor, over the oppressed, above all over people of darker skins.

Most South African writers, including some Afrikaners, have taken aboard a cargo of modern ideas and attitudes. People like Smuts and van der Post, of earlier generations, and Brink and Breytenbach among moderns, look at the world, if not as Englishmen, as West Europeans. The Dutch Reformed Church has now, with its abandonment of the endorsement of apartheid, come back into line with the Calvinist Churches of Holland, Scotland and France. The set books for English students at Stellenbosch University include the works of such fashionable authors as Salman Rushdie. Even the National Party government and its press and the SABC have a body of attitudes much like those of a rather conservative part of Europe: Bavaria, for example, or Belgium. The Afrikaner establishment has rather reluctantly moved with the times.

Bosman wrote of the humbler Boers, the kind of people who today no longer vote for the National Party but for the Conservatives, and who may even support the para-military right. He wrote of the farmers in the Marico; political roughs in Pietersburg who carved up their opponents with bicycle chains; of miners who marched down Jeppe Street to boo the *Rand Daily Mail*. The same people today are in angry mood, posing a worse threat to Botha than the most angry blacks. At the general election of 1987 they overtook the Progressives as the main opposition party. In two by-elections in the Transvaal in 1988 the right wing hugely increased their majority. They could, in the near future, replace the National Party in office. As the Marico farmers in Bosman's stories thought they had been betrayed by old Paul Kruger, so their descendants think they have been betrayed by Botha. The young roughs of Pietersburg may soon be wielding their bicycle chains or the modern equivalent against the candidates of the National Party. The poor whites of Johannesburg go to meetings, not to boo the *Rand Daily Mail* (it ceased publication years ago) but calling for the enforcement of the Group Areas Act. These are all Bosman's people.

Bosman is just as revealing about the Johannesburg phenomenon. He understood and expressed the absurdity of this vast city which sprang into being quite suddenly in the empty high veld. In Australia and the United States there were mining camps that flourished a few short years and then turned into ghost towns, or quaint little historical relics, like Ballarat. Only Johannesburg kept growing. It goes on growing even now that the gold has expired within its environs. Far from preserving the relics of early days, Johannesburg constantly tears down and renews its fabric.

Johannesburg is the hub of the Transvaal which has 75 per cent of the wealth and industry of all South Africa, which in turn has 75 per cent of the Gross National Product of all the continent, south of the Sahara. Without Johannesburg, all South Africa and some of the rest of Africa would collapse in ruins.

Johannesburg is unique in Africa, a huge city of Europeans, comparable in wealth and power to the cities of the United States and Australia. Other South African cities like Cape Town, Port Elizabeth and Durban were entrepots and administration centres where most of the whites were the middle or governing class. Only in Southern Transvaal is there a large, white working class. But for Johannesburg, South Africa might now have the same kind of racial mix as the present Zimbabwe. Whites still run much of Zimbabwe's agriculture, though the farmers are only a few thousand in number. In cities the size of Harare (the former Salisbury) or Bulawayo, some tens of thousands of whites remain as businessmen, professional people and government servants, but they are only a small minority. Most of the whites in Zimbabwe's cities are first or second generation in Africa.

There is another all-important distinction between Johannesburg and the smaller cities of southern Africa. The others, though built by the whites, now serve as a focal point for the non-whites in the region, as for instance Port Elizabeth to the Xhosas, or Bulawayo the Matabeles. But Johannesburg sprang into being far from any centres of population either for whites or blacks. There were a few thousand Boers in the Southern Transvaal, and scattered and often migrant groups of Tswanas and Sothos. The blacks, who over the years came pouring into Johannesburg and now populate townships the size of Soweto, have come from all parts of the Republic and the surrounding states. The citizens of Johannesburg come from all nations and now belong to none. This is true for the blacks as much as the whites.

Johannesburg, this city without a nation, frustrates all efforts to bring peace to South Africa. It is like a boil on the body politic. Within ten years of its birth, in 1886, Johannesburg went to war with Pretoria in the Jameson Raid. Three years later, the British embarked on the Boer War to keep their hold on Johannesburg. The phenomenon of Johannesburg, just as much as the character of the Boers, now stands in the way of a peaceful solution, or any solution, to what ails South Africa.

The statesmen and political analysts pore in vain over the map of South Africa to find an arrangement preserving the freedom and interests of the different ethnic groups. The Zulus might be given a share of power in Natal, the Xhosas in Eastern Cape, the Coloureds in Cape Town. The Sothos, Swazis and Tswanas already have their separate states to which could be added parts of the present Republic. The Afrikaners who wanted to keep their own separate republic, might be given a chunk of the Transvaal. And so speculation proceeds until someone always poses the question: 'And who's going to get Johannesburg?' For he who controls the wealth of Johannesburg is in effect the ruler of southern Africa. No one ethnic group could hold it against the jealousy of the others. If the present Republic kept its present boundaries, the politicians who then ruled Johannesburg, whoever won power in Soweto, would attract the hostility of the rest of the country. Moreover, the wealth of this purely capitalistic city would not continue under a socialistic or corrupt regime, the kind of regime which exists in most of the continent. The blacks of Johannesburg know this just as well as the whites.

The altitude of more than 5,000 feet and the brilliant sunshine give to Johannesburg a heady feeling of hope and adventure. The African men in their flash three-piece suits, and their dumpy womenfolk in berets, look confident and alert for the main chance. It is a busy, hustling city. You rarely see beggars, the destitute or defeated. Life is hard for those without work, but those in a job have money for beer and tobacco. It is still now as a hundred years ago, a wide-open city to anyone with effrontery, and luck, and his wits about him. This is increasingly so for the blacks as well as the whites.

It was one of Bosman's fantasies to equate Johannesburg with the fabulous lost cities of Africa such as Prester John's Kingdom, Monoma-tapa and King Solomon's Mines:

> It's a queer thing . . . that for so many hundreds of years, when the interior of South Africa was still unexplored, that there should have been a legend of a Golden City. And people were so convinced of the existence of this city that they even went searching for it . . . even marked it on their maps . . . and at most they were only a few hundred miles out.

Upon this Golden City depends the fate of southern Africa. As long as Johannesburg prospers, Southern Africa prospers. Should Southern Africa fall into chaos, all the wealth of Johannesburg would pass into legend along with Prester John's Kingdom, Monomatapa and King Solomon's Mines.

SELECT BIBLIOGRAPHY

[Note: all books were published in London unless otherwise stated]

Barnes, Leonard *Caliban in Africa* (1930)
Benson, Mary *The Struggle for a Birthright* (1966)
   Nelson Mandela (1986)
Bosman, Herman Charles *Mafeking Road* (1948)
   Cold Stone Jug (1949)
   A Cask of Jerepigo (Johannesburg 1957)
   Unto Dust (1963)
   Jurie Steyn's Post Office (Cape Town 1971)
   A Bekkersdal Marathon (1971)
   Willemsdorp (Cape Town 1977)
   Makapan's Caves (1987)
Campbell, Roy *The Wayzgoose* (1928)
   Light on a Dark Horse (1951)
Chalmers, John A. *Tiyo Soga* (1879)
Chaudhuri, Nirad C. *The Autobiography of an Unknown Indian* (1951)
   Thy Hand, Great Anarch! (1988)
Cohen, Louis *Reminiscences of Kimberley* (1911)
   Reminiscences of Johannesburg and London (1924)
Davenport, T. R. H. *South Africa. A Modern History* (1977)
De Klerk, W. A. *The Puritans in Africa* (1975)
Epstein, Edward Jay *The Diamond Invention* (1982)
First, Ruth and Scott, Ann *Olive Schreiner* (1970)
Fisher, John *The Afrikaners* (1969)
Fitzpatrick, Percy *Jock of the Bushveld* (1907)
Flint, John *Cecil Rhodes* (1976)
Frank, Katherine *Voyager Out* (1986)
Gray, Stephen (Editor) *Herman Charles Bosman* (Johannesburg 1986)
Green, Timothy *The New World of Gold* (1981)
Harrison, David *The White Tribe of Africa* (1981)

Harrison, Mary *Winnie Mandela* (1985)

Jackson, Stanley *The Great Barnato* (1970)

Kruger, Rayne *Goodbye Dolly Gray* (1959)

Kuzwayo, Ellen *Call Me Woman* (1985)

Leipoldt, Christian *300 Years of Cape Wine* (Cape Town 1952)

Lewinsohn, Richard *Barney Barnato* (1937)

Ludi, Gerard *Operation Q-018* (Cape Town 1969)

Ludi, Gerard, and Grobbelaar, Blaar *The Amazing Mr Fischer* (Cape Town 1966)

Meiring, Jane *Thomas Pringle* (Cape Town 1968)

Moodie, D. C. F. *The History of the Battles and Adventures of the British, the Boers and the Zulus in South Africa* (1888)

Morris, Donald R. *The Washing of the Spears* (1968)

Official Handbook of Cape Town (Cape Town 1909)

The Oxford History of South Africa (Oxford, 1969)

Pakenham, Thomas *The Boer War* (1979)

Plomer, William *Turbott Wolfe* (1926)
   The Autobiography (1975)

Porter, Bernard *Critics of Empire* (1968)

Pringle, Thomas *Narrative of a Residence in South Africa* (1835)

Ransford, Oliver *The Great Trek* (1972)

Robbins, David and Hartley, Wyndham *Inside the Last Outpost* (Pietermaritzburg 1985)

Roberts, Brian *Cecil Rhodes and the Princess* (1969)

Rosenberg, Valerie *Sunflower to the Sun* (Cape Town 1976)

Rosenthal, Eric *The Stars and Stripes in Africa* (1939)
   Gold! Gold! Gold! (1970)

Sachs, Bernard *Herman Charles Bosman as I knew him* (Johannesburg 1971)

Sampson, Anthony *Black and Gold* (1987)

Sisson, Terence *Just Nuisance, AB, His Full Story* (Cape Town 1985)

Smith, Wilbur *The Power of the Sword* (1986)

Strydom, Hans *For Volk and Führer* (1984)

Thompson, George *Travels and Adventure in South Africa* (1827)

Troup, Freda *South Africa. An Historical Introduction* (1972)

Uys, Pieter-Dirk *No-one's Died Laughing* (Johannesburg 1986)

Van der Post, Laurens *A Walk with a White Bushman* (1986)
   Yet Being Someone Other (1986)

Waugh, Evelyn *Remote People* (1931)
   A Tourist in Africa (1960)

West, Richard *The White Tribes of Africa* (1965)
   The White Tribes Revisited (1978)
Wheatcroft, Geoffrey *The Randlords* (1985)
Winter, Gordon *Inside BOSS* (1981)
Woods, Donald *Biko* (1978)
Wright, David *Roy Campbell* (1961)

ACKNOWLEDGMENTS

The author and publishers would like to thank the following for permission to reproduce extracts from the publications mentioned, although unfortunately in a few cases it has not been possible to trace the present copyright holder to whom they apologise for any omission: International Defence & Aid Fund for South Africa, *The Struggle for a Birthright* by Mary Benson; Human & Rousseau (Pty) Ltd, a number of quotations from the books of Herman Charles Bosman; the words from *An Instant in the Wind* by André Brink are reprinted by permission of Faber & Faber Ltd © André Brink 1976 published by W. H. Allen; Francisco Campbell Custodio and Ad. Donker (Pty) Ltd, for the lines from Roy Campbell's *The Wayzgoose* and *Creeping Jesus* and the extract from *Light on a Dark Horse*; John Farquharson Ltd, for *The Autobiography of an Unknown Indian* by Nirad C. Chaudhuri; Nirad C. Chaudhuri and Chatto & Windus Ltd, for *Thy Hand, Great Anarch!* by Nirad C. Chaudhuri; Penguin Books Ltd, for *The Puritans in Africa* by W. A. De Klerk (© W. A. De Klerk); Stanley Jackson and William Heinemann Ltd, for *The Great Barnato* by Stanley Jackson; Gerard Ludi and Tafelberg Publishers Ltd, for *Operation Q-018* by Gerard Ludi; Rupert Hart-Davis, for *The Autobiography* of William Plomer; thanks to W. J. Flesch & Partners of Cape Town, for permission to quote from *Just Nuisance, AB* by Terence Sisson; Laurens van der Post and Chatto & Windus Ltd, for *A Walk with a White Bushman* and *Yet Being Someone Other* by Laurens van der Post; Gerald Duckworth and Peters Fraser and Dunlop, for *Remote People* by Evelyn Waugh; A. D. Peters and Co, for *A Tourist in Africa* by Evelyn Waugh; Penguin Books Ltd and Tessa Sayle, for *Inside BOSS* by Gordon Winter (© Gordon Winter, 1981).

INDEX

Nandi, mother of Shaka, 119–20; death, 123–4
Natal, 91–6; *see also* Durban
Natal Witness, The (newspaper), 110, 116, 127
National Automobile and Allied Workers Union, 66
National Congress Youth League, 77
National Party: Jews and, 170
National Union of South African Students (NUSAS), 85, 114
National Union of Mine Workers (NUM), 184
necklaces, necklacing, 63–6, 98, 113, 189
Nguni people, 67
Nico Malan theatre complex, Cape Town, 23
Nissen, Christian, 167
Nxumalo, Gugu, 123
Nyerere, Julius, 125
Nzo, Alfred, 113

Oberholzer, Constable Willem, 161
O'Brien, Conor Cruise, 28
Ojukwu, Omeka, 125
Oppenheimer family, 146
Oppenheimer, Sir Ernest, 148
Oppenheimer, Harry, 170, 181–3
Orange Free State, 134–5
Ortega, Domingo, 107
Orwell, George, 106
Ossewabrandwag (OB), 54, 166–8
Ossewatrek *see under* Great Trek
Owen, Wilfred, 130

Pakenham, Thomas: *Boer War*, 129–30, 157
Palestine Liberation Organisation (PLO), 171, 173
Pan African Congress, 76
Parys, 134–5
Pass Law, 21
Pembroke Castle (ship), 17
Pietermaritzburg: described, 109–10; unrest and violence in, 116
Plomer, Charles, 99–100

Plomer, William, 99–102, 104–7, 110; *Turbott Wolfe*, 101
Port Elizabeth: described, 62–3, 154; unrest in, 63, 66–7, 72
Post, Laurens van der *see* van der Post, Sir Laurens
Powell, Robert, 118
Pretoria: described, 154–6
Pringle, Thomas, 69–71, 100
Prockter, Lewis, 58–60
Progressive Reform Party, 181
Pugsley, Rev Ernest, 96

Q-018, Operation, 82, 84

Raborife, Norman, 185
Ramogale, Jack, 191–5
Rand Daily Mail, 80, 82–3
Rapport (newspaper), 56–7
'Republic Intelligence', 82
Rhodes, Cecil, 17, 26, 146, 149–50, 157–9; administration, 51–2
Ritter, E. A.: *Shaka Zulu*, 117, 120, 123
Rivonia plot and trial, 74–5, 78–81, 83, 113
Robben Island, 16, 70
Robbins, David, 110
Roberts, Field-Marshal Frederick Sleigh, 1st Earl, 131, 133
Robinson, John, Bishop, 59
Robinson, Sir Joseph B., 151–3, 177
Roos, Tielman, 102
Roosevelt, Theodore, 47
Rosenberg, Linda, 41–2
Rosenberg, Valerie, 200
Rostron, Frank, 165
Rousseau, Jean-Jacques, 140, 142
Rubusana, Rev Walter, 76
Ruskin, John, 15, 45
Russell, David, 201

Sachs, Bernard, 200–2
Sachs, Solly, 202
Sackville-West, Vita, 106
sanctions, 113
Sauls, Freddie, 66–7
Scargill, Arthur, 184